THE TRAINING OF PART-TIME TEACHERS
OF ADULTS

Department of Adult Education, University of Nottingham
in association with The National Institute of Adult Education

During the period of the Project:

Brian Graham was Senior Lecturer, John Daines and Terry Sullivan were Lecturers in the Department of Adult Education, University of Nottingham. Pauline Harris and Fran Baum were Research Associates appointed to the Project.

Alan Charnley was Senior Research Officer, the National Institute for Adult Education.

NOTTINGHAM STUDIES IN THE THEORY AND PRACTICE
OF THE EDUCATION OF ADULTS

THE TRAINING OF PART-TIME TEACHERS OF ADULTS

T. B. GRAHAM J. M. DAINES T. SULLIVAN
P. HARRIS F. E. BAUM

Department of Adult Education, University of Nottingham

ISBN   0 902031 79 1

Typeset and designed by Burns & Smith, Derby.

CONTENTS

FOREWORD

The case for training teachers no longer has to be argued in primary, secondary and much of further education. In higher and general adult education, however, it is still often assumed by providers that expertise in a subject is qualification enough for teaching it.

The great majority of teachers of adults work part-time in that field, some doing no other paid work, some having full-time occupations which involve no teaching, others teaching full-time some other age-group for which they have been trained. The quality of the adult education service depends largely upon the skills of this army of part-time teachers, most of whom have received little or no training as teachers of adults. To some, their commitment seems too slight to make training worth their while; some cannot find, or are unaware of, available training courses; others, trained for work with younger learners, consider themselves equipped to teach students of all ages.

The view expressed in the *Russell Report* (1973) that ". . . appropriate training specifically for work in adult education is essential for all full-time and as many as possible part-time staff. . ." is still far from being realised. However, substantial progress has been made since the appearance of the second ACSTT (FE) Report in 1978 and information on the work of the Regional Advisory Councils and the LEAs in their areas has been collected in 1980 by ACACE and in 1981 in a DES survey, on which the present Report has been able to draw.

The need for a different kind of study has emerged. Not enough is known about the detailed working of training courses, the views of providers, the background, aims and methods of trainers, the expectations and experiences of trainees and the impact of training upon them, their students and the adult education service as a whole. This study was specifically commissioned by the Department of Education and Science and the scheme developed by the Department of Adult Education of the University of Nottingham and presented in association with the National Institute of Adult Education. The work was carried out under contract, and it should be noted that the findings which are here presented do not necessarily represent the views of the DES.

Such a study could be attempted only in the context of a circumscribed programme of work. For reasons which appear in Chapter 2 *(The Provision of Training)*, the East Midlands Region was seen to be suitable and the title chosen for the DES Report was: *The training of part-time teachers of adults, with particular reference to the East Midlands*. The Steering Committee met first in May, 1980; the first research associate was appointed in June 1980 and the second in September. The completed report was delivered early in February, 1982. Though the area was limited geographically, the field of research proved impossibly broad. Constraints of time, manpower and finance narrowed the scope of the study to a detailed examination of the work and working of Stage 1 and Stage 2 courses (in terms of the ACSTT (FE) Report) and associated City and Guilds 730 courses, with brief assessments of the modest training programmes of the Responsible Bodies in the area and the specialised training offered by a number of organisations. It was originally intended to include some general evaluation of the benefits of training in its effect on teaching behaviour and also to attempt some measurement of the efficiency and effectiveness of training through Cost Benefit Analysis but, it became apparent that these operations were beyond the resources of the project, and attention was, therefore, concentrated on more 'illuminative' considerations.

In this area the study has unearthed and placed on record, making generous use of quotation from our informants, much material which should contribute to the understanding of training needs and processes. Chapter 2 presents the policies of LEAs in the East Midlands as providers against the background of national provision and in an historical perspective of the Region. Chapter 3 *(The World of the Part-time Teacher)* draws together data on the provenance of part-time teachers, their precipitate entry at the deep end of adult education, their problems — (especially that of isolation) — and their ways of meeting them. Chapter 4 *(The Trainers)* uncovers much fresh material on the commitment of trainers, their aims and methods, their occasional doubts and the benefits which they see themselves, as well as their trainees, deriving from the training experience. Chapter 5 *(Learning to Teach: the Trainees)* shows the complementary perceptions of the trainees, sometimes close to those of the trainers, sometimes at variance with them, and bringing out what they see as the principal benefits of training: raised confidence, additional teaching skills and some relief of the sense of isolation.

The Report makes it clear that the training of part-time teachers of adults is valued by providers, trainers and trainees who share the view that it improves the quality of the service. Gaps and shortcomings remain: subject specialism is unevenly catered for and is not without importance, however successful the classes may be socially; teachers may relapse into isolation after training in the absence of follow-up and support in teaching Centres; the problem of combining the advantages of nationally recognised awards with the claims of sensitivity to local needs is far from being resolved. Above all, the harsh economic climate has cramped the efforts of dedicated workers struggling to raise quality where they cannot prevent a decline in quantity.

It is hoped that this book, in all but minor detail the DES Report, may lead to a greater appreciation of the importance of training part-time teachers of adults, to a deeper understanding of its principles and practice and to the more effective use of the resources which may be devoted to it in the future.

Elizabeth Monkhouse
Chairman of Steering Committee

ACKNOWLEDGEMENTS

We wish to acknowledge the generous co-operation of all LEA Officers, Principals, Heads of Centres, Part-time Teachers and Adult Students. The assurance of confidentiality precludes a more exact identification of those who gave of their time. We would also thank the Specialist Subject Organisations and Associations and the Responsible Bodies for providing us with such valuable information. Without the help of all these people there would have been no project.

We are grateful for the support and encouragement given by members of the Steering Committee. In particular we would like to record our gratitude to Dr. Elizabeth Monkhouse and Mr. Konrad Elsdon who gave unstintingly of their advice and expertise.

We would also like to thank Mrs. Hilary McCreedy for her help and quiet efficiency and Mrs. Jean Nightingale for so painstakingly typing the report. Finally we commend all those colleagues and friends who in their several ways gave us much encouragement and assistance, both in carrying out the research and writing the report.

The Authors

Steering Committee

Mr. D. W. Brown	Secretary, North West Regional Advisory Council for Further Education
Mr. J. Cammack	Department of Education & Science
Dr. A. H. Charnley	(Secretary), Senior Research Officer, NIAE
Mr. J. M. Daines	Department of Adult Education, University of Nottingham
Mr. T. E. Dawson	Adult Education Advisor, North Yorkshire
Mr. K. T. Elsdon	(Assessor), HMI
Mr. T. B. Graham	Department of Adult Education, University of Nottingham
Prof. H. A. Jones	Pro-Vice-Chancellor, University of Leicester (to 1/9/81)
Dr. E. Monkhouse	(Chairman) formerly Senior Lecturer, Department of Extra Mural Studies, University of London
Mr. R. Ruddock	Senior Research Fellow, Department of Adult Education, University of Manchester
Prof. M. D. Stephens	Department of Adult Education, University of Nottingham
Mr. A. K. Stock	(Treasurer) Director, NIAE
Mr. T. Sullivan	Department of Adult Education, University of Nottingham
(Mr. M. Warburton	ACACE)

ACKNOWLEDGEMENT

Introduction

The original aims of this research project focused upon the training of the part-time teachers of adults. It was proposed not only to provide a statistical picture of the personal characteristics of trainers, trainees and teachers of adults but more importantly to give an account of the variety of the training provision and to examine the attitudes and opinions of all those concerned in the training schemes under consideration. It was also intended to provide and test measures of the effectiveness and efficiency of the training provided.

We planned to consider the characteristics, motives and aspirations of teachers, their perceptions of training received and of training in general. We intended to elucidate from the 'providers of training' (the Responsible Bodies, Specialist Training Agencies as well as the LEA employers) their perceptions of the value of training, present costs, perceived benefits and future trends. We further planned to look in detail at the training process, seeking the attitudes and opinions of both trainers and teachers in training towards the experience and its subsequent effects. Lastly, we intended to seek information from class members about their valuations of both courses and teachers and to collect data relating to dropout rates and student willingness to bear costs of their own travel and course attendance. Thus we intended to study both the process of training and the outcomes of that training on both trainee and student.

Part of the original methodology of the research was rooted in the technique of cost-benefit analysis (CBA). In the event, the measures of benefit (student willingness to bear costs) proved impossible to collect as originally conceived and, therefore, CBA had to be dropped from the project. (See Appendix 1: "CBA: Collecting the Data"). Thus, there was a change in the orientation of the project away from a mixed quantitative—qualitative design and towards that of a qualitative study. The only quantitative analysis attempted was a multiple regression model of teacher characteristics and class dropouts. The results of this analysis have been published under a separate title [1].

The qualitative aspect of the study began with two objectives. First it set out to provide complementary and explanatory evidence of the quantitative analysis; secondly to provide an in-depth analysis of the attitudes and opinions of all those involved in the training of part-time teachers of adults. To this end, responses were to be sought from the training providers (the LEAs, Responsible Bodies and specialist Subject Agencies), the people who taught on such courses (the trainers), men and women currently studying East Midland Stage 1 and Stage 2 programmes and from teachers currently teaching adult education non-vocational classes. With the change in orientation, a wider and more analytical survey of the training of part-time teachers by means of interviews where possible, supplemented by the descriptive statistical data.

We were faced with the problem of identifying a conceptual framework which would serve as the basis for the enquiry. There appears to be little consensus on the theoretical underpinnings of the training of adult educators. There is a lack of agreement about the solutions to many of the basic questions in the training field, especially in the area of the analysis and evaluation of 'good' adult teaching. There remains much uncertainty as to how teachers best acquire and develop a set of skills and attitudes consonant with such models. Whilst general

[1]*Human Capital Theory and Adult Education* ed. J. E. Thomas, University of Nottingham Department of Adult Education.

guidelines and statements of intent about the structure, objectives and content of training courses exist (various Regional Advisory Councils, the Advisory Council on the Supply and Training of Teachers), the complex process of how individuals learn to teach is yet poorly understood. However we did have the basic concept that training is about change; the process of training is how these changes are brought about and its outcomes are the consequences of such training. It is against this background that the areas of enquiry were defined in an attempt to uncover and illuminate those facets of training which trainee teachers respond to and interact with. Thus, a range of questions was asked on areas including the policy and provision of training, course objectives, organisation and management, course content, methods and evaluation. Trainees and teachers were asked about training expectations, motivations, benefits and effects; students were asked about their classes. In retrospect, some of the detailed points included may appear rather arbitrarily chosen but the degree to which the project was exploratory made a pragmatic perspective unavoidable, and our informants were to be trainees, complemented by the views of their course trainers and those responsible for overall training policy. Yet, if only some of the major questions asked find acceptance, the answers to such questions may serve to extend the present limited understanding of the training of adult educators.

CHAPTER 1

The Project: Design and Methodology

This Chapter sets out the structure and methodology of the procedure used and states the definitions and parameters employed. A survey of relevant literature has not been included in this report. The interested reader is directed to the NIAE Monograph "Training the Educators of Adults", 1982, in the "National Institute's Review of existing Research in Adult and Continuing Education."

SECTION 1: STRUCTURE AND METHODOLOGY

The research structure set out to provide an analytical survey of attitudes and opinions of all those concerned with the training of part-time teachers of adults, and some examination of the process and outcome of such training. The methods to be employed were questionnaires, semi-structured interviews, class visits and the collection of relevant documentation from both local and national sources.

Adult educators are taken to be those who organise and teach non-vocational classes sponsored by Local Education Authorities and Responsible Bodies (the Universities and the Workers Educational Association). For the purpose of this research the major point of focus has been upon part-time teachers employed in the LEA non-vocational educational service. Non-vocational classes are taken to be those adult classes which do not have any major vocational focus or aim to prepare students for public examinations. (See Appendix 5 for examples). Literacy and allied classes are not included in the category of 'non-vocational' subjects. Training is taken to be any deliberate attempt to improve the teaching expertise of the part-time teachers of adults; its activities can range from award bearing courses to conferences and class visits. School teachers who possess a Qualified Teacher's Certificate of Education (including PGCE and B.Ed.,) have been considered to be untrained teachers of adults throughout.

The main system of training considered was the East Midland Scheme which is made up of three hierarchical stages: Stage 1, Stage 2 (plus the combined Stage 2 and City and Guilds 730 Certificate) and Stage 3 (the Certificate of Adult Education provided by the Universities of Nottingham and Leicester). The geographical/administrative areas studied were the four East Midlands Counties, Nottinghamshire, Derbyshire, Lincolnshire and Northamptonshire. The original plan included Leicestershire but at the time of data collection major reductions were being undertaken in the funding of the Adult Education in that county leading to restructuring and reorganisation of the service. It was judged that at such a time the research would have proved particularly sensitive and difficult within such a changing situation and in consequence this county was not included in the project.

Figure 1 sets out the research area as a set of five stocks of data arranged in 'blocks'. The purpose of the diagram is to identify the various respondents and the sources of information, the type and nature of the information sought and to indicate the methods by which this data was collected.

1

Figure 1: Outline Research Design

Block 1 Providers	Block 2 Trainers	Block 3 Trainees	Block 4 Teachers	Block 5 Students
4 LEA Representatives 1 C & G Representative 3 R B Representatives Other Subjt.-based Training Providers (S)	LEA running 1980-81 S1 S2 S2/C & G 730 (S3)	LEA Courses attending 1980-81 S1 S2 S2/C & G 730 (S3)	LEA pt. nv classes teaching 1980-81 S1 trained (S2 trained (S2 C & G 730 trained S3 trained Other trained Untrained	LEA pt. nv. classes enrolled 1980-81 Training level by Subject category
Policy on Training (I) Provision of Training (I) Training Budget (S)	Numbers & location (S) Personal charact's (Q) Attds. to Training & teaching (I)	Numbers & Courses (S) Personal charact's (Q) Attds. to Training & teaching (I) Effects of Training (M)	Number (S/Q) Personal charact's (Q) Attds. to Training & teaching (I) Classes taught and location (Q)	Personal value of classes (1) Attitudes towards Teachers (I) (Attendance) (S)

Where: Bracketed figures show main method of data collection.

I = Interview   S = Survey/letter
Q = Questionnaire   M = Monitoring Schedule
Tr = Training   C & G = City & Guild 730 Course.
$S_1/S_2/S_3$ = E M Regional Training Schemes

The Providers   (Block 1) are four of the five Local Authorities in the East Midlands and the Responsible Bodies (the Universities of Nottingham and Leicester and the East Midlands District of the WEA). The LEA representative was in each case the nominee of the Chief Education Officer and drawn from those senior officers having concern with Adult Education; the RB representatives were the staff having responsibility for adult education training. The City and Guilds Institute of London also provided a nominee, who, in common with all others, was interviewed in private. The administrators of certain subject-based training schemes were contacted by letter and invited to submit written evidence of their training objectives, provision and procedures, together with a statement of their attitudes towards the training of adult educators. (See Appendix 2 for listing of Organisations and Associations contacted).

The Trainers   (Block 2) are those people who were concerned directly with training adult educators on Stage 1 and Stage 2 training courses run within the survey area during the period September 1, 1980 to March 31, 1981 inclusive. Each course leader was interviewed and asked in addition to provide written descriptive information of his/her course. All those who worked as trainers on courses other than at a peripheral level were asked to complete a questionnaire. Several other course tutors who had been substantially involved throughout their courses were also interviewed. There were some 20 interviews and 25 questionnaires.

The Trainees   (Block 3) are those who were attending an East Midlands Regional Training Scheme course during the period September 1980 to March 1981. Although there are three levels of course normally available, Stage 1 (S1), Stage 2 (S2), and the Stage 2 courses run in parallel with the City and Guilds Course for Teachers (S2/730) and Stage 3 (S3), there was in fact only one Stage 3 course running during the period of the project. It was judged that to use this course, in its third and final year, would provide an unbalanced picture, particularly as it was the first to be run in that county, and in consequence no trainees were interviewed. All other courses were visited and trainees requested to take part in the project by filling in a questionnaire and completing a series of monitoring schedules both during and after their course. They were also asked if they were willing to talk to us and where possible a man and a woman from each course were interviewed. Some 12 training courses with 160 trainees were contacted, producing about 100 questionnaires and 25 interviews.

The Teachers   (Block 4) are those who were teaching non-vocational adult education classes during the academic year 1980-81, begun in the Autumn or Spring terms. The identification of these teachers allowed a direct written request to be sent to all, asking for the completion and return of a questionnaire and for a willingness to be interviewed. A follow-up request and duplicate questionnaire were sent to non-respondents. From the total returned, approximately a 50% rate, a stratified sample of those willing to be interviewed was employed — level of training or non-training against subject category taught. Interviews were carried out either face to face or by telephone (a proportion 3:1), the same schedule was used for both. The reservations concerning how representative any sample of a population is unless it is truly a random selection are as relevant to this study as to any other. Thus all interpretation has to be viewed in the reality of an attempted *population* survey with a less than total response. The sample may or may not accurately represent the whole. The target population was thought to be about 3,700; a questionnaire return of 1800 was achieved and some 65 interviews carried out.

The Students   (Block 5) are those enrolled and who attended non-vocational adult education classes in the Session 1980-81, taught by teachers in Block 4. Students played a rather less important role in the project than had been originally envisaged. There had been an intention to try to discover whether students' impressions in general, and of methods used in

3

particular, varied between classes of trained as opposed to untrained teachers. In the event the scale of this particular undertaking was beyond the resources of the project and it was not attempted. There was also an intention to secure data on benefits for the CBA but as recorded elsewhere this had to be abandoned (see Appendix 1). Nevertheless, a number of classes were visited and students invited for interview. A sample of 35 students from some 20 classes were interviewed either by telephone or face to face. The information they gave about themselves, their class and their teachers has been used to illuminate the account of 'the World of the Part-Time Teacher'.

SECTION 2: THE MAJOR INSTRUMENTS

The Questionnaires

Three separate questionnaires were designed, for Trainers, Trainees and Teachers. Though similar in most respects in terms of personal details of age, experience and qualifications they were different in certain specifics of past, present and future involvement in training activities. The content of each questionnaire was designed to provide a statistical description of the personnel involved. In the case of both trainees and teachers additional data of current and intending training commitments were sought together with the identity of those respondents willing to be interviewed. The major content areas are shown in Figure 2.

Distribution of these instruments proved relatively easy in the case of both the Trainers and the Trainees as the vast majority of these recipients were met personally either before or during the first visit to each training course. Questionnaires were returned in stamped, addressed envelopes and where necessary a reminder was given by telephone. Teachers in Block 4 proved less easy as their identity was not always directly forthcoming. Some adult education officers supplied not only names but addresses of teachers within their area whilst others only provided a list of the names of teachers who were working in a particular centre. In certain other instances, Area Principals and Centre Heads chose to distribute unaddressed packets containing the explanatory letter, questionnaire and stamped addressed envelope to their teachers by means of their own particular networks. These differences in distribution did not severely affect the response rate; follow-up was certainly facilitated where the approach by name was possible. After an interval of some three months, those teachers who could be identified as non-respondents were circularised with a second request plus a further questionnaire.

The Interview Schedules

A separate interview schedule was devised for each of the first four blocks following an overall aim of seeking reciprocal and complementary information from the separate groups of personnel. That is to say, each block was to be questioned upon broadly similar and overlapping themes. Modifications were made to suit their particular knowledge and experience in an attempt to identify and evaluate the differing attitudes and opinions of each. Figure 3 shows the major content areas. Typically, a provider's interview lasted about two hours, and a trainer's somewhat more. The other interviews were rather shorter, a trainee's taking perhaps an hour, and a teacher's slightly less. There were 'separate' interview schedules for trained and untrained teachers. The former included a short series of questions concerning attendance at adult education teachers' training courses and the benefits judged to have accrued from them. Untrained teachers were asked about their reasons for non-attendance at such training courses.

4

Figure 2: Questionnaires — Major Content Areas

Trainers (Block 2)	Trainees (Block 3)	Teachers (Block 4)
Name, age and centre address	Name, age, course address	Name, age, centre address
Teaching experience (f.t. & p.t.) Current A E teaching inc. p.t. Work experience in teaching subject Formal (acad.) qualifications Teacher training courses attended.	Teaching experience (f.t. & p.t.) Current A E p.t. classes Work experience in teaching subject Formal (acad.) qualifications Teacher training courses attended.	Teaching experience (f.t. & p.t.) Current A E p.t. classes Work experience in teaching subject Formal (acad.) qualifications Teacher training courses attended.
Involvement in training courses Involvement in other training activities Support and training as trainer	Previous course 'drop-out' Involvement in other training activities Financial assistance	Previous course 'drop-out' Involvement & value of other training activities
Involvement in present course (Role, contact & prep. time, teaching methods, objectives)	(Current involvement known)	Any current training course
	Attendance at future courses	Attendance at future courses.
Further comment	Further comment Willing to be interviewed	Further comment. Willing to be interviewed.
(LEA staff-job specification)		

5

Figure 3: Interview Schedules — Major Content Areas

Providers (Block 1)	Trainers (Block 2)	Trainers (Block 3)	Teachers (Block 4) T & U.T.
POLICY, influences, aims & objectives, monitoring. Provision, target groups. Integration with other prov's. Standardisation & complementary courses. Demand.	POLICY, involvement in formulation, target groups, Demand. Selection complementary training courses. COURSE objectives. Relation to other levels. Determination, value, support in centres.	ADMISSION, selection. Motivation for attendance general vs. subject course. OBJECTIVES, (determination) SUPPORT — Course & Centre	POLICY, LEA encouragement & recognition, requirement for training. Motivation for non-attendance vs general support & follow-up — ATTITUDE, reasons
RESOURCES, training budget, changes in expenditure — effects. STAFFING, responsibility staffing pool, trainers selection training and support.	MANAGEMENT & ORGANISATION admin, staffing, moderator. PROFILE, involvement & other job description training, support, motivation.	Course ORGANISATION & MANAGEMENT, Group compos., Trainer characteristics.	TEACHING, OTHER WORK, SATISFACTIONS Problems, *acult of* child teaching STUDENTS, attendance, motivation value, change, learning difficulties SUBJECT, experience & qualifications content/skill changes.
EVALUATION, benefits, criteria, effectiveness.	EVALUATION of objectives, methods. MONITORING & ASSESSMENT criteria, methods. Trainee expectation, motivation.	EVALUATION, involvement benefit, recognition. Model. MONITORING & ASSESSMENT relevance. Problems, time. EFFECTS, expectation, change, value.	Expectation, value, application — Possible benefits of training
	CONTENT, selection, ACSTT 1/2, learning difficulties. TEACHING METHODS, choice Trainee participation, experience, class visit.	CONTENT, value, choice TEACHING METHODS, suitability, novelty, experience, participation demands.	
Developments of training	Further developments.	Personal development, further support & training	Attendance at future courses. Other alternative provision. Contact with other teachers/advisors'.

The interview procedures employed within the four blocks were broadly similar. Appointments were made to suit the respondents, usually at the place of work of the providers and trainers, or at the homes of trainees and teachers. By agreement, all interviews were tape recorded with a guarantee of anonymity. A proportion of the teachers' interviews were carried out by telephone partly to facilitate the physical collection of data and partly because it was judged that some respondents might be more willing to talk on the telephone than be visited by a researcher in their own homes. In fact one fifth of all those teachers willing to be interviewed opted to do so only over the telephone.

The Student interviews were of a rather different nature from those of the 'professionals', having more to do with the personal benefits and satisfactions derived from attendance at classes than with an evaluation of training or indeed teachers. They were asked to give some account of the activities which typically took place in their class and to give their opinions about the qualities of good adult teachers. The major content areas were:

> Reasons for attendance; a description of a typical class; personal progress, expectations, benefits and satisfactions; possible improvements; qualities of a good teacher of adults.

Most interviews were carried out by telephone, this being the choice of many of the students who agreed to be interviewed, though some were willing to give personal interviews. The proportion of telephone to home conversations was 4 to 1. Again, all interviews were recorded.

The Monitoring Schedules

It was recognised from the outset that any observational evaluation of classroom teaching or of training courses was quite impracticable. Even had an adequate and acceptable instrument been available, the project had neither the resources nor the trained manpower for such an undertaking. It was decided that some monitoring of trainees' progress as indicated by their own self-descriptions made during and after their training courses might provide a useful indicator of change. Such reported change, brought about by the training experience, would of itself be some evaluation of the training if an imperfect one.

Four instruments were designed and used, though some modifications were made to their exact wording and the times of application in the light of experience.

(a) 'Teaching Inventory': a free response item which required trainees to list, and rank, on a three point scale of importance, their criteria of good adult teaching. The request was placed in a context of "a visit to a class in the same subject that you teach". This was filled in twice: the first no later than two weeks from the commencement of the course and the second at its finish (or the cut-off date of late March, 1981, whichever was the sooner).

(b) 'Schedule I': in effect, a sessional diary. Trainees were asked to write a short paragraph briefly outlining their thoughts and feelings following each meeting of their training course. The immediacy of their reactions was stressed. In the case of the two Counties where the residential weekend played a major part in (some of) their courses, particularly at the Stage 1 level, the schedule was modified to allow for separate responses to be made to consecutive sessions.

(c) 'Schedule II' (2 versions): this proposed a series of questions and statements to trainees seeking attitudes, motivation and evidence of professional change. Two complementary versions were applied, one within the first two weeks of the course and the second on its completion (or by March, 1981). The key words used or implied were:

7

Attitude to course; course objectives; participation; self confidence; recognition of experience; blocks to learning; expectation; anticipated change; trainer empathy to problems.

In the second version, the key words were:

Motivation for attendance; expectations met; problems experienced; challenge of ideas; anticipated change; relevance; value to teaching.

The Teaching Inventory 'list' was normally completed at the Course and collected. The first version of Schedule II was supposed to be returned by post with the questionnaire; the second version and the 'diary' (Schedule I) were meant to be brought to a final course session for collection. Rather few were, and the request for a subsequent return by post produced not many more!

SECTION 3: PROCEDURE

It would be inappropriate to give a lengthy account of the procedure employed though one or two of the more important aspects are noted here. An indication of some of the problems encountered during the active research period may be helpful in providing a context in which to read the research findings that follow.

Structure of the Service: Without intending any adverse criticism a major constraint upon the early stage of the project was the diplomacy which had to be exercised to secure *entrée* to collect the data. All the LEA Directors of Education gave permission for the project to be mounted within their Authority and for their staffs to be approached and their help sought. As a first step it was necessary to determine and comprehend four separate organisational structures. Subsequently, responsible staff within each structure, and at every level, had to be identified. Each had to be acquainted with the aims, purposes and demands of the project and more critically, their agreement and co-operation secured before any contact could be made with personnel at a more junior level. Thus Adult Education Officers had to be approached before meeting with trainers, Centre Heads before teachers and so on; all had to be contacted, sometimes by telephone, most often directly. It was fully appreciated that this was the only and proper procedure to adopt and the resultant goodwill and co-operation that it engendered were of considerable value. The process took a great deal longer to achieve than was originally anticipated, and valuable time and energy were lost in consequence,

Attitudes towards the research: The vast majority of LEA personnel, both full and part-time, were more than willing to give time, thought and energy to the demands made upon them by the project. Some in particular were exceedingly generous and were ever ready to help. A small minority, however, questioned the whole *raison d'être* of the research. Where these people were involved in training courses it was less than helpful since some held the *entrée* to trainees on these courses. Though it should be emphasised that such contrary voices were few they did not ease the establishment of good relationships with others in the field nor aid the collection of data.

Data collection: Within two or three of the blocks there were some problems involving the actual collection of data. In 'Providers' (Block 1) the statistical data centrally available about part-time teachers and indeed County training activities, were rather sparse. There was no common or consistent method of costing or recording expenditure on training courses, and training budgets of the previous few years were not as readily available as might have been hoped. In 'Trainers' (Block 2) some trainers had difficulty in making sufficient time available for the various demands made upon them by the project, though the vast majority were most willing to help. More serious was the discovery in Block 3 that though the majority of trainees in training were quite anxious to help, the project requirements placed too great a demand upon them. They were in the main quite unable to complete the monitoring instruments left with them, largely because of the other pressures of their course and their own class teaching. In 'Teachers', (Block 4) it transpired that many untrained teachers appeared to believe that they had little or nothing to offer to a consideration of training because they themselves were untrained. Although the documents sent to them tried to indicate the reverse, it must be assumed that a substantial number did not respond to the questionnaire, partly because of this belief and partly because some of the questions may have appeared threatening to them. There certainly were a number of untrained teachers who completed the questionnaire and returned it yet refused to be interviewed, and of these a few stated that they believed they had no competence to discuss the training of adult teachers. In the Teachers' block (Block 4) there was also the over-riding problem of identifying the total population of teachers within the four counties. Since there were no complete lists of part-time teachers, some certainly received two or more questionnaires where they taught in several Centres and there may also have been a residual who were not reached at all. An indication of the data collection problem associated with 'Students' (Block 5) is given in Appendix 1.

Response patterns: It is by no means a novel finding that interviewees tend to give those responses which they believe interviewers wish to hear. As far as can be judged this effect was marginal but there were instances where it was evident. Rather more commonly noticed was the strong cohesiveness which existed within adult groups and with their leader. The friendship/bond which was universal between students and their class teachers was strong and highly protective. It must be recognised that this may well have inhibited some of the critical appraisal of learning and teaching that might have been hoped for, particularly from training courses. In addition it may have led some trainees to 'echo' their trainers' attitudes and opinions rather than consider and report their own.

Timing of the project: In terms of the breadth of coverage of the training field it cannot be denied that the project suffered from the economic climate current during the period of data collection. Feelings of general depression and lack of morale were apparent at all levels within the service. The training course provision of most counties was less then previous years, Adult Education Centres had been shut and class provision reduced. Fewer teachers were coming forward for training and not a few apparently doubted the value of undertaking training with the perceived decrease in the likelihood of teaching opportunities. Under these conditions the information gathered, and commented upon, is from a rather depressed community and does not reflect the beliefs and enthusiasm more usually associated with Adult Education.

It may be noted as a footnote to this section on procedure that the statistical analyses of the descriptive data obtained from both Trainees and Teachers were carried out by computer programme using SPSS and that practically all the taped interview material was transcribed verbatim for ease of handling in the subsequent qualitative analyses.

In summary, the original design of the project was intended to evaluate the effects of the training of the part-time teachers of adults, to attempt a description of the teaching personnel of the Adult Education Service and to examine their attitudes and opinions. Both the process and the outcome of training were to be studied. Experienced problems of data collection led

9

to a redefinition of the quantitative/qualitative balance to an all qualitative approach with subsidiary statistics, though using the original design framework. Set out as five 'blocks', Providers, Trainers, Trainees, Teachers and Adult Students were separately surveyed by interview and except for 'students' also by questionnaire. Allowing for the inevitable set of practical problems that such an endeavour produces, a set of complementary and overlapping information on training and teaching was produced, covering many of the important aspects of the training field. This wealth of information was subsequently analysed and reported.

CHAPTER 2

The Provision of Training

This chapter describes the training provision of the part-time teacher of adults from a national viewpoint and from the perspectives of local authorities, individual institutions and specialist organisations who are responsible for the provision of training. The first section considers the current national training scene within England and Wales; the second section sets down a brief account of the history of one such training scheme — the East Midlands Region. The remaining three sections look in turn at the major providers of adult teacher training: the Local Education Authorities, the Responsible Bodies (the Universities and the Workers Education Association,) and the Specialist Subject Training Associations/Organisations. In the case of the LEAs and the Responsible Bodies only East Midland institutions are described. The majority of Specialist Training Agencies are national bodies although a proportion of them have active training interests in the East Midland region.

SECTION 1: A REVIEW OF TRAINING OF PART-TIME TUTORS IN ENGLAND AND WALES (1981)

The purpose of this section is to place the research findings within the overall national contexts. All ten Regional Advisory Councils, together with selected Local Authority Officers and Heads of Adult Centres, and representatives of Responsible Bodies and Voluntary Associations generously provided the necessary information.

Schemes

Although the training of part-time teachers in adult education was well established in some areas of England and Wales, interest quickened in 1978 following the report of the Advisory Committee on the Supply and Training of Teachers on the Training of Adult Education and Part-time Further Education Teachers.

The training schemes applied by most local education authorities followed the guidelines suggested by Regional Advisory Councils which formed models for or were based upon the recommendations of ACSTT. These schemes usually offered three stages: Stage 1 of about 36-40 hours, Stage 2 of about 100 hours and Stage 3 of about 500 hours including supervised practice and seminars. Occasionally introductory courses of eight hours were also provided. Stages 2 and 3 were often offered as a series of modules. Some local education authorities preferred to follow the syllabus of the City and Guilds of London Institute, Course 730 and in one Region and in many areas it virtually replaced Stage 2. Other areas offered combinations of RAC-suggested courses and the C & G Course 730. In one area a pilot scheme was in existence, using City and Guilds Course 942 (the Certificate in the Teaching of Adults) which consisted of a common core, plus options in specialist subjects and for specialist groups such as teachers of the physically handicapped.

Schemes for part-time tutors connected with Responsible Bodies and Voluntary Associations often had specialised objectives which took into account the specific traditions and mores of the body or association in question. Some of their training provision, like that of some LEAs dated back to the 1960s or even earlier, as was the case of the University of Oxford Extra-Mural Department's residential course for tutors. On the whole the voluntary bodies and associations seemed to prefer one-day courses, usually run as 'workshops', although some, as for example the National Federation of Women's Institutes, provided courses of a slightly more substantial nature. In some areas part-time tutors teaching for voluntary bodies could enrol on courses provided by the LEA, but in other areas the LEA courses were already over-subscribed or the fee charges were unattractive. Nevertheless, as some part-time tutors taught groups of students in both the LEA and the voluntary sector, there was some degree of cross-fertilisation of pedagogic ideas.

Provision

There was in mid-1981, considerable variation in provision between and within, Regional Advisory Council areas. In nearly all regions the guidelines for Stage 1 courses were agreed by the RAC and in a few regions there was a consistent pattern of provision at this level by individual Local Authorities. However, in most regions there were some authorities that were not offering Stage 1 courses at all. Fewer RACs had agreed Stage 2 guidelines and the pattern of provision by individual authorities varied considerably. It was about the nature of Stage 3 courses and their validation that the differences were most marked. For example, some Regions appeared to be adopting a system in which Stage 3 was equivalent to a Certificate in Education (Further Education) course whilst others were contemplating a special arrangement with universities to validate a new Certificate in Education (Adult Education). In the event only two regions have settled for a course at this level. The actual provision of Stage 3 courses was, therefore, very limited and in mid-1981 only one course was operating in England and Wales.

Curriculum and syllabus objectives

In one Region, the major objectives set out for trainers included:
— giving teachers as much practical experience of as wide a range of interactive and didactic methods as is practical and appropriate in the time available;
— devising ways in which the content and method of the modules could be scrutinised and evaluated by teachers. . . and to provide the necessary encouragement for teachers to apply the same measures to their own work;
— seeking to maximise opportunities for teachers to teach and to learn from each other. . . and . . . where in a supportive group atmosphere, teachers share insights into, and understanding of, each other's work;
— arranging appropriate tutor-supervised classroom teaching linked to the basic module and also encouraging teachers to visit and assess each other after each module.

In another Region, the guidelines tended to be more specific; for example, thirteen methods were listed under the title: 'Teaching Methods with Adult Students'. This was however more a question of emphasis, and the basic approach to adult education in both the guidelines quoted was the same. In another Region, the impression was that the basic philosophy emerged from practice in Further Education Colleges rather than from Adult Education experience. Such differing emphases resulted in varying approaches to methods of training, particularly in recommendations about the balance between the student-centred and the subject-oriented approach. Most guidelines wanted teachers to diversify teaching methods, to use learning and teaching aids selectively, and to recognise the strengths and weaknesses of interactive modes of learning and other forms of learning experiences. It was clear that the guidelines issued by the majority of RACs and the consequent curricula and syllabuses were thoughtful documents; if there were dangers they lay in the execution. This was particularly the case in trainers' desire to meet students' 'needs' which resulted in an unwillingness to confront students with material "which they cannot readily see as having immediate bearing on their current practice".

Assessment and certification

In general, part-time adult tutors who undergo training are assessed on the evidence of their practice on the job and their course work; there is evidence that some course teams attempted to involve students in the overall assessment process so that this became the norm. There were many approaches to assessment and little proof that one is more effective or efficient than another. Arrangements for certification differ between the regions. Satisfactory completion of Stage 1 led to certification either by RACs, LEAs or both jointly; Stage 2 by RACs, though in conjunction with LEAs in a few cases; and Stage 3 by validating bodies. Only when Stage 3 is a Certificate in Education (FE) course will the certification be nationally recognised. Since a C & G Course 730 award is so recognised, many area providers saw an advantage in encouraging part-time tutors to go forward from Stage 1 to C & G Course 730. We were informed that the 'Certificate in the Teaching of Adults' (C & G Course 942), as an adult education oriented course, has added attractions for those specialising in adult education. The pattern of certification is clearly not fully established or even defined throughout England or Wales.

Training the trainers

To date, most of the training of part-time tutors has been in the hands of experienced adult educators, such as Local Authority Advisers, Adult Education Centre Heads and University Tutors. As most of the provision in England and Wales is at Stage 1 or its equivalent, the quality of the trainers has proved satisfactory, but all our evidence suggested concern for the future, particularly for Stages 2 and 3. Financial stringency has led to a fall in the number of Local Education Authority advisers; because of Centre self-financing schemes, Centre Heads were hard pressed to find time for training, either for themselves or for would-be part-time tutors; and pressures on University staffs were increasing. It was suggested from nearly all sources of information that the provision of training for trainers was insufficient to maintain the present quality of staff and inadequate to cope with any possible expansion of training of part-time tutors.

One area reported that, by devising a system of 'support tutors' for trainees, and by establishing that training was as an important part of a Centre Head's duties, the quality and quantity of trainers was being maintained; nevertheless, even in this case, it was reported that it was desirable to improve the quality of trainers as a whole.

Demand for courses

In England and Wales overall, adult education student enrolments had fallen since 1978/79 although one area reported an increase in enrolments of 2% in 1980/81. It follows that a fall in the number of part-time teachers would be expected and perhaps, a fall in the number offering themselves for training. The position was complicated in that in some areas the fall in the total numbers of part-time teachers had been accompanied by a fall in the proportion of untrained teachers; in other areas the decrease in the total number of teachers had resulted in a marked increase in the numbers willing to be trained. In a few areas, 'to be trained' was an explicit condition of employment; in many more training was actively encouraged. As an example, in one Region the numbers attending part-time teachers' courses reached a peak in 1974/75. In that year, about four times as many part-time teachers were being trained compared with 1967/68, and twice as many when compared with 1978/80. Within that Region, between 1979/80 and 1980/81, in some areas the number of part-time teachers on courses increased by up to 54% whilst in other areas the numbers fell by between one-half and two-thirds; the total number in training remained about the same.

If we change the base date from 1974/75 to the dates when some Regional Councils implemented the Advisory Committee's recommendations then most of the evidence suggested that current demand for training was buoyant. We estimate about 4000 serving part-time adult education teachers were being trained in the period 1980/81 in England and Wales to at least Stage 1. An unknown number attended short courses; most proceed to a Stage 2 course. There was a general impression that between 10 and 20 per cent of those taking Stage 2 had expressed *a desire* to take the Stage 3 section qualifying for a Certificate in Education, but in the view of one area with experience of parallel courses some three years ago, only about five per cent would *actually* go forward beyond Stage 2.

Though the general view was one of cautious optimism so far as the provision and the demand for training was concerned, there was one Region which registered "pessimism". Most Regions pointed to differences between areas within their Region but, nonetheless, claimed that the demand for training had proved surprisingly high and for that reason morale was usually good. Indeed, in some areas there were teachers waiting for vacancies on courses. Though the results of the Advisory Committee's recommendations seemed to point towards the establishment of a national system of training opportunities for part-time teachers, local responses in the context of financial stringencies were so varied that so far as any particular teacher was concerned, training possibilities depended upon where he or she lived.

Distribution of courses

Table 1 shows the distribution of courses provided for both teachers and trainers in the nine English RAC Regions. They derive from a 1981 DES national Survey on 'The Provision of Training for part-time Teachers in Further Education in Relation to the Recommendations of the Second Report of the Advisory Committee on the Supply and Training of Teachers' (FE Sub Committee).

The regions are:

North	— N	East Anglia	— EA
Yorkshire & Humberside	— YHCFE	London & Home Counties	— LHC
North West	— NW	South West	— SW
East Midlands	— EM	South	— S
West Midlands	— WM		

Table 1: Table Showing the Distribution of Courses Provided in the 9 RAC Regions

Course Type	Region	1980-81 Courses	1980-81 Trainees	PRE 1980-81 Courses	PRE 1980-81 Trainees	Contact Hours excluding TP	Remarks
Stage 1	N	3	50	4	80	36	
	YHCFE	13	150	204	5,737	36-40	
	NW	70	1,556	"many"	?	40+	Some earlier courses unrecorded
	EM	10	120	80	1,500	36 — 40	
	EA	12	214	13	239	36+	
	LHC	23+	459+	65	1,438	30 — 40	
	S	9	133	22	380	36	
	SW	4	60	8+	160+	35 — 36	
Stage 2	YHCFE	4	40	?	?		Some early Stage 2 unrecorded
	NW	10	150	10+	150+	120	
	EM	4	60	44	622	70 — 100+	
	EA	5	75			70 — 100	
	LHC	1	15	2+			
	SW	5	75				
	S				60+	100	
Stage 3	EM	1	9	3	30	Orig. 300 Now 370+	
CGLI 730/942 linked to scheme	EM	6	86	38	673	120	
	EA	2	30			120	
	LHC	16+	260+	52	877	120	
	S	5	70	?3	?55	120	
	SW						
Total ACSTT follow-up		204+	3,612+	550+	12,001		
CGLI 730 (1979/80) course *not* linked to ACSTT II schemes		212	416				
Total of all modes		416+	4,028+				

15

Table 1: (Continued)

Course type	Region	1980—81		PRE 1980—81		Contact hours excluding TP	Remarks
		Courses	Trainees	Courses	Trainees		
	YHCFE	1		1	?	?	Plus unrecorded earlier work.
Trainers	NW	1	19	5	75	1 x 20;	4 — 5 days residential
	EM	1	8	4	100	1 x 20;	
	EA	1	24	1	25	4 x 100 — 150	
	LHC	1	39			c 80	
						100	
	YHCFE						No precise information but activity
Supervisors	NW	1	25	1+	25+	6	3 regional one-day; many local
	EM						
	LHC	some					
	SW			?8+	?120+	5 — 18	
Induction	YHCFE						Some local activity
	NW						Some local activity
	EM						Many local courses
	LHC						
	EA	?1	?15	?6+	?120+		
	WM					?12	Some local activity
Bridging							Few specific courses being held; growing demand from QTs to join normal courses under schemes.
	N						
Subject Refresher	YHCFE	1	30	2	60	16 — 18	Details not available but many held
	NW						
	EM						
	LHC						
	SW						
	S	14+	250+	many	?	1 day upwards	

The survey also provided two distribution maps of ACSTT II schemes, LEA provision, etc. Some of this information is presented as a single distribution map, Figure 4.

    — of regions, showing types of ACSTT II schemes in being or in preparation, substantial trainers' courses, University Departments closely involved in RAC schemes and/or providing advanced courses for FE personnel, and other HE Institutions similarly involved

    — of LEA 'areas', showing ACSTT II

Ⓣ Substantial trainers' course(s) held	⊖ Stage 1 courses
◬ University offers advanced course(s) in AE/FE	⊞ Stage 1 and 2 courses
▲ University ditto and active in RAC scheme	③ Stage 3 courses
▲ HFE Institution active in RAC scheme	

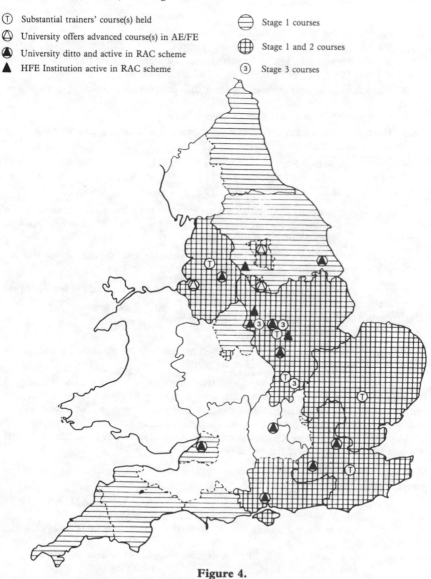

Figure 4.

17

The same survey reported the arrangments made under the regional schemes. A summary of this information is given here:

1. The RAC has adopted a scheme and there is some training provision, however small or limited:
   (a) Across the whole of FE at least in principle: 4 of 9 regions (N, YHCFE, NW, S).
   (b) For general adult education only: 3 of 9 regions (EM, EA, LHC).
   (c) In process of converting scheme from (b) to (a): 1 of 9 regions (EM).

2. RAC is developing a scheme:
   1 of 9 regions (SW).

3. RAC has no scheme and is taking no current action:
   1 of 9 regions (WM)

4. All or a majority of LEAs in region participate in Scheme at least to Stage 1:
   6 of 9 regions (YHCFE, NW, EM, EA, LHC, S).

5. Individual LEAs in regions without a scheme offering provision equating to Stage 1 or above:
   Wolverhampton, Staffordshire, Dorset, Avon, Cornwall, Devon.

6. LEAs thought to have made *NO* specific provision to at least Stage 1, nor to do so in co-operation with others, by regions:

N	5 of 9	EM	0 of 5	LHC	0 of 27
YHCFE	0 of 11	WM	9 of 11	S	2 of 5
NW	2 of 17	EA	0 of 5	SW	3 of 7

7. Scheme (whether general or AE only) is working or being planned in the context of a regional analysis (current or relatively recent) of numbers and characteristics of teachers employed, and of their training needs:

   4 of 9 regions (EM, EA, S, SW). In addition some individual LEAs elsewhere are gathering or have gathered such information for their own areas.

8. The scheme currently takes account of the training needs of all kinds of FE Staff (not only or mainly AE):
   (a) In principle: 4 of 9 regions (N, YHCFE, NW, S).
   (c) In *substantial* practice: 0 of 9 regions.

9. The scheme provides specifically for part-time teachers' characteristics and access through the organisation of Stage 3 or its planning:

   This is the case for all 3 course locations/institutions (all in EM region) where Stage 3 courses have been held so far, and is intended in the region (NW) which is closest to making provision. Some existing or draft schemes do not appear to take account of this requirement and seem to confuse the differing clientèles and conditions of accessibility appropriate for part-time teachers with those properly accepted for full-time staff catered for under the First Report of ACSTT (FE).

10. The schemes involves one or more of the following organisational features at one or more stages:

    (a) Regional planning of provision: 5 of 9 regions (YHCFE, NW, EM, EA, LHC).
    (b) Regional moderation: 5 of 9 regions (YHCFE, NW, EM, EA, LHC).
    (c) Built-in links to validation for actual/potential Stage 3: 3 of 9 regions (YHCFE, NW, EM)
    (d) Permanent structures to facilitate meetings, co-operation and development of trainers: 6 of 9 regions (YHCFE, NW, EM, EA, LHC, S).

11. The scheme has been or is supported by substantial trainers' courses:

    4 of 9 regions (NW, EM, EA, LHC).

12. The scheme benefits from productive links with appropriately experienced staff in universities/public Sector HE.

    6 of 9 regions (NW, YHCFE, EM, EA (from neighbouring region), LHC, S).

SECTION 2: THE EAST MIDLANDS REGIONAL SCHEME OF TRAINING

In order to set the current research project in context, some mention needs to be made of the background of the tutor training scheme in the East Midlands Region. It is not intended to be in any sense an exhaustive account and indeed only records the more significant developments. Nevertheless, it is hoped that these paragraphs will provide an appropriate historical orientation.

The concept of training for part-time teachers of adults is not new and the schemes we have today have been gradually evolving during the last thirty years. Since the 1950s short courses and conferences have been organised by a number of LEAs. The traditional pattern of many of these early initiatives often consisted of an address by the Director of Education, a briefing on administrative procedures, a set lecture by a visiting speaker and discussions in subject groups. These meetings were popular and useful in that they brought teachers together and provided them with a chance to exchange ideas and experience. They were limited in both content and purpose.

The more professional present day pattern took its origin from courses conducted by Manchester University for LEA institutions in its region. Experiments and pilot courses of the kind and substance now known through the second ACSTT(FE) report started in the West Riding of Yorkshire in 1962. The resulting scheme was adopted by the rest of Yorkshire three years later and officially instituted by the Yorkshire Regional Advisory Council for Further Education in 1966.

During this period members of Her Majesty's Inspectorate came to play an increasingly significant role in training. Concern to develop training activities spread in the Inspectorate from 1961 and a number of their papers (OFE memos) were widely circulated. In connection with these national initiatives, a national survey of training for adult educators by Responsible Bodies was conducted in 1963-64 and the subsequent report particularly referred to RB involvement with LEA training. The findings were widely circulated and training came to play a more important part in the Department of Education and Science Salisbury courses for full-time adult education staff. The national survey also led to significant negotiations with Professor Harold Wiltshire, then Professor of Adult Education at the University of Nottingham, and there was a continuing link between these national activities and those of the Nottingham University Seminar for Adult Educators which was also working on ways of developing tutor training.

The late sixties were an expansionist period in adult education. Full-time staff were optimistic and many people were excited about being involved in the professional development of adult educators. A number of key developments took place during these years which helped create an ethos for training, which in turn provided part of the impetus for what was to occur in the East Midlands. Some of the important training initiatives that took place between 1965-1970 were as follows:-

1965 The University of Nottingham offered the Diploma in Adult Education and became increasingly involved in developing adult education as a subject.

1966 The National Institute of Adult Education Report on 'Recruitment and Training' was published.

1968 The BBC's first adult education training programme, Teaching Adults, was broadcast (April — June). This was accompanied by the publication 'Teaching on Equal Terms' (BBC 1969).

1968 An Inspectorate survey of LEA adult education training was conducted. This was intended as a national exercise but its intensity varied greatly in different parts of the country. As a result the findings were never fully collated or published nationally. However, the fact that the survey was carried out raised the level of consciousness in the field and new developments were sparked off.

1969 The University of Nottingham established the Certificate in Adult Teaching Course. This was provided in conjunction with Leicestershire LEA for teachers of design-based subjects.

1970 A Department of Education Short Course which became known as the Cambridge Conference took place. Its proceedings were published under the title 'Explorations in Adult Learning and Training for Adult Education'. The most active trainers from the East Midlands were either there or at least involved through correspondence.

1970 The Nottinghamshire LEA organised a short 'Training the Trainers' course as soon as 'Explorations' became available.

From this milieu the East Midlands Regional Scheme of Training evolved.

A number of other important factors contributed to the development of the scheme from the early days. One was a Regional Advisory Council Consultative Committee for Adult Education, in which the Universities and the LEAs were equally involved and used to working and co-operating with each other. Another was a regional adult education seminar for full-time staff which had been meeting regularly to study various aspects of adult education. This seminar was originally sponsored by Nottingham University but later was transformed into the East Midlands Regional Institute for Adult Education. A third was a Regional Advisory Council Officer who was deeply interested in adult education developments. He had not been long in the post and was in the process of defining his areas of responsibility. His comments more clearly illustrate the point:

> I think what you need is somebody prepared to keep it going. If I had been inundated with work at that time, maybe some of this wouldn't have happened. That is just a fact. If somebody has a bit of time it's easier. At that time I'd just arrived and hadn't been given a clear remit. I just happened to tackle teacher training in Further Education and Adult Education.

In addition, the northern fringes of the East Midlands Region border on to South Yorkshire, which by now had a fully fledged scheme of courses for its part-time staff. The enthusiasm generated in Yorkshire sparked off a demand for training among East Midlands tutors.

In 1969 the East Midlands Seminar for Adult Education had established a Working Party of adult educators which was given the task of examining regional training provision. Also in the same year, the Regional Advisory Council was pressed to interest itself in training and this became the policy of its Consultative Committee on Adult Education. Subsequently, the Consultative Committee established a working group to look at training. Membership of both working parties was the same and it was decided to merge them into a single body under the Regional Advisory Council. How the embryonic scheme emerged from the work of this group is succinctly described by one of its leading architects:

It (the newly established group) engaged itself in a lengthy process of curriculum development and the study of pilot work on the ground. When it finally reported to its parent Regional Advisory Council Committee its report was accepted there and, eventually, by the Regional Advisory Council itself, so that it carried the whole regional weight of representative, administrative and professional approval. This in turn, meant that Authorities felt at least justified and probably under pressure to allocate resources to the work according to their means, but doubtless much more substantially than they would have done without such an imprimatur. An equally important factor was that the working group who had done the thinking, planning and pioneer work, had in that process turned themselves into a truly regional training team, working across institutional and Authority boundaries, but serving them all.

The Advisory Council accepted the scheme in 1971 and from that stage, development accelerated considerably. (See Appendix 3). In essence the proposal provided for training to take place in three stages. Stage 1 was to be provided and assessed by LEAs themselves but according to the RAC recommendations. It was felt that 36 hours of tuition would be a minimum and on completion of the course, trainees would be given an LEA Stage 1 Certificate. It was, therefore, intended to be localised, brief and to concentrate on basic teaching techniques.

A number of pilot courses at this level were held in Nottinghamshire, Derbyshire, Leicestershire and Lincolnshire and an important feature of this build-up was the readiness of individuals and authorities to make training resources available, but at a pace commensurate with a concern for maintaining standards. It was during this early phase of the scheme that those involved learned one of their most important lessons.

That as soon as training at this level was provided demand for it and for more advanced work rose dramatically. (1)

They resisted the clamour for a more rapid provision of courses until they felt they had the confidence, expertise, and resources to tackle the next stage. The general pressure of demand continued and eventually this led to the introduction of pilot courses at Stage 2 level.

Stage 2 courses required at least 60 hours of course attendance and a further 30 hours' supervised teaching practice. Teaching skills were to be developed to a greater extent than on Stage 1 and a more thorough treatment of content was thought possible. The problem with this level was to work out the means of assessing the course which, although provided by LEAs, led to a Regional Advisory Council Certificate. To deal with this, the Regional Advisory Council Consultative Committee substituted for the original pioneering Working Party an Assessment of Training Sub-Committee, whose terms of reference were defined as relating almost exclusively to Stage 2. The main purpose of the Committee was to consider applications for Stage 2 courses and to appoint moderators to monitor their planning and subsequent progress.

The problems and difficulties of learning how to moderate courses across the region were successfully overcome. Not only did the number of Stage 2 courses continue to rise but there was also an insistent, albeit minority, demand for some form of post Stage 2 qualification. To estimate this the Assessment of Training Sub-Committee conducted a survey of holders of Stage 1 and Stage 2 Certificates in 1974 and the replies were encouraging enough to warrant

---

(1) K.T. Elsdon "The East Midlands Scheme", in *Adult Education*, Vol. 46, No. 4. p.243.

establishing a pilot course which would eventually become Stage 3 of the scheme. Following negotiations with Nottingham University, this finally emerged as their Certificate in Adult Teaching. The first part-time course was introduced in conjunction with Derbyshire LEA in 1975 and three years later the same course was offered in Nottinghamshire. The University of Leicester currently provides an equivalent course for Northamptonshire LEA. Stage 3 was a much larger undertaking, requiring 350+ hours of contact time with 100 hours of supervised teaching practice. Academic standards, content and work demands were much higher than on Stage 2. The course was to be validated by the appropriate University, but teaching and organising shared by joint University/LEA course teams.

Throughout the early years of the scheme, the main bottleneck was the shortage both of skilled trainers and supervisory staff at centre level. Resources of trained staff from the original group soon proved insufficient; consequently a number of 'Training the Trainers' courses were established to cope with the problem. The Department of Education and Science' national advanced course for trainers, which was held in Nottingham in 1972, was a a large scale attempt to assist and a number of adult educators from the region made use of the opportunity. The next major development of this kind was the Area Training Organisation/Department of Education and Science provision for trainers; courses of this nature were held annually in the East Midlands between 1972 and 1974. Since then, no other regional initiatives have been taken for trainers, although one LEA organised its own course during 1980-81.

These early Training the Trainers courses were crucial in helping develop a number of enthusiastic individuals into a regional training team which formed the working core and administrative base of the scheme, at both regional and LEA levels. Members of the team learned to operate across boundaries by means of mutual assistance and course moderation. Trainers' courses also fostered the active co-operation of LEAs, Universities and eventually some Polytechnics on an equal and co-operative basis.

The issue of training local staff to supervise their part-time staff was not so easy to resolve. Spasmodic attempts were made by a few LEAs to provide short courses, but they were not on a large enough scale and the problem left a major gap in the scheme. Little was done until 1977 when the Consultative Committee for Adult Education set up a Working Party to examine the 'Role and Training of the Part-time Head of Centre'. The interim report was published in 1978, but has not resulted in further action.

It is worth noting, that whilst the Yorkshire Regional Advisory Council (later Yorkshire and Humberside) was the originator of the regional training concept, the East Midlands Advisory Council, once started, forged ahead very rapidly indeed and quickly overtook its northern neighbour. This helped to create a momentum which was unique in the country. Yet the scheme was not established without many obstacles and problems, as one of those who were closely involved has noted elsewhere:

> There were individual and inter-authority disagreements and tensions; the occasional risk of dulling initiative by having too much committee talk and structure, the trainers' course that lost its staff by a chapter of accidents, went to pieces and left a heritage of local weaknesses; the occasional tendency to neglect subject expertise and development for professional growth; the effects of economic stringency on tutors in training who suddenly found themselves unemployed and could not even obtain teaching practice. And many more [1].

---

[1] K.T. Elsdon, "Some Possibilities of Regional Co-operation in Adult Education; unpublished paper for *DES Course N88*, 11-14 July 1977 p5.

The problems were temporary and do not appear to have affected the principle of regional co-operation, for within a short period of four years, a three stage training scheme had been thought through and implemented.

The early creative phase of the Scheme, between 1971-75 was followed by a period of maintenance, adaptation and review. Between 1975 and 1980, few major initiatives were taken; LEAs continued to develop and provide Stage 1 and Stage 2 courses, and demand remained constant for a third level course. During this phase, one of the problems that people became aware of was the danger of the scheme ossifying, and the Assessment of Training Sub-Committee constantly encouraged and supported experiments and new approaches which would maintain the spirit, impetus and change of the early years. For instance as one of the RAC officers notes:

> There have been experiments with Stage 2 amongst the more committed authorities that have moved things along or away from the original model, and these have been alliances with the City and Guilds 730 course which have changed the face of things . . . Experimentation and adaptation have occurred. It just isn't recorded, or sufficiently understood and known.

Valuable insights were gained into the operation of Stage 2 courses from a detailed analysis of 22 moderators reports which was published in 1977.

Because of the lack of regional co-ordination of Stage 1 work, the same process was not developed for the basic courses. The same RAC Officer's comments:

> We probably know all too little about Stage 1 courses. From hearsay, one guesses some of these are a bit more haphazard then they were in the early days and at least seen by some as not providing the right material for feeding into Stage 2. But we know all too little about that.

The pace of change in adult education generally and training in particular began to accelerate in the late 1970s. The need for a critical review of the regional scheme in the light of what was happening was becoming increasingly recognised once the Further Education Sub-Committee of the Advisory Council for the Supply and Training of Teachers published its recommendations on the training of full and part-time staff in adult and further education, (ACSTT 1978). Though not officially adopted by the Department of Education and Science, the Report soon gained wide acceptance as the basis of local and regional Training Schemes. Even though it was to a great extent based upon the East Midlands model, it acted as a spur to thinking about future developments in the region. (See Appendix 4). Other factors which prompted the review were the newly validated arrangements for the training of full-time Further Education teachers and the scale of reductions in expenditure on Adult Education. A sub-group of the Assessment of Training Committee was asked to initiate the work and a draft report was presented in 1980. This is currently being discussed.

The numerical achievements of the scheme in the East Midlands region between 1971 and 1981 are as follows:-

Table 2: East Midland Courses for Part-Time Teachers (1)

	Courses Provided	Trainees
Stage 1	90	1,620
Stage 2	48	682
Stage 3	4	39
City & Guilds +		
Stage 2	44	759

Courses for Trainers

	Courses Provided	Trainers
	5	108

SECTION 3: THE LOCAL EDUCATION AUTHORITIES

The preceding section on the evolution of the Regional Scheme described the development of current policy, the influences which shaped it and its present form. What emerges is a picture of a region with a longstanding commitment to training teachers in adult education and a now well-established scheme for this. This section concentrates on current training practice and policy in the region, primarily at the provision of Stage 1 and 2 courses since they constitute the major part of the present effort in the four counties. It looks at the constraints on this provision, and alternative forms of training that LEAs would like to be able to provide. Whilst the terms 'policy' and 'practice' have been used, it was not always easy to decide which was being described, especially as 'policy' is not always clearly formulated and available. Although looking at 'practice' implies some view of 'policy', in the current climate of cutbacks this is more likely to represent a much reduced form of their policy than LEAs would ideally like to see.

The organisation of Adult Education and training in the East Midlands

Adult Education is organised differently in each county, and these differences affect the organisation of training. In one county Adult Education is based on the Further Education Colleges and each college has a department responsible for adult education. In the other three counties, adult education is provided through a network of adult education centres, often with part-time Centre Heads, grouped under 'tutors' or 'organisers' responsible for all the centres within a particular area. In one of these counties some, and in another most adult education is provided through community schools or colleges.

These differences are to some extent reflected in the provision of training. In one county the initiative for training comes from the Further Education Colleges. If an adult education department wishes to put on a training course the college applies to the appropriate education officer who administers the training budget and who ensures that the final spread of courses gives as many people as possible in the county an opportunity to train. In another, the area tutors are responsible for providing Stage 1 training for anyone who needs it in their

---

(1) Source: The 1981 DES national Survey on 'The Provision of Training for part-time Teachers in Further Education in Relation to the Recommendations of the Second Report of the Advisory Committee on the Supply and Training of Teachers (FE Sub-Committee).

area; if demand is low they may offer a course in conjunction with another area tutor. Stage 2 courses are at present offered at County level through FE colleges. In the remaining two counties the initiative for training comes from higher up in the hierarchy of the authority. In one of them, training is the responsibility of two Area FE Organisers who have a considerable degree of autonomy as to how they spend the money allocated. The other puts the responsibility in the hands of a training department for Adult Education. Despite these differences throughout the region, Stage 1 courses are staffed by adult educators who have developed a training role, rather than by teacher trainers from Universities and Colleges of Higher Education. Where courses are offered in FE colleges, other college staff may become involved. There is a strong feeling amongst LEA Officers that trainers should have first-hand experience of the world in which part-time teachers have to work.

> We see it as important that these part-time teachers are trained by people who know what goes on in the Centres.

> They have to have the credibility in the eyes of their students that they know what they are doing. . . We need people who are alert to the changing circumstances of the service who themselves are prepared to keep up to date with what's going on.

> We have a small nucleus of people who we consider are able to do the training thing, and we tried to increase that number by putting on the Training the Trainers course. By and large the main criterion we use, well we need somebody who's got the AE ethos here (points to heart).

Integration of Adult Education training with other training available

In addition to the training considered in this report, there are two other main types of similar work. One is specialist training provided by bodies outside the LEAs. The other is of a more general kind designed to cover the needs of staff employed in both the Further Education Colleges and the Youth Service.

Clearly there is a danger that there could be a great deal of overlap and duplication of effort and resources and in many instances this tends to occur. Co-ordination of LEA training work with subject specialist organisations has been limited. Some of their qualifications (e.g. coaching certificates) carry exemption from Stage 1 and there have been arrangments to make the regional scheme's courses an integral part of the training programme of a few subject organisations. These have not been consolidated and the links between LEAs and subject bodies remain tenuous and unstructured. All LEA officers interviewed consider that there is a considerable potential for further co-operation and integration if the common ground between the forms of training can be identified and the difficulties of organisation can be overcome.

Of the general training offered by other bodies, City and Guilds is by far the most widespread. In the counties surveyed, holders of the City and Guilds 730 award who wish to go on to Stage 3, are rated equivalent to those who have a Stage 2 Certificate. Two counties have chosen to offer Stage 2 in conjunction with City and Guilds 730, which gives teachers a nationally recognised teaching award for further education, together with a course having a particular emphasis on adult education. One LEA representative noted that it will help improve the professional status of part-time teachers.

> If the Stage 2 course content is such that it overlaps with something like City and Guilds, I see no reason at all why the teacher shouldn't go on to take that certificate if it improves their credibility in the eyes of other people.

Whilst recognising the advantage of a national award, the other counties had rejected this alliance. The main anxiety seemed to be that City and Guilds 730, being a course primarily for Further Education teachers does not take account of the wider variety of situations within which adult education teachers have to work. There was some fear that working to meet the requirements of this national award may limit and constrain the autonomy and flexibility of regionally organised courses. Some of the concerns about the City and Guilds course are apparent from these comments by LEA officers:

> The City and Guilds as an outside body could be making demands on us in terms of the course, which we might not be prepared to adhere to.

> I think City and Guilds works in some places and in some places it doesn't, and obviously the key factor is the staffing and their attitudes to what they perceive adult education meaning.

Despite these doubts, the City and Guilds course has changed considerably since the regional scheme was established in the early 70s. It has dropped its assessment by examination, moved some way towards a validating rather than examining role, created opportunities for exchange of ideas between course tutors and acknowledged the need for a course which is more flexible and meets the particular need of students. Nevertheless City and Guilds 730 remains a course which caters for a wide range of people. Those who teach in many different situations — in Further Education colleges, in hospitals, the forces, public service and industry — and those who want to teach in more than one kind of post-school education find it provides a good preparation. On the other hand teachers who are specialising in adult education sometimes find it less appropriate.

Adult education is closely linked with Further Education and the Youth service — in LEA structures these areas are usually the responsibility of the same officer. There has been only limited integration of training in these three services. One LEA administrator saw the possibility:

> The services have been drawn together in some senses, they are now under the two hats . . . worn by one professional, and it may well be that in the future there will be links because I think there are clear advantages in the methodology — for instance that the Youth Service use, and perhaps there have been cross influences of that kind on the sort of courses that we've run in the county, but they have been influences rather than integration.

Another thought differently:

> We had some experiments in the early seventies where we tried training youth workers and adult education teachers together. I don't think it was successful. . . There wasn't enough common ground. . . we have taken the point of view that adult education teaching is a specialised area of work and we haven't tried to really join it up with other forms of training.

Two counties do allow people teaching adults outside the authorities' adult education service to use Stage 1 and 2 courses if they wish, while the other two tend to keep Stage 1 and 2 exclusively for their own adult education teachers. Notably, the training of FE college staff has remained quite separate. Despite this lack of integration, exchange of ideas on training between these groups is recognised as beneficial, and this is made possible to some extent by the fact that some adult education trainers also work on other kinds of training. It is worth noting that moves to integrate adult education training with that of Further Education College teachers is now under way in the Regional Advisory Council.

Resources

Training opportunities are very much constrained by the resources available, and apart from one authority, training budgets seemed to be modest. No-one explained clearly how the sums allocated for training had been arrived at; they seem to have remained relatively unchanged for some time except for increases to take account of inflation. In two counties there were decreases in line with general cuts in educational expenditure. These sums did not seem to have been recently reassessed, so for those now responsible for administering the budget it is much more a question of deciding what training would be possible within the resources granted, rather than assessing training needs and budgeting to meet them. The reality of the current situation is highlighted by the following comment from one senior LEA administrator:

> On the one hand there is the professional part of you saying that training courses, or refresher courses, or one day courses for students on particular aspects of the curriculum are important and curriculum development and on-going monitoring is vital; the administrator in me says, 'yes, that's all well and good but somebody has to pay for it and we haven't got the money to do it'. In a world where everything was available, then I would want to see as many opportunities for people in the adult field to get together to swap ideas and learn of new ones, but in the real world of ever-growing financial constraints coming on we've got to cut our cloth according to the budget.

Also LEAs have to work within the limits of staff available:

> I don't think the needs for training were looked at. This was done in the County Treasury Department and we've had enough money to do what we can, with the staff resources we've got. So short of appointing new staff out of that money, there's nothing much.

Current provision

LEA officers responsible for adult education mentioned three different but related forms of training which in principle they believed should be available for part-time teachers:

(a) general training courses (Stages 1, 2 and 3 of the regional scheme)
(b) informal training and support from Centre Heads
(c) contributions to costs of attending courses other than those provided by LEAs.

(a) Stage 1, 2 and 3 Courses: All counties try to maintain provision of these courses which form the backbone of their training. In two of the four counties surveyed there is a strong expectation that all teachers employed by the county will take Stage 1. There are often people who are exempted e.g. qualified school teachers; teachers taking short courses; and people holding other kinds of teaching qualifications and pragmatically, teachers of shortage subjects. In the other two counties, training is encouraged rather than expected. In all the counties Stage 1 and 2 courses have remained within the regional scheme, and therefore have basic similarities, but there have been some changes in style and emphasis within counties, and some more experimental approaches within this basic format.

At present these courses do not have currency everywhere outside the region; they only tend to be recognised whenever there are comparable schemes. One way of overcoming this might be to have a system of national awards for part-time teachers in adult education, however, almost all the LEA officers we spoke to seriously questioned a national scheme. Whilst they felt that it might be useful in giving the certificates and adult education greater status, and indeed be appreciated more by the teachers themselves, they had serious misgivings about the loss of flexibility and the standardisation this might imply. The arguments were cogently made by two different LEA officers:

> Again I am thinking of the part-time teachers themselves, to whom a national award would be a good thing. However, if as a result of introducing such a certificate, that meant that strictures were put on the actual scheme of work to the extent that it became alienated or divorced from the real needs of the part-time teachers, then I wouldn't support it. No training is of real value unless it relates to the needs of people who are undergoing it.

> If you are an educationalist you mush look for experimentation, new ideas and new approaches. . . within any course there must be an opportunity for people to develop along routes which were not planned. . . you must not confine people within the bounds of a set syllabus or scheme of work, and say, sorry, we can't go outside that because it isn't in the scheme. These courses should be designed as educational experiences and it worries me that national awards could inhibit this approach.

Rather than standardisation of content, methods and approach (other than in a most general sense), they seemed to prefer a system enabling national recognition of regional awards. This they argued could be an inter-regional process, similar to Stage 2 moderation, ensuring that the equivalent courses would be comparable. The point that was made time and again was that the initiative should remain within the regions, an opinion best summed up by the LEA administrator who said:

> In my view the region is the right body for the award, but the currency, ought, if possible, to be a national currency, the training should be done at local level and, therefore, the answer to standardisation is it's not necessary as long as there is validation. It's validation we want not standardisation.

The problem of currency and status of the award was felt to be particularly pressing in the case of Stage 3, which demands a great deal from teachers who embark on it. Both the regional Scheme and ACSTT II stipulate that the scheme should lead to a properly validated Certificate of Education. Trainers and trainees involved appear to have met the criteria but neither of the Universities responsible for these courses has yet made arrangements for the appropriate award. Indeed at all levels of training, these are problems of transferability to courses leading to the Certificate of Education, and this may well affect motivation. This raises questions about the links between teacher training in adult education and other sectors of training.

> The regional scheme for training full-time teachers in FE will lead to a CNAA certificate which will be recognised by the DES, meaning that the teacher is then recognised as a teacher within the service, wherever he might go and wherever he might teach. This must be the ultimate objective. I think what we should be aiming for is to fit in as a part of FE and HE. I think that you ought not to be running adult education on the outside of the education service all the time, it is an integral and important part of the whole service. I regard it as part of FE . . . everybody is given an opportunity for education from 16 to 80 or 90. Therefore, you need a natural system of qualification or certification. Teachers must have this status. (LEA officer).

(b) Training and Support at Centres: All authorities expect Centre Heads to take a responsibility for supporting and helping teachers in their centres, both as a back-up for those attending training courses and in an on-going staff-development role for others. They see Centre Heads as the obvious people to take on this more informal training role because they are the only ones regularly in contact with part-time teachers. They are ready to admit that this does not always happen in the way they would like to see.

> We're unhappy to a degree about the back-up to Stage 1 and 2 courses. Now that's not to say we can necessarily do much about it, we are very poorly staffed in this county.

Three important reasons seem to contribute. Centre Heads do not always have time. It is recognised that often they have a very heavy workload, and are rather thinly spread on the ground. As one person interviewed put it:

> Perhaps the authority is to blame because it expects too much of these people.

Further there is the rather diverse nature of the Centre Head's job as manager, administrator, trainer etc. Some Centre Heads working under pressure do not manage to get beyond their clerical and managerial duties. Some authorities now make it clear to Centre Heads at interview and in their job contracts that training at centre level is part of their responsibility; however, they do not allow adequate staff-time for the purpose. In any case two of the authorities have now abolished the post. Finally, none of the LEAs seem to offer much support or training for Centre Heads themselves. One reason why some Centre Heads may prefer to concentrate on other aspects of their work may be uncertainty about how to tackle their training role.

(c) Funding Attendance on non-LEA Courses: There is a limit to resources and the full-time teacher seems to benefit at the expense of the part-timer. As one senior administrator said:

> Part-time teachers tend to be a bit under privileged in that sense owing to some reluctance to spend limited in-service training money on them.

It is the policy of some authorities to re-imburse only half the costs of attending courses and this can still mean considerable expense for staff. LEAs had helped with attendance at courses leading to Diplomas in Adult Education and M.Ed. for full-time staff and the Loughborough Design Course for part-time teachers. It seems that resources restrict these opportunities, especially in the current economic situation.

Representatives of the LEAs emphasised several areas where they saw a need for more training:

> — induction courses, including courses for qualified school teachers beginning to work in adult education
> — subject training — both to develop the teachers' knowledge of their subject, and to develop their skill in teaching it
> — on-going training for part-time teachers
> — training for trainers

Induction Courses: At present, Stage 1 acts as a form of induction course for those who take it. Some LEAs felt separate provision of shorter induction courses should be made to give all new teachers a brief introduction to work in adult education, including those exempt from Stage 1. This type of course could be planned to meet the needs of particular groups — the most often mentioned need being for some kind of 'reorientation' course for qualified school teachers entering adult education.

Subject Training: The four counties involved in the East Midlands regional scheme have placed their emphasis in training on offering general courses for teachers of all subjects. Only Leicestershire, which has remained outside the scheme, has chosen to organise training around the skills and teaching of particular subjects in adult education. The counties in the scheme say that they assume subject competence as a condition of appointment and therefore they have put little emphasis on subject training. When resources were more plentiful they organised a considerable number of weekends and day courses for teachers of particular subjects. In some areas, they have worked alongside subject training organisations, like the Keep Fit Association, who have incorporated the Stage 1 into their training programme. This is an area of training which the LEAs feel needs to be expanded — both in the updating and developing of subject knowledge, and in its teaching. They foresee considerable difficulties in the staffing of such courses — both in the expense and in finding people with a suitable combination of subject expertise and adult education experience.

> But it's not the money that's short, strangely enough, it's the trainers, suitable trainers. I mean when one thinks of the need to upgrade ladies' soft crafts in terms of design rather than just making soft toys or whatever, where do we find somebody who's going to be effectively able to train these people? We haven't got the people around in this county.

One possibility might be through closer co-operation with suitable subject—specialist organisations (a strategy adopted most extensively in Leicestershire):

> It would be highly desirable if LEAs could encourage these specialist groups with finance and so on to develop subject expertise. . . it might be more economical to the LEA sometimes to give a small grant to a voluntary body.

On-going training for part-time teachers: LEAs see the regional scheme as the major part of their on-going training programme for teachers. Unfortunately, the other parts often cannot be implemented. Some of these have already been mentioned — induction courses, support and guidance in the centres where teachers work, and subject-based training. A wide range of other ideas were given that would help teachers to keep in touch and learn with and from other teachers in ways that would break the isolation of part-time staff and develop and keep alive the momentum achieved on training courses. The nub of the problem was highlighted by this LEA representative:

> They are isolated, they are insecure, because they never know from one year to the next whether their job will be there or not. . . You provide one-day courses, conferences for them, the support is immense, tremendous, because they feel this isolation and insecurity and they want to learn from their colleagues. . . we don't do enough of this.

Training for Trainers: Training is needed both for Centre Heads involved in 'informal' training and for trainers involved in the more formal courses. A variety of suggestions emerged here, from more informal opportunities, to allow people within the county or region to get together at conferences at an inter-regional level. Only one county has recently offered a substantial course for trainers and this is obviously another possibility at county or regional level. Some counties are currently helping to finance a number of adult education staff who are involved as students on university higher degree courses. The following com-

---

[1] In the year following the Research, one county has in fact re-introduced complementary subject based 'modules' at Stage 1 level run as additional provision to the 36 hours.

ment from one administrator echoes the general LEA attitude to the problem of supporting trainers:

> Well I think there is a need for greater support of trainers. I would guess it is along the lines for the opportunity to cross-fertilise with other people in the region or even on a wider front. I still regret that, for instance, on our particular Training the Trainers course, there was never a recall, because it is only after a certain time that people actually doing the training, that one's ideas gell and you want to go back and say well look this is the way we've gone, which way have you gone, and yes, I think there is an unfulfilled need there. I mean the East Midlands Regional Institute for Adult Education one time held a conference on this and that was very useful, although it was too short. I think what it needed, although the chances of getting together this sort of thing now are receding still further, is three or four day conferences, made up entirely of people who have been involved in training.

To implement all these ideas would require considerable resources. Sometimes it could be more efficient and potentially more stimulating for an LEA to work with other organisations such as specialist training bodies or with other LEAs in providing training especially where small numbers of people, widely dispersed, are involved. Other approaches such as linked one-day schools, 'packaged' training materials or a modular course approach may sometimes be more suitable than the usual format of training courses. Although the LEAs seem satisfied with Stage 1 and 2 courses which form the major part of their training, there were some hints that this may be a good time to review training needs. A large part of training effort has gone into these courses for some time now and as one person suggested there may be a case for identifying other training 'needs' before these become 'demands'. As a larger proportion of an LEA's part-time staff become trained certain administrators feel it may become increasingly necessary to look hard at the existing provision of courses and perhaps shift the emphasis to other forms of training before the impetus of the present style of work reaches its peak and falls away.

> I know Stage 1 and Stage 2 are quite successful. It's very hard then to say 'let's sit back and rethink it all again. . . we've got a good Stage 1 and Stage 2 but it's no good letting it go until it peaks and drops and then try and rethink it. We ought to be examining all the way along to see which way we're going.

It was argued by a number of LEA officers that current training schemes should also be examined in order to make sure they were encouraging new approaches to, and new forms of, adult education. These would meet the changing needs of students as well as help cope with the constraints imposed by reduction in public expenditure. The difference between this ideal and the reality of the situation in which LEA administrators find themselves is highlighted in the following quotation by one of their number:

> I'd like to get people together and start thinking of new ways of approaching Adult Education away from the traditional 36 weeks evening course in whatever. One college had very successful weekends and one day courses, I'd like that to spread and it can only spread if full and part-time staff get together. Unfortunately, I can't provide the opportunity for people to get together — it's very sad.

How do LEAs look at the benefits of training? The representatives spoken to all referred to improvements in the service that can be provided. Primarily they see this being achieved by improving the quality of the teachers employed — by increasing their understanding of the philosophy or ethos of the adult education service, by making them more aware of the implications of how they work, especially for their students, and by helping them to improve the structure and organisation of their classes. While such benefits are hard to prove, they did not seem to question that these are the effects of training. Some LEA spokesmen were aware of the fact that they had made no attempt to assess benefits and that to a large extent their assumptions about the effectiveness of training were based on 'hope' and 'blind faith'. This emerges from the following quotations from two senior staff:

> Courses are designed to get the teacher to understand the whole philosophy of adult education and to help adults to develop themselves. On top of that, we hope that the teacher has developed a certain degree of technical skill. . . in other words, we just hope that the quality of work in the classroom has improved.

> I think it is important in Adult Education that we should seek to improve our image in terms of being able to say both locally and nationally, we are not doing something trivial. We have seriously attempted to train our staff so they can offer the highest possible teaching. I know that's an instrumental thing, but it's an important objective.

The same officers went on to argue that other instrumental benefits to LEAs themselves might result from these changes, for example, the number and range of courses on offer, the number of students attending or the number of complaints received. No evidence was offered in support of any of these points but one officer did illustrate his case in the following manner:

> Take cookery for instance, the trained teacher is much better in organising the use of equipment, so that we don't get lots of complaints next morning. . . Also, I've never been called in to look at a class with a really nasty complaint from the public, of a teacher who's been through the training scheme.

In a time of financial cut-backs, LEAs seem very conscious that they must be offering a high standard of adult education class to justify the large fee increases imposed in 1980-81. Training was perceived as an important means of helping provide value for money within this context.

> I think basically it is the policy of the authority to endeavour to improve, wherever possible, the quality of the service that is offered, particularly where the fees are getting higher and when anybody pays for anything they expect a good service at the end of it. Our courses for part-time teachers can help us in this task.

SECTION 4: THE RESPONSIBLE BODIES

The other major providers of Adult Education in the East Midlands, the Responsible Bodies, in total employ just over 600 part-time teachers. A senior member of each of the bodies concerned, two University extramural departments, one WEA district, was interview-viewed, in order to determine their policy and attitudes to training and the extent of their activities in this field during the 1980-81 session. The responses were interesting in that they underlined the autonomous nature of each institution, yet at the same time highlighted some of the prevalent Responsible Body attitudes to training. From the evidence, it appears that none of the three bodies had a clearly formulated training policy for their part-time staff. One is currently working "towards a much more coherent policy", another was much more vague in its intentions, whilst the third had attempted to introduce a more structured scheme but had not succeeded in implementing it. Thus:

We had a quite comprehensive scheme worked out, a sequential scheme starting off with a briefing conference, moving through to a more formal bit of training, then for those who wished it a more extended piece of training, roughly analogous to Stage 1, 2, 3 in the LEA scheme, and culminating for those who want it in the Certificate in Adult Teaching. But because of the opposition to it, both explicit and implicit (by that, I mean some staff just don't co-operate) — the whole thing has vanished into limbo.

This case highlights one of the dilemmas faced by Responsible Bodies. The majority of their full-time staff appear to be willing to provide support for part-time staff on a one-to-one basis, yet they seem cautious and hesitant about establishing their own formal courses for adult teacher training. Consequently, the emphasis of their provision is on an individual basis using written back-up materials, class visits and 'general support' whenever required. This is how two bodies perceive their function:

Individual resident tutors, will spend a lot of time helping individuals on an individual basis. I suppose supervision has become the dominant mode, rather than explicit training courses. All new tutors ought to be visited early in their teaching career with us, and given whatever help and guidance seem appropriate and possible. So visiting and supervision of that sort, and one-to-one guidance and general support I think is the main vehicle.

Full time members of staff would be giving quite a lot of help and support, informally e.g. seeing new teachers, talking about what was required, advising on production of a syllabus, talking about some of the problems of teaching adults, also visiting them and in some instances, offering them an opportunity to visit their own classes.

An example of how this support is carried out, is illustrated by this comment:

We needed to establish from the start that we are there as supports. So we argued very strongly the handbook shouldn't be sent to part-time tutors, but be handed to them by the full-time members of staff, when he first meets them or once they have agreed to take the course. A bit of time should be spent talking about it and linking it to the future.

And the rationale underlying this approach is best summed up by this person who clearly expresses an emotional commitment to training:

We accept our social responsibility for part-time tutors, we think that part-time staff will perform much better if they, in fact, are emotionally committed to us as an institution. We put a great deal of effort into this.

Other examples of support included pre-sessional meetings for new tutors, occasional meetings for certain subject tutors and experimental workshop type courses (12 hours) concerned with highly practical aspects of teaching, making use of closed circuit television. None of the Responsible Bodies in our survey provided or participated in longer courses, even to Stage 1 level.

Why this training should be limited to an informal and individual approach is not easy to determine. From respondents' comments it appears to be the consequence of a number of inter-related factors, particularly full-time staff attitudes and the way in which Responsible Bodies organise themselves and allocate their responsibilities. The very scattered location of their clases throughout the East Midlands counties does not easily lend itself to bringing part-time teachers together. Moreover it is apparent from our study of LEA part-time staff (see Chapter 3), that teachers of academic subjects who already possess paper qualifications have a tendency to resist training. Only one organisation explicitly expects all its full-time staff to take responsibility for helping part-time tutors and this is laid down in their job description.

> That's part of our job-contract, to help and support part-time tutors. It is loosely worded, but it is there. . . it is expected that we will undertake, help, support and give guidance.

This clearly pays dividends for in the same organisation a group of full-time staff have established a working group called "Part-time Tutor Training and Assessment". So far they have produced a handbook for part-time tutors and are currently trying to work out a set of guidelines to help the full-time staff in the initial evaluation of part-time staff. The handbook is an indication of the effort made to convey some principles of adult teaching to tutors who do not have regular contact with the full-time staff. The other two bodies have not gone so far in specifying their expectations. Instead, there is a much more general expectation that the appropriate staff should be involved, which in practice means that the work is done by those who believe in it and are willing to take it on. This whole problem is compounded by the lack of formal organisational structures for deciding upon and implementing training policy. The manner in which Responsible Bodies tend to work is illustrated by the following:

> We have no central control of this, we don't have a pattern, we don't have a system and we don't have a committee which organises things. We have a staff tutor in subject X and if he has only 4, 5 or 6 tutors working for him in this subject area, then it is up to him to decide whether informal chats or occasional class visits are the way of doing it, or whether in fact, if he has got 20 part-timers, he might be keen to run a seminar on an occasional basis. It is left to individual tutors to decide what they wish to do and what initiative they want to take.

Within each body, attitudes of individual members of staff vary tremendously between those who firmly believe in the value of providing opportunities for tutors to learn about teaching and those who don't. The flavour of the range of views is apparent from this comment:

> Here we have a wide variety of opinions, one extreme reckons that we could set up a system that would apply to all part-time tutors. At the other extreme is somebody who believes there is nothing in this and what you do is to appoint tutors and let them develop their own style and technique. And if it doesn't work sack him. So there is a continuum of views; everybody is at a different point.

It is interesting to note here that an analysis of these interviews revealed that the arguments against University and WEA provision of training for their part-time tutors were much stronger and clearer than were the arguments in favour. The latter were virtually non-existent. A rather defensive stance is adopted in order to rationalise the lack of impetus in their provision. The following comment is an example of a commonly held view amongst Responsible Body staff:

> Training may be threatening in two ways. It's threatening, or thought to be threatening, to the recipients, the part-time teachers, and it's threatening and may be more so, to our staff who might be involved to be appearing to be offering something to people who may be senior colleagues. It's threatening to the teacher as well as to the recipient

— I think that might be the root of it. I think we may be saying something about ourselves in the sense that most of our staff see themselves as subject specialists and not as experts in the theory and practice of education. They would be happy to talk about their subject, but far from happy — or even far from interested to discuss how it should be taught.

Such an opinion may arise from the fact that many of the staff of the Responsible Body themselves never received any training and are diffident about becoming trainers themselves. Someone with an academic training may well feel unqualified to train someone in another discipline, though he may think his experience enables him to advise informally another teacher in the same subject. These attitudes do not only limit Responsible Bodies from adopting a more structured approach to the training of their part-time tutors; they also tend to hinder the possibility of their working more closely with LEA training programmes. This was evident from the responses to the question whether Responsible Bodies encouraged their part-time staff to use LEA courses: there is some comparative evidence from some few areas elsewhere in the country that part-time Responsible Body tutors are joining regional training schemes run by LEAs of their own volition. Absolute numbers are small but they are growing. There is no evidence to suggest that there are any parallels in the East Midlands region:

No, we are not involved in long and closely intermeshed LEA training courses.

To my knowledge, there has been no passing on — although the possibility has been hinted at from time to time. I have asked colleagues involved in the LEA training programme why the scheme for LEA staff is not appropriate for our tutors? I don't think I've ever got a really satisfactory answer.

The following comment perhaps might help understand why:

We felt it may be possible to recommend certain of our tutors to use the LEA scheme, but only those who are guaranteed a fair amount of teaching, because it is so time consuming. Also certain aspects of the LEA scheme are fairly closely tied to the needs of their tutors and the much more formalised setting in which they operate. There's a lot of common ground obviously, particularly on the more philosophical as opposed to the practical/organisational side. How do adults learn? What are the problems of learning for them? Teaching methodologies in Adult Education. All that is common and there would be no problems at all. I suppose what we probably are looking for in the long term is some flexible arrangement by which some of our tutors can use the appropriate bits, instead of saying "all or nothing".

Even though this is an optimistic view the same respondent went on to express his worries about LEA Courses:

I think all of us have a fear of being trapped in a highly formalised system that will give us no room for manoeuvre, particularly in a system that is not appropriate to us . . . Another criticism of the LEA, from what I have heard from colleagues, is that they have the impression the LEA system is geared at validating, then that is it. Once you are accredited, we can more or less wash our hands of you. My own feeling, is that is probably a harsh view. But certainly one thing we are strongly trying to tie to this is the idea of on-goingness.

This comment provides a good example of the Responsible Bodies' lack of knowledge of LEA training provision and their lack of understanding of the Regional Scheme and its content.[1]

Other views were less specific, yet the lasting impression given by these respondents was that the Responsible Bodies see themselves as separate and distinct units. Moreover, they perceive identifiable differences between themselves and the LEA in terms of function and support of part-time teaching staff. Consequently they do not recognise what they see as the highly formalised training structure of the LEA sector as either appropriate or practical within their own setting.

SECTION 5: THE SPECIALIST SUBJECT TRAINING ASSOCIATIONS/ORGANISATIONS

There is a wide variety of specialist subject qualifications available to LEA part-time teachers. This type of training, which lays great stress on the development of subject expertise and knowledge, is provided by an increasing number of bodies, especially in the arts and crafts areas and sport. In general they tend to work in isolation from the LEA training field. Little was generally known about such organisations who provide specialist training, or about the quality and range of the qualifications they offer. A short-term enquiry conducted early in 1980 by the University of Surrey for the Advisory Council for Adult and Continuing Education, helped to identify 44 of the organisations contacted. This enquiry was summarised in the Advisory Council's discussion paper, 'Specialist Training for Part-time Teachers of Adults (April, 1981). The other organisations were noted from responses to the teachers' questionnaire.

Fifty-one bodies were contacted by letter, and after explaining our objectives we asked them for:

(a) details of courses which they considered to be complementary or alternative to LEA training programmes
(b) their views about LEA training courses
(c) their views about ways in which they would like to be involved in future developments in the training of part-time teachers

Thirty-four (62%) replies were received and their responses categorised as follows:

— Nineteen responded as requested; some more comprehensively than others
— One sent a detailed response but their work is primarily in London and the Home Counties
— Fourteen were not directly involved in the training of part-time teachers

An analysis of this material was undertaken. The main features of replies from the 19 bodies who responded positively are set out in tabular form as Table 3 (i) and 3 (ii).

---

[1] During 1981, two conferences convened by the WEA in Birmingham and attended by university extra-mural and WEA staff from England, Wales and Scotland suggest that recognition of the need to train part-time tutors is growing in the RB sector. Though a number of participants expressed the view that existing Stage 1 courses would not suit RB tutors in approach or organisation, they acknowledged the need for something more systematic than the kind of arrangements discussed in this chapter. A pilot scheme, involving three universities and two WEA Districts is now under consideration with a view to meeting the needs of academically qualified tutors teaching in scattered locations and perhaps becoming recognised as a Stage 1 course.

Table 3(i): Specialist Subject Training Associations/Organisations — knowledge of training activities

Organisation	Qualification offered	Course Details fee: length: entry requirements	Course emphasis	Courses provided in East Midlands 1980-81	Other forms of support provided for members	Knowledge of LEA training schemes in East Midlands	Views about such schemes	Attitudes to co-operation with LEAs	Involvement in future developments in training
Keep Fit Association	Basic Keep Fit Association	Standard LEA non-vocational course fee	46 hrs Keep Fit knowledge & Skills	1 Basic Course in one county	Membership of the Association	Sound knowledge because many members of the Association have taken basic LEA training courses	"Our teachers have found existing schemes very helpful, especially when working alongside teachers of other subjects"	"It is necessary to obtain LEA Stage 1 in order to gain the Keep Fit Stage 1. Therefore in the East Midlands we have always had good co-operation with LEAs".	"Wish to be fully involved in future developments of LEA schemes".
	Basic Keep Fit Association Award (must also take an LEA Stage 1)	80 hrs minimum Membership of a Keep Fit Class £50	20 hrs teaching practice	1 Stage II Course held at regional level	Conferences and Rallies at national and regional level				
				1 course for teaching the elderly	Annual Summer school		"Existing schemes are good where they operate"		
	Stage II Teachers Award (must also take an LEA Stage 2/C & G730)	80 hrs minimum Completion of basic course or its equivalent	14 hrs elements of teaching		Social events		"If Stage 1 teachers take the LEA Course after completing our Basic Course, they find they have already covered some of the work".		
					National magazine booklists, information leaflets and diaries.				
	Trainers Award	4 yrs. approx. 300 hours Keep Fit Association Stage II award, considerable practical experience of teaching Keep Fit.	As above		Short 'taster' courses for those wishing to take the Basic Award				
					Courses for those working with special groups				
					General refresher courses				

Organisation	Qualification offered	Course Details fee: length: entry requirements	Course emphasis	Courses provided in East Midlands 1980-81	Other forms of support provided for members	Knowledge of LEA training schemes in East Midlands	Views about such schemes	Attitudes to co-operation with LEAs	Involvement in future developments in training
Slimnastics Association	Slimnastics Teachers Certificate (Teachers can use the designation T.S.A.)	£23.50 8 weeks; 30 hrs at least Participation for at least 2 years in exercise classes, one year of which must have been in Slimnastics classes.	Mainly a Slimnastics and development of skills in this subject Out of 9 subjects on the syllabus, two are devoted to teaching skills.	One course; this has drawn teachers from the East Midlands and the East Anglian Region	T.S.A. Qualified teachers are included on a Slimnastics Teachers Register Refresher courses Seminars Continuing assessment to obtain annual renewal of the teaching Certificate issued by the Association. Teachers manual (140 pages) Leaflets and books	Chairman of the training Committee has completed a Stage 1 course. One of the founders has recently completed City & Guilds 730		"Our own community education offices co-operate in every way possible". "Very willing to co-operate with LEA Staff".	
Royal Life Saving Society	Teachers Preliminary Certificate Course Teachers Certificate Advanced Teachers Certificate				—Membership of R.L.S.S. —Publications and details of courses	No immediate knowledge of courses offered by LEAs		"To my knowledge there is no co-operation or co-ordination". "We do not have any contact with LEAs regarding courses we or they operate in the East Midlands: we do liaise with the Sports Council".	

Organisation	Qualification offered	Course Details fee: length: entry requirements	Course emphasis	Courses provided in East Midlands 1980-81	Other forms of support provided for members	Knowledge of LEA training schemes in East Midlands	Views about such schemes	Attitudes to co-operation with LEAs	Involvement in future developments in training
Amateur Swimming Association	Preliminary Teachers Award	Entry fee £2.00, at least 16, undertaken an appropriate course of training	On teaching & learning. Not specifically geared to the teacher of adults. Tends to emphasise the teaching of children.		Publications and information about courses	"I have no information on the LEA Schemes".		"As far as I know there is no conscious effort to co-ordinate LEA training courses with any of ours — but this may go on in some parts of the country".	"I am sure the A.S.A. would be quite happy to become involved in future developments of training providing the training was in addition to our own. However, it is necessary for us to have much more information on what training courses are involved, before we could give a definite reply to any consequence".
	Teachers Certificate	Entry fee £5.00 30 hours at least 18; holders of Preliminary Award							
	Advanced Teachers Certificate	Examination fee £5.00 30 hours holders of ASA Teachers Certificate							
English Basket-ball Association	Preliminary Teachers Award	Minimum 8 hrs – £3	6 sessions: 1 devoted to class organisation		National courses for players, teachers & officials.	"Schemes not known".			"We would like to be involved in the development of training of teachers who will be involved in teaching sport. The Association would like to be kept informed of future developments in the training of teachers in adult education".
	Teachers Award	Minimum 16 hrs – £3	16 sessions: 1 devoted to simple teaching, coaching						
	Coach's Award Senior Coach Award	Approx 50 hrs £6 £9	Teaching on the course appropriate to school and Youth Club groups						

Organisation	Qualification offered	Course Details fee: length: entry requirements	Course emphasis	Courses provided in East Midlands 1980-81	Other forms of support provided for members	Knowledge of LEA training schemes in East Midlands	Views about such schemes	Attitudes to co-operation with LEAs	Involvement in future developments in training
British Amateur Gymnastics Association	For men, 5 grades of coach. For women 6 grades ranging from Assistant Coach to Senior Coach.				Annual Handbook Information on competitions and other events Publications list Regional and national courses.	"Very limited I am unfamiliar with the LEAs Adult Training Scheme in the East Midlands".		"Yes, LEA trainers do co-operate, but I am afraid this is at a reasonably low level."	"I am afraid the only way our organisation could be involved in the future development of training of teachers in non-vocational adult education is to offer courses as part of the scheme for those wishing to be qualified in the P.E. side of education. But we would want to be as helpful as possible in what appears to be a profitable scheme for a large section of the community".
Swing into Shape	Swing into Shape Teachers Certificate	£50 30 weeks, 60 hrs 180 hours attendance as a member of a Swing into Shape Class. (credit exemptions for exercise qualifications)	Mainly the development in 'Swing into Shape'	1 course	Register of teachers and classes Rallies Detailed information sheets Consultant medical adviser Regular meetings at social events	Detailed knowledge of course in one LEA. The Senior Tutor has completed a Stage I course and a Stage II City and Guilds 730. A number of other teachers have also completed Stage II/City & Guilds 730.	"Found them of some use; useful in ideas, but the ideas relevant to Swing already have been covered by us in our training". "I think people who are teachers who are not part of any organisation will find them very important and very valuable. But if organisations such as ours have anything about them, they will have absorbed what is taught and put it into their own training".	"I advise our girls to take the LEA basic course and I will go on advising them to do the LEA scheme. But I don't think it is necessary that I do. If the LEA insisted on a minimum of Stage I then we would be willing to accept, because our members want to measure up to what is required of them". "I doubt if anyone would want to go on to Stage III".	"Would like to be consulted about future developments".

Organisation	Qualification offered	Course Details fee: length: entry requirements	Course emphasis	Courses provided in East Midlands 1980-81	Other forms of support provided for members	Knowledge of LEA training schemes in East Midlands	Views about such schemes	Attitudes to co-operation with LEAs	Involvement in future developments in training
Royal Yachting Association	Royal Yachting Association & Department of Trade Yacht-Master Cert. preferably with an instructors endorsement.	£700 4 years Yachtmaster offshore cert. + experience	Organisation of practical cruising courses and methods of practical instruction	None	Annual weekend Yachtmaster Instructor Course in Cowes Informal regional meetings for part-time teachers 11 page pamphlet on Instructional Techniques R.Y.A. Members Manual. Regular information about all courses and conferences.	"Not known"		"There is no specific LEA/RYA co-ordination but our instructor courses are held in high regard by several LEAs".	"We would like to be closely involved in future developments, in order to strengthen our schemes, to meet demands from more discriminating adult students. If we know more about local courses, we could do more in the way of encouragement for instructors to attend courses. Alternatively we could use the expertise of those who train adult teacher trainers, to strengthen our own instructor training programmes".
English Bridge Teachers Association	English Bridge Teachers Association Ordinary Level Diploma. Advanced Level Diploma Honorary Diploma	£27.50 20 hrs Evidence of ability in Bridge. Familiar with course syllabus £25 20 hours Preferable to have Ordinary Level Diploma	Bridge techniques but reference is made to the skills required to teach Contract Bridge		Newsletter 15% discount on Bridge books Advisory service providing help on any teaching problem.	"I am afraid I know nothing about them"	"LEA courses are of no practical help to teachers of contract bridge". "An LEA course gives no guarantee whatsoever that the person concerned has either the knowledge or ability to teach Bridge".	"I don't personally think co-operation would help in any way. The co-operation we so urgently need is twofold – refusal of LEAs to employ any but registered E.B.U. Diploma holders and exemption from their training schemes".	

Organisation	Qualification offered	Course Details fee: length: entry requirements	Course emphasis	Courses provided in East Midlands 1980-81	Other forms of support provided for members	Knowledge of LEA training schemes in East Midlands	Views about such schemes	Attitudes to co-operation with LEAs	Involvement in future developments in training
Pre-School Play Group Association	There is no nationally recognised course, although the term *fieldwork course* is now accepted as appropriate for courses defined to: "strengthen the playground movement by ensuring a team of workers skilled and experienced at all levels of playground work. This team of workers includes tutors".	No fee Average 6 days Been a student on a Playgroup Foundation Course	Four elements (i) communicating with adults; (ii) playgroup practice and management; (iii) a wise philosophy of playgroup movement; (iv) human relationships and human development	—1 short course for tutors — Resource groups in each of four counties. —Regional one-day conferences. —1 day Seminar for tutors of longer playgroup courses	Resource groups self-directing informal learning groups, used before tutors attend formal sessions Regional training conferences and residential weekends Tutors Register in each county General Study days General P.P.A. publications including the Associations' magazine 'Contact'. Branch meetings	Great deal of knowledge of each LEA's courses	"In its region P.P.A. tutors are encouraged to attend LEA Courses when available. (This view is not held nationally for in *some* cases LEA courses are deemed unsuitable). Some tutors have found Stage 1 unsatisfactory, dull and bad teaching practice, but enjoyed and learned more from Stage 2". "In another county, a few have taken Stage I and found it valuable, challenging and a useful yard stick in measuring ones ability against others". "Whilst in another, Stage 1 has been enjoyed least. Stage 2/City & Guilds 730, has proved most useful."	"There is a greater need for co-operation between LEAs and the PPA. Few approaches have so far been made to discuss co-operation or co-ordination with counties in the region, although contact has been with individual trainers who have contributed to the Resource Groups". "One tutor has done Stage 3 and found it the most meaningful and productive of all".	"PPA members in each county, would welcome close links with LEAs and the chance to be involved in and considered in timing of courses. They would like to receive direct notification and publicity on current and future Schemes of Teacher Training". "Feel that LEAs should make more effort to co-operate with each other, regionally and nationally". "We would like to see recognised Fieldwork Courses of at least 120 hours, with a direct link with LEA Courses. Consultation in Course design and a PPA link tutor for such courses is considered essential". "On the whole, in this region we feel our courses are complementary to LEA Schemes".

Organisation	Qualification offered	Course Details fee: length: entry requirements	Course emphasis	Courses provided in East Midlands 1980-81	Other forms of support provided for members	Knowledge of LEA training schemes in East Midlands	Views about such schemes	Attitudes to co-operation with LEAs	Involvement in future developments in training
National Federation of Women's Institutes	Demonstrators Certificate Instructors Certificates in Crafts Drama Producers Certificate Home Economics Instructors Course	21 hours	For example in Instructors Certificate content is as follows: Role of the teacher in adult education Reasons why students attend Simple visual aids Planning a course Techniques of teaching and learning		Local meetings Courses/conferences at the Women's Institutes own residential Denman College.		"Most of the National Federation of Women's Institutes schemes seem to be comparable with the proposals for Stage 1, but with probably more emphasis on subject knowledge and less on methods of teaching. All LEA schemes lay great emphasis on institutional provision, formal teaching studies and college environments. The WI tutor felt this was not appropriate for tutors working in rural areas with limited facilities."	"It is hoped in the long run, that the N.F.W.I. might gain approval from the appropriate bodies to introduce a scheme of training, equivalent to A.C.S.S.T. Stage I for WI members involved in teaching adults, which would be recognised by LEAs as an acceptable basis for taking LEA Stage II courses".

Table 3(ii): Specialist Subject Training Associations/Organisations — training activities

Organisation	Qualification	Course Details fee: length: entry requirements	Course emphasis	Other forms of support provided for members	Views expressed about LEA schemes
Squash Rackets Association	Part 1 Coaches Award	12 hours			
	Intermediate Coaches Award	15 hours			
	Advanced Coaches Award				
Lawn Tennis Association	L.T.A. Assistant Coaches Scheme				
	Part I	18 hrs minimum £4.60 exam fee			
	Part II	40 hrs minimum £9.20 exam fee			
British Judo Association	B.J.A. Coaches Award (in addition there are: County Coaches Award Senior Coaches Award)	12 hours pre-examination course Entry: 18 yrs 3rd term or over	Out of 6 elements in the syllabus, 1 is devoted to 'Coaching a Class in Competitive Skills'	Books Papers & Articles Films	
Football Association	Preliminary Coaching Certificate	Minimum of 15 hrs	Out of 11 topics one is concerned with Techniques of Coaching and Organisation	Courses Books Films	"I find it of considerable interest and I find it ironic that schemes such as are described by the LEAs have expanded rapidly, yet there is little known about them and how they are influencing the people they are meant to help". "Certainly there is a need for co-ordination between those involved in the LEA training schemes and National Coaches such as myself".

Organisation	Qualification	Course Details: length; entry requirements	Course emphasis	Other forms of support provided for members	Views expressed about LEA schemes
Institute of Iyenga Yoga	Iyenga Yoga Teachers Certificate	36 weeks practical Yoga 30 weeks teachers training 30 weeks teaching method & teaching practice (the latter is frequently done in conjunction with the appropriate LEA)		Demonstrations 1 day schools Newsletter Social events	
International Dance Teachers Association					"The members of this association are qualified by examination. These are conducted by examiners drawn from a panel from over 100, all of whom have been appointed, for the past 30 years or so, by open examination and interview. All examinations are conducted to set syllabuses, which have been proved by let and practice over many years to be acceptable. They are of course, updated regularly". "Training for these professional examinations, is normally done on what might be termed an apprenticeship basis by existing teachers in the private sector. And while we run refresher courses, we do not run specific training courses for teachers. I am in no doubt that my members would assert that, while acknowledging that some tuition conducted by teachers not trained in these methods is adequate, most found in the maintained sector are inadequate and superficial".

Organisation	Qualification	Course Details fee: length; entry requirements	Course emphasis	Other forms of support provided for members	Views expressed about LEA schemes
St. Johns Ambulance	First Aid Lay Instructors Certificate	20 hours A valid first aid certificate	4 hrs on aspects of teaching and learning. 6 hrs practical work in which students prepare and take a lesson.	Class Secretaries Handbook 31 pages: includes such themes as Aims of the Course, preparation, first evening. Visual Aids. Manual for Instruction 50 pages includes sections on how to learn, planning a lesson and variety in teaching.	
Royal Society of Arts.	Teachers Certificate in Shorthand Teachers Certificate in Typing Teachers Certificate in office procedures Diploma in the Teaching of Secretarial Studies Certificate in the Teaching of English as a foreign language to adults Certificate in the Teaching of English to Adult Immigrants	Minimum 150 hrs plus 10 hrs minimum teaching practice Holders of the 3 certificates above who submit an extended essay. Minimum of 100 hours Not less than 100 class contact hours.			"The Board would certainly hope to see its certificates recognised within the Haycock Structures and communications have been made with Regional Advisory Councils about this".

One of the most striking features of many specialist training bodies is the emphasis given to the establishment and maintenance of standards of subject competence. Standards are not easy to specify; and examination of course documents indicated that they tend to be expressed through clearly prescribed levels of practical skills and theoretical knowledge. In a few instances the criteria for obtaining some basic award were minimal; a few hours' attendance or the payment of a fee appeared to be sufficient. On the whole, the majority of respondents have identified a specific set of skills and a body of knowledge which people are expected to acquire before being deemed suitable to hold their qualification. Requirements for course entry and the criteria for, and methods of assessment, are clearly and unambiguously set out and strictly adhered to.

It is interesting to note here that these factors were identified by some LEA personnel as issues which would have to be worked out when developing and defining national standards for adult teacher training courses. LEA trainers are also aware that levels of subject competence, however defined, must also influence admission to Stage 3 Courses. On the other hand, some specialist bodies have expressed concern at occasional lapses in the LEA field over appointment of tutors whose competence may be low, hence their admission to Stage 1 may be questioned.

As far as many subject-based training schemes were concerned, those trainees who do not match up to the expected course requirements do not receive the award. The project did not attempt to examine evidence of pass/failure rates; the one example that did come to hand illustrates what maintaining standards means in practice. One association with two awards, gives these figures for 1980:

Out of 90 people who entered for the first level award 43 passed
Out of 29 people who entered for the more advanced award 9 passed

In both courses students were told why they had failed and they were encouraged to try again the following year. Many associations attempt to safeguard standards by exercising some form of quality control. For instance one group is so committed to keeping its members 'up to scratch' that each person is assessed annually before his Teaching Certificate is renewed. Another group periodically re-examines holders of its award, whilst others offer annual refresher courses. 'Exercise' bodies in particular work hard to maintain their standards of competency.

Another striking feature of these organisations is the back-up and support they provide for their members. This takes many different forms and an analysis of all they provided in 1980 indicates the following distinct categories:

— meetings, such as refresher courses, conferences, summer schools, rallies, demonstrations, competitions and specialist courses where people have an opportunity to practise and learn new skills and to discuss new ideas and approaches. Through these meetings members are encouraged to raise the standards of their performance in their specialisation as well as to improve their teaching techniques.
— regular social events and business meetings.
— printed material concerned with

(a) keeping up to date with the subject
(b) teaching: an increasing number of groups publish handbooks about teaching techniques
(c) information about the events referred to in (i) above
(d) keeping in touch with what is happening elsewhere in the association and with what other people are doing. This usually takes the form of a newsletter or magazine

    (e)   syllabuses and training course details
— teaching materials, especially films
— advice with teaching problems
— a register of those who are qualified to teach a particular subject

The importance of these activities should not be underestimated. They are necessary not only in terms of keeping up interest in a subject but also in terms of maintaining morale and breaking down the sense of isolation felt by many people who are employed part-time by LEAs. Because members of these associations keep in touch with each other and are informed and kept up to date with developments they experience a sense of community and identity. In this way, many of the specialist training bodies have overcome some of the difficulties identified by many part-time tutors, as discussed in Chapter 3. All these activities emphasise the willingness of teachers to devote their own time and money to in-service education and training.

Although the majority of such organisations provide some form of training for their members, it was evident from this survey that there was a distinct difference in their provision of tiered progressive awards. From the 19 organisations surveyed, eight, all sports bodies, provided three or more different grades of award, two provided two grades and a further eight provided one grade only. The preliminary award in a triple grade series is worth noting because it serves the purpose of helping people assess whether they would like to go on for further qualifications without losing too much time or money. All the organisations appear to subscribe to the concept of continuing education. Most take the view that qualifications are not an end in themselves and there is a need to go on developing new skills and to learning new ideas. The differences in their provision are probably attributable to factors such as the size of the association, finance and the numbers of experienced staff. Only one body does not provide a certificated award. It depends on LEA courses where they are available, though it questions the concept of certification and the 'ladder structure' approach to training.

From the evidence it appears that very few 'Training the Trainers' courses are provided by the organisations included in our survey. Only one organisation identified this as an area of concern; it regularly provides a substantial course for those of its members who wish to develop expertise in teaching others how to teach.

Nearly all the specialist organisations expressed a desire to know more about and to understand LEA training programmes. The majority of their comments revealed almost a total ignorance about training developments in the LEA field. A few associations which have local branches and county and/or regional committee structures and whose members had first hand experience of LEA training courses displayed some knowledge.

Four organisations expressed firm views about LEA basic courses. They reported that some of their members found Stage 1 "useful" and "relevant" especially when it was shared with teachers of other subjects. Another group found Stage 1 "dull" and "unsatisfactory". Perhaps in this case Stage 1 work had already been covered in their own training. It is significant that the response from the same group to their Stage 2 training was much more positive and members expressed unanimous praise for their course. The sole criticism of LEA training arose from one association, mainly because they considered that courses:

> Are of no practical help to teachers of. . . An LEA course gives no guarantee whatsoever that the person concerned has either the knowledge and ability to teach our subject. . . Our courses go beyond LEA training in that they concentrate on the teaching of. . . a very specialised subject.

It is important to note here that those who see little value in LEA schemes or know little about them appeared to have a limited understanding of the differences between subject competence and teaching skill; specialist training schemes predominantly stressed subject rather than teaching competence. Consequently they tend to concentrate on the development of subject expertise without recognising the need for more clearly defined elements of training in adult teaching and learning skills.

LEA training schemes have evolved in isolation from training done by specialist bodies and there have been few attempts to co-operate with each other or to co-ordinate their programme. Why this should have developed in such a way is now a matter of history but some of the reasons given by the subject associations may help us understand the nature of the problem:

— LEA training structures either at County or Regional level do not match easily with the manner in which all the different specialist bodies are organised, so it is not easy to provide a forum for discussion or a body for moderating or validating courses
— specialist teaching awards and training schemes do not equate neatly with Stage 1 and Stage 2 courses
— many specialist training bodies provide awards based on approved national standards. Again the difficulty is how to equate these to regional teaching awards
— many of the organisations providing specialist training are voluntary associations which do not wish to see their independence threatened by LEA training schemes. Because of this "reservation and nervousness" and "uncertainty" have been expressed about working more closely with LEAs
— LEA schemes tend to be geared to meet the needs of teachers of adults who will be working in a classroom situation. To specialist trainers, their work is not so closely focused, for their courses are intended for 'instructors', 'coaches', 'demonstrators' and 'voluntary leaders', who will be working in a number of widely different environments.

In spite of these difficulties, many subject organisations recognise the advantages of working in much closer co-operation with LEAs. There has been little exchange of expertise between LEA trainers and those involved in more specialised forms of training. If this were to take place some feel that mutual benefit could be derived from the process. For example, LEA courses could benefit from the subject expertise of members of training bodies particularly when considering the subject needs of teachers at Stage 2 level. Specialist trainers could use the expertise of trained adult educators on their courses. In addition, some specialist trainers would like to develop a working partnership with LEA staff through which they could establish complementary and integrated schemes of training. In principle many specialist training associations would welcome closer links with their LEA counterparts and expressed a strong wish to be kept in touch with and consulted about future initiatives which could affect their members.

CHAPTER 3

The World of the Part-time Teacher

*Training aims to improve the expertise of the teacher. Thus, the training processes describ-
ed in this report can only be fully appreciated if they are set against the wider background,
the world of the adult teacher. The purpose of this chapter is to describe this context and illustrate the realities of the day to day experiences of adult non-vocational teachers. The information is based upon accounts provided by part-time teachers and their students.
Following a short statement about the sample, the chapter is organised into eight sections.
They are:*

Profile of Part-time Teachers
The Teachers, their Satisfactions and Motives
Part-time Teachers in their Centre
The Classroom
Teaching Approaches
Attitudes to, and Effects of Training
The Untrained Adult Education Teacher
Overview

Teachers' perceptions and attitudes towards teaching, learning and training are supplemented by the views of students indicating what they want from adult education and how
they feel about classes they have attended. Emphasis is placed on findings relating to training
showing the present extent of extra-course training and training needs as perceived by
teachers.

Sample Details: Questionnaire Survey: The project attempted to reach all teachers
teaching non-vocational part-time adult classes within the survey area. Unfortunately the
rather imprecise numbers provided by County Officers of their part-time teaching strengths
meant that no exact count of how many teachers had been reached was possible. One indicator of this overall uncertainty is the comparison between the 64% return rate of one
County where home addresses were used and that of 41% of another County where unnamed
envelopes were given out by Centre Heads to an uncertain number of teachers.

Table 4: Response Rate to Teachers Questionnaire

	County A	County B	County C	County D	TOTAL
Distributed	1190	928	573	1049	3740
Returned	496	383	366	546	1803*
	42%	41%	64%	52%	48%

*(includes 12 unattributed)

Teachers who did not reply to the first request were sent a reminder some three months
later. This had the effect of raising the return rate from 35.5% to the final 48% (County increases were 6%, 18%, 15% and 17% respectively). There were a total of 255 unusable questionnaires which left a sample of 1548 for subsequent analysis. There were no significant dif-

ferences between the first return from 1105 teachers and the second of 443 in terms of whether the teachers were trained or not though a minor trend was observable: the proportion of untrained teachers returning questionnaires did rise slightly in the second mailing, from 28% to 31%. It may be that within the total population more untrained teachers failed to make a return and in consequence the obtained sample over-represents trained teachers, but this is entirely speculative.

Interview Survey: Teachers were asked to indicate on their questionnaires their willingness to be interviewed, and whether by telephone or in person. Of the 1548 respondents, 37% (576) refused or gave no answer. Of the remaining 972, the majority 34% (521) had no preference for either method whilst equal numbers chose 'in person only', 14% (216), or 'telephone only', 15% (235). A sub-sample of teachers were interviewed according to their level and type of training and the subject areas which they were teaching. Table 5 gives the distribution of the 63 interviews which were used in the subsequent qualitative analysis; ten further interviews had in the main to be discounted generally because of technical failures.

Table 5: Teachers Interviewed by Training and Subject

	Arts/Crafts and Skills	Sports/ Exercise	Academic	Total
Adult Educ. Training	22	6	6	34 (54%)
Prof. Teacher Training	3	3	0	6 (9%)
Subject Training	2	5	1	8 (13%)
Untrained	10	2	3	15 (24%)
Total	37 (59%)	16 (25%)	10 (16%)	63

Where: Adult Education Training means E.M. Regional Scheme, S1, S2, (S2/C & G), & S3

Prof. Teacher Training means qualified teacher's Certificate in Education (School)

Subject Training means courses/awards of specialist training agencies.

SECTION 1: PROFILE OF PART-TIME TEACHERS

There were nearly twice as many women as men in the sample of 1548, 64%: 35%. The average age of teachers was in the late thirties:

Table 6: Age of Teachers

20 – 29 years	30 – 39 years	40 – 49 years	50 – 59 years	60 + years
13% (204)	36% (561)	25% (381)	17% (256)	8% (117)

(Total: 1519, with 29 non-respondents)

All teachers were by definition teaching part-time non-vocational adult education classes for an LEA. The majority, 61% taught only one class though a fifth, 22% taught two. Of the remainder, 9% taught three such classes and a similar number of teachers 8% had four or more. Turning to the length of a class, a third, 33% lasted a single term with a small minority 4%, running for less than seven weeks. However, the majority, 62% ran for longer than one term, typically 20-22 weeks.

Practically all of the 1548 teachers taught only one subject, 91%. The remaining 9% were recorded as teaching two or more subjects. The types of subjects taught by the teachers in the sample are indicated in Appendix 5: Table 7 shows the data categorised into four major subject areas.

Table 7: Subjects taught by Teachers

Arts & Crafts	Skills	Sports	Academic
30% (464)	22% (337)	31% (473)	18% (274)

(Total: 1548)

For the purpose of handling the data, some classification of teaching subjects had to be decided upon. 'Sports/Exercises' and 'Academic' were self-delineating. 'Arts and Crafts' were a little arbitrarily defined and included those adult classes which dealt with such subjects as flowers, textiles, painting and so on. However, there was a variety of subjects which included those to do with motor vehicles, DIY, secretarial subjects and musical instruments; these did not fit easily under the existing headings. An additional classification was, therefore, employed — viz. 'Skills'

The respondents' teaching experience was distributed over the variety of School, Further Education and Adult Education work, both full and part-time. Some 38% of the sample had taught full time in either primary or secondary schools, the vast majority for less than ten years. Rather fewer had worked full time in FE Colleges, 4%, though double that number, 9%, reported that they had had part-time FE experience. In both cases, the length of service was nearer five years than ten. The pattern of teaching experience in part-time, non-vocational adult education is given in Table 8.

Table 8: Teaching Experience in Part-Time Non-Vocational AE

	N	%
Up to 1 year	263	18
2 or less	188	13
3 — 5 years	378	25
6 — 10 years	374	25
11 — 20 years	234	16
21 — 30 years	38	2
More than 31 years	14	1
TOTAL	1,489	100

(with 59 non-respondents)

It can be seen that the vast majority of teachers have taught classes for less than ten years, and half for less than five.

One fifth of all respondents reported that they had neither work experience nor qualification in the subject they taught. It should be recalled however, that for many subjects taught in Adult Education no formal qualifications are available although high levels of expertise exist. Some 25% of all teachers had some form of subject qualification. A further 44% stated that they had both subject qualifications and teacher training within their subject. Less than 8% claimed work experience only and the remaining 5% either gave no answer or stated that the question was not applicable to their subject.

Table 9: Types of Training

	County A No	%	County B No	%	County C No	%	County D No	%	Total No	%
A.E. Training in combination:										
Adult Education	112	24	90	34	104	22	50	15	356	23
A.E. & Prof. T.T.*	5	1	0	0	3	1	3	1	11	1
A.E. & Subject Training	35	8	28	10	18	4	8	2	89	6
A.E. & Subject & Prof. T.T.*	3	1	1	—	1	—	1	—	1	—
Total A.E. Training	115	34	119	44	126	27	62	18	462	30
Professional & Subject Training:										
Prof. T.T.*	138	29	64	24	152	32	115	35	469	30
Prof. T.T.* & Subject Training	23	5	9	3	21	5	14	4	67	4
Subject Training	51	11	36	13	39	8	51	16	177	12
Other (not classified)	5	1	0	0	1	—	2	—	8	1
Total Prof.* & Subject Training	217	46	109	40	213	45	182	55	721	47
No Training:										
None recorded	97	20	42	16	134	28	89	27	362	23
No answer	—								3	—
Total (%)	469	100	270	100	473	100	333	100	1548	100
A.E. Training by Stages:										
Stage 1	58	37	60	50	67	53	28	45	214	46
Stage 2	9	6	2	2	1	1	3	5	15	4
C. & G. 730	39	25	25	21	11	9	16	26	91	20
Stage 2/730	2	1	3	3	0	0	6	10	11	2
Stage 1 & Stage 2	37	24	10	8	44	35	2	3	93	20
Stage 1 & Stage 2/730	4	3	15	13	0	0	6	10	25	5
Stage 3	6	4	4	3	3	2	1	2	14	3
Total A.E. Trained (%)	155	100	119	100	126	100	62	100	462	100

*where 'Professional Teacher Training' = Qualified teachers Certificate in Education (School)

53

Forty three percent (664) of teachers in the total sample held some formal academic qualifications, either a Degree, HNC/HND, ATD or a qualified school teacher's Certification of Education. Some 4% held qualifications relating to their full-time profession and 16% had City and Guilds Subject Certificates. Of the remainder, 11% held GCE Certificates while another 12% reported other qualifications of various types including 18 craft apprenticeships. One sixth of the whole, 16% either entered nothing under this heading or reported "no qualifications".

A consideration of the teaching qualifications of the whole sample (Table 9) shows that about one third, 30% had obtained at least one Regional Scheme Adult Education Teacher's Certificate; some held this in addition to a qualified school teacher's certificate and/or a specialist subject qualification. Another third, 34% had undergone teacher training without adult education training though 67 of these teachers (4% of the whole sample) also had specialist subject training. Of the remaining third, 12% had subject training only and a further 23% had none at all. Table 9 shows this breakdown by Counties and by Regional totals. Some differences are observable as between counties: County B for example not only has the highest proportion of teachers who have undergone some form of teacher training, 84%, but it also has the highest proportion of Adult Education trained teachers 44%. County D with practically the lowest trained force, 73% has also the lowest Adult Education trained group, 18% and the highest proportion of qualified school teachers, 35%. Subject training remains relatively constant throughout though the proportion in County C, 8%, is relatively low.

The distribution of types of teacher training within the total sample may be further realised in terms of sex and age. Not only are there twice as many women in the sample as men, but women far outnumber men in having undertaken adult education training. Thus, 38% of all women in the sample had Adult Education training compared with 15% of the men, a ratio of nearly five to one. Women in the sample are somewhat less likely to be qualified school teachers, 31% of all women compared with 42% of all men, but they are less likely to be totally untrained, 19%: 31%. There was no difference in terms of subject training, 11%: 11%. A breakdown of training by age shows that not only are half the total sample of teachers in their twenties and thirties but also that qualified school teachers make up the largest single proportion of this younger age grouping, 51% and 42% respectively. Those older than forty are less likely to be qualified school teachers, typically less than one fifth within each decade; they are, however, more likely to have had adult education training. Thus, 43% of those in their fifties have attended adult education training courses. Subject training levels remain relatively stable throughout, again at less than a fifth.

Considering in more detail the 30% (462) of the sample who gave details of their adult education training — Table 9 also shows the levels of training achieved by County and gives the totals for the combined Region. Stage 1, 2 and 3 are the three hierarchical stages of the East Midland Regional Training Scheme with Stage 3 (S3) being the responsibility of the Universities of Leicester and Nottingham. The City and Guilds 730 Teachers' Certificate may be offered alone, or as in some areas as a joint course with an S2, (trainees receiving both awards). Nearly a half of all these Adult Education trained teachers had undertaken Stage 1 training; a further 26% (106) had gone straight into a second level course, either City and Guilds 730, Stage 2 or joint S2/C & G 730. Another 25% (118) followed their Stage 1 training with some form of Stage 2, and a few teachers, 3% (14) had studied at the highest level, Stage 3. There do not appear to be any major discrepancies between counties though County C, whilst having the highest proportion of its teachers with Stage 1, 88% (111), also has the lowest proportion of Stage 2 teachers 45% (45). County A with 59% (93) has the highest proportion of second level trained teachers. It is noteworthy that half the overall number of trained teachers are Stage 1 trained, one quarter Stage 2 trained, one quarter with both and just a handful with a Stage 3 qualification.

There are some interesting points to be seen in the comparison between types of teacher training undertaken and subjects taught. Table 10 below shows the detailed breakdown of training by subject category. The highest proportion of adult trained teachers taught in the Arts/Crafts category, 41%, the lowest 16% were those in the Academic grouping. Not surprisingly perhaps the Academic category had the highest proportion of qualified school teachers, 57%, and Skills had the lowest, 27%. It was the Sports/Exercise category which had the greatest proportion of teachers who recorded that they had some form of teacher training qualifications, 86%. Over a third of these teachers had taken subject training, 36%; of the whole sample taken together (1548), 9% had undergone training as sports coaches and a further 6% had Exercise Training. Adult teachers of the physical subjects were the least likely to be completely untrained, 14%, compared with the 24%, 24% and 35% of the other three categories.

Considering the 30% (463) of the sample who had undertaken adult education training, teachers who taught either Arts/Crafts or Sports/Exercise were more likely to have undertaken Stage 1 training, 24%, and 28% respectively, than those teaching Skills, 19% and certainly those teaching Academic subjects, 12%. Sports/Exercise teachers were much less well represented at Stage 2 level, 11%, as were teachers in the Academic category, 9%. It was the Arts/Crafts and the Skills teachers who had the highest proportions of second level training 27% and 15% respectively. Stage 3 trained teachers were predominantly Arts/Craft specialists. Sports/Exercise teachers are the most likely to be qualified with some form of teacher training, qualified school teachers are best represented in Academic subjects though the least trained in Adult Education and Arts/Crafts teachers have the highest proportion of adult education training.

Respondents were asked if they had ever attended a training course and subsequently dropped out. Of the total sample, 4% reported having left an adult teachers' training course whilst 1% had left school teacher training courses, and another 1% had left a subject training course. Practically all gave "personal reasons" as the cause.

A further question dealt with teachers' intentions to undertake additional teacher training. Exactly half of the total sample 50% either said that they did not intend to take any such training or gave no answer. Of the other half, only 6% definitely stated that they were going to undertake additional training with the remaining 44% admitting to "possibly" only. There was no unequivocal identification of the types of courses which would be attended by the 762 respondents to this question with 56% either stated that they didn't know or gave no answer. The remainder were evenly split between the regional training scheme, 20%, which included 2% who opted for the City and Guilds 730 courses, and the 19% who chose a subject-based course. A further 5% stated that they wanted to obtain a Certificate of Education. It should be noted that these figures include those teachers who have already undergone some training.

Teachers were finally asked to state what staff support and training activities they knew of in their area. Over half the total sample, 56% either said that they knew of none or gave no answer. A further 13% stated that there was none available in their area. Only 31% affirmed that there were training opportunities and activities relatively close to them.

The range and variety of teachers' personal and professional details make it difficult to identify general characteristics. An indication of the main points may be provided by attempting to draw a simple portrait of 'the typical teacher'.

The typical part-time teacher of adults is a woman in her late thirties who teachers a single subject to one non-vocational class. Her subject is likely to be handicraft (arts, crafts or skills) and it is probable that she will hold some subject qualification. She may have taught in areas

Table 10: Types of Training by Subject

	Arts/Crafts N	%	Skills N	%	Sports N	%	Academic N	%	Total N	%
A.E. Training in Combination										
Adult Education	176	38	70	21	71	15	39	14	356	23
A.E. & Prof. T.T.*	4	1	1	—	3	1	3	1	11	1
A.E. & Subject Training	8	2	12	4	68	14	1	(1)	89	6
A.E. & Subject & Prof. T.T.*	1	0	0	5	1	0	0	6	—	—
Total A.E. Training	189	41	83	25	147	31	43	16	462	30
Professional & Subject Training:										
Prof. T.T.*	140	20	87	26	91	19	151	56	469	30
Prof. T.T.* & Subject Training	3	1	5	1	57	12	2	1	67	4
Subject Training	18	4	39	12	112	24	8	3	177	12
Other (not classified)	2	—	2	1	3	(1)	1	—	8	1
Total Prof.* & Subject Training	163	35	133	40	63	55	162	60	721	47
No training	112	24	118	35	65	14	67	24	362	23
No answer									(3)	
Total (%)	464	100	334	100	475	100	272	100	1548	100
A.E. Training by Stages:										
Stage 1	68	15	35	10	91	19	20	7	214	46
Stage 2	5	1	3	1	6	1	1	—	15	4
C. & G. 730	65	14	17	5	5	1	4	2	91	20
Stage 2/730	4	(1)	1	—	2	—	4	2	11	2
Stage 1 & Stage 2	31	7	25	8	27	6	10	4	93	20
Stage 1 & Stage 2/730	8	2	2	1	12	3	3	1	25	5
Stage 3	9	2	0	0	4	1	1	—	14	3
Total A.E.	190	41	83	25	147	31	43	16	463	100

*where 'Professional Teacher Training' = Qualified teachers Certificate in Education (School)

other than adult education though her main experience is part-time non-vocational adult work in which she will have worked for three to five years. Her formal education is likely to have gone beyond GCE level. It is likely that the typical teacher will have undertaken adult education teacher training and Stage 1 and Stage 2 are equally probable and she is most unlikely to have left a training course prematurely. She may or may not undertake further training. She is unlikely to know of, or be able to draw upon adult staff support beyond formal training courses.

SECTION 2: THE TEACHERS, THEIR SATISFACTIONS AND MOTIVES

Entry into teaching, and job satisfaction

The accounts given by teachers of how they became teachers of adults suggest that recruitment was usually informal and based on a variety of contacts. Of the 63 teachers interviewed only one reported that she had been appointed after responding to an advertisement. Other paths by which individuals came to teach adult education classes were:

Student taking over from teacher who had to retire for some reason (e.g. moving, ill, etc.)
Approached by college because of skill
Doing teacher training course and was asked
Relative already taught at Centre
Contacted Centre to offer services
Knows Adult Education organiser and asked by him/her
School teacher taking class at own school

Both surprise and concern were expressed by many teachers at this *ad hoc,* even casual method of recruitment. Typical of this view, was the teacher who confessed:

To be quite honest, I was surprised that Mr X asked me to do this course without knowing whether or not I could teach, because it could have been a complete failure.

Indeed some concern was expressed by a proportion of respondents about the general lack of 'quality control' and assessment of standards of their work. This view was neatly summarised by the remark:

In many ways I think they're very, very lax in their assessment of teachers. I've never had an inspector or anything during a class in 5 or 6 years. . . I could be doing anything. They know the course title, they know the attendance figures, but they don't know what on earth goes on during it.

The varied backgrounds and interests of part-time adult teachers suggests that they were attracted to work in adult education for a variety of reasons. The word that most easily came to the lips of teachers when asked what they felt they got out of adult education was "enjoyment" and whatever additional reasons were given, this was certainly the predominant one. Obviously this suggests a high level of job satisfaction. No matter what level of training the teacher had reached, the emphasis on the pleasure gained from teaching was still affirmed. This basic enjoyment was accounted for by the respondents in terms of the satisfaction they gained from the two chief inter-related roles they saw themselves as performing in the classroom viz

— the teacher as a subject specialist
— the teacher as a social enabler

For many, one chief source of enjoyment was to be able to pass on knowledge and skills involved in their particular subject. Teachers liked to encourage beginners and took pleasure in the progress they made. As one teacher said:

I like seeing beginners, who've never come before, they spark off and you can get them going on something and see they're really enjoying it, that's the part that's good.

Similar comments were made by many others who showed pride in the achievement of their students and satisfaction in seeing the benefits their students gained from their class, whether it was the ability to relax in the case of Yoga classes or excitement at being able to make something with their own hands.

Teachers recognised and appreciated that teaching their subject increased their own knowledge of it.

It's taught me an enormous lot, you've always got to be prepared to learn and you can learn a tremendous amount from your students.

Teachers also found that their teaching stimulated them and encouraged them to try out novel ideas, to keep in touch with current trends and to keep their skills up to date. This view was summed up by an experienced pottery teacher:

It keeps me on the ball. . . I think you can stagnate, you become very satisfied with what you do. When you have to teach somebody else, it also makes you look to yourself and keep your own hand in.

Another source of satisfaction to many teachers was that of working with people and helping them with their problems and difficulties, what may be called a social enabling role. Teachers mentioned that some students appeared to attend primarily for social reasons; for example to make new friends, to meet people, even to have a regular evening away from home and on occasion to help cope with bereavement. Teachers saw their students as individuals from a variety of backgrounds bringing a whole range of personal factors into the classroom with them. The more perceptive teachers recognised that social needs may have to be satisfied before some students will start learning. Fulfilling and coping with such demands of students gave a great deal of satisfaction to some teachers. It is clear from the accounts of how they worked, they recognised that they had a number of roles to play. These can in fact vary from being a social worker/counsellor, to leading and managing groups in order to create a friendly atmosphere. It was not always clear from the way they spoke whether they saw the role of 'social enabler' as an end in itself or as a means of being a more effective teacher generally.

Like their students, many part-time teachers felt they derived social benefits from their teaching, benefits quite distinct from the financial reward. Women in particular, who might otherwise have been tied to the house found teaching an interesting and stimulating outlet that allowed them to meet a wider range of people and to add an important dimension to their lives. This was described as:

Mental stimulation, the socialising of it. . . just simply to have the break from the normal house routine.

I enjoy it, in my evening class there are lots of people who are interested in different kinds of things. . . it's not just teaching the subject but the contact with them and their reaction to the world.

The teachers themselves

Though every teacher has individual motives for and finds unique benefits from teaching besides that of financial reward it may be convenient to present the information given by our respondents in a simple typological framework. In order to do so four categories have been chosen but it recognised that they are over-simplifications and that they interlock and overlap. Such categorisation is a useful way of distinguishing the different perceptions of teaching and training provided by our respondents. The four categories employed bear marked parallels with the routes by which teachers come to adult education, and it is surely no accident that the attitudes and opinions they express should be related to their own previous experience.

The four categories identified in the study are:

1. Qualified School-Teachers
   They may be divided into those teaching the subject that they teach at school and those teaching a different subject. (See also 2 and 4).

2. Subject Enthusiasts
   Individuals who have a particular interest to which they devote a good deal of their time and which they enjoy teaching in order to pass on their enthusiasm

3. 'Professionals'
   Individuals who are teaching a subject which forms their full-time employment.

4. 'Apprentices'
   Individuals who started the subject by attending adult education class and have become increasingly expert at it, finally taking up a post as teacher.

The main characteristics of each type of teacher are outlined below with some indications of their training needs.

1. School Teachers   The chief satisfaction school teachers gained from teaching adults derives from the differences between teaching adults and children. Evening class teaching was often perceived as being more relaxed and rewarding than school teaching. Teachers appreciated the 'keenness' of their adult students and valued the chance to meet people outside the world of school education. Teaching adults was seen as less stressful than day-school teaching. There was a freedom to experiment with new ideas. For teachers who had retired from school or taken years off to have children, adult education offered an attractive way of keeping in touch with education.

The training needs of this group of teachers differ from those of the other three categories. While they had all received pedagogic training some at least recognised the importance of further adult education training whether or no they had undertaken any. Many more believed that adult education teaching was different from school teaching. One main reason reported by school teachers for not taking adult teacher training was lack of time. This may be a less than accurate description but the reason offered was a reluctance to devote free time in order to obtain a qualification considered to be of 'marginal' value to their main career. As one young teacher commented:

> My main priority is to become a good secondary teacher. I do this adult education as a bonus system.

There was a feeling that the most beneficial time to go on a course would be before they started teaching adults:

> I think it would have been better had I had some form of course before I was thrown in at the deep and because I've learnt by making mistakes.

Though in the main it was felt that such training might not be worth the time and commitment it would require. One teacher mentioned that he would appreciate having an outsider assess his adult teaching and make suggestions as to how he could improve his method. The qualified school teachers whom we spoke to who had experienced adult education training were very keen on such 'additional' training. One felt the benefits were very clear-cut and believed that all teachers needed to go on courses; another felt very strongly that individuals should be trained specially for adult education and more generally that refresher courses were important to stimulate new ideas.

2. Subject Enthusiasts   Another important category of teachers are those whose enthusiasm for a subject which they had taken up as a hobby had developed in to real expertise, and teaching it had permitted them to continue their own interests whilst passing on knowledge of their subject to others. One way an individual might come to start teaching his/her hobby is illustrated by a teacher who explained:

> I took squash up as a pastime, a hobby which gradually developed into, shall we say, a full-time hobby. I found myself teaching other beginners just accidentally.

Typical of some teachers in this group was a woman teaching "Pressed Flowers" who was new to teaching. It was clear from her interview that her hobby was very important to her. She said:

> I've been doing it for about eight years. After a couple of years I felt, 'right I'm going to get somewhere with this'. . . I began to develop my own designs then and that was when everything really took off. I'm very much self-taught.

This teacher felt she was learning as she taught and said that she had commented to her students:

> If you find something that I haven't pressed, please press it and tell me how you get on because I'd like to know as well.

She saw her role as passing on her experience to her class and attempting to stimulate enthusiasm in them at the same time. One of the essential qualities of a good teacher to her was "the ability to impart the idea of enjoyment of the subject".

Occasionally, enthusiasm for a subject was not simply one of sharing it with others but served a more instrumental function. For instance one experienced bridge teacher expressed the view that one of the main purposes of his class was to provide new members for the Bridge Club, of which he seemed to be a leading member. This extended to the point that at the end of the beginners' class there was a special evening at the Bridge Club to integrate these people into the Bridge Club. Asked what he hoped students would get out of the class, he said:

I hope primarily that they will support the local Bridge Club in particular and the game in general.

A common feeling among many 'subject enthusiasts' was that the training offered by their subject association was the most appropriate. It was often thought to be more relevant to the teaching of that subject than the general scheme offered by the local authority. Thus, a ballroom dancing teacher when asked about the value of local authority courses said:

> Well, I would say they might be fine for other types of teaching but they certainly would be no good to anyone in the dancing profession.

Some people who were primarily subject enthusiasts had been on general training courses. In some cases they found the experience useful, especially when they had no subject association to which they could turn. However, they still saw general training as subordinate to the development of subject skills. Often such courses had been attended because they were compulsory. Thus a machine knitting teacher said she had done a Stage 1 course "because I was told to" and that the only thing she had wanted to get out of it was "the ability to teach in adult education in this county". She had no intention of continuing with the regional scheme and could see no point in doing so.

3. Professionals   Some adult teachers teach a subject closely related to their full-time occupation. In quite a number of cases such teaching was conceived of as an extra — usually for financial gain — and this appears to be the case far more often than for other groups. Examples of the subjects taught by these teachers are Golf, Car Maintenance and Typing. Members of this group were likely to be uninterested in general adult teacher training and felt that their professional competence was sufficient training for teaching the subject. Teaching was generally viewed very much as a 'sideline' and not as a major part of their life. Many people in this group had a qualification in their subject gained through an apprenticeship or at a college. Sometimes they had taken a City and Guilds teaching qualification in conjunction with their subject qualification.

An extreme example of the attitude towards adult education evidenced by certain individuals in this group was given by a golf professional. He saw himself as doing the "evening institute" teaching almost as a favour. He summed up the main benefit to himself, thus:

> I think most of the professionals hope (that) what we get out of it is to sell the beginners half a set of golf clubs.

He did not feel he had any difficulties with his teaching and learning problems were conceived very much in terms of problems with the subject rather than as general learning problems. He explained why he felt training was not relevant to him:

> Well it depends how much it is going to cost in time and money. . . If I were, doing Evening Institute classes for 20/30 hours per week, you would go on a thing, but for the money you get out of it, it's going to be a big inconvenience, . . .

Another example from this group was a teacher of electronics, a chief production engineer, who wanted to teach in order to keep up to date with electronic components. The teaching was of clear benefit of his full-time job yet he felt he would not give the time to train because:

> The adult education I take very seriously and enjoy doing it, but to be honest there's not much return from it, and I would rather do a course that would benefit my full-time career.

Finally, the example of an artist who taught for the local authority demonstrates that 'professionals' saw their teaching in a different light from that of other groups of teachers. He did not see himself as a teacher but rather as he put it as "the master". He preferred to teach students who had a certain competence and commitment to the subject rather than beginners.

> There are one or two where I've suggested they'd be better in the recreational classes that the ordinary schools run. We do try at the art college to run a more experienced student type of class.

He did not dismiss training out of hand, but it was evident that he did not really see any need to undertake any. He said:

> I don't know really. Probably a little help in the technique of teaching. But for all I know my technique might be all right. If it wasn't I don't think I'd get people wanting to come in to the class.

It is teachers from this group who are likely to be most resistant to training. They see adult education as a small, rather incidental and unimportant aspect of their lives and consequently feel it not worthwhile to give up time to go on a training course.

4. Apprentices   Some people come into adult education 'through the ranks'. They attend a class themselves developing sufficient expertise until they themselves are asked to teach or do a training course. It is from this group that the teachers who were most keen to do the regional scheme came. This may be because the aims of the scheme are most in tune with what they wanted from a training course, that is, confidence, basic teaching skills and the status of having done an official teaching course. Teachers in this group appeared to see adult education as assuming an important place in their lives and they were likely to derive a sense of achievement and pride from their work. Often they seemed to find self identity through their teaching and believed it broadened and improved the quality of their lives. A typical route by which teachers represented in this group progress from being a student to being a teacher is illustrated by one person who started as a student in a crochet class and subsequently took both Stage 1 and Stage 2. In addition she had been on a number of weekend specialist courses to widen her craft experience. She continued to attend an adult class each year as a student. One Keep Fit teacher had also started as a student and had taken over from her teacher without any other training, though later she:

> Went on as many courses as I could get myself on to and took it from there.

This teacher was typical of people in this 'apprenticeship' group: she thought very highly of the regional training scheme and felt that the Stage 2 had been "great, a fantastic course". Even though people in this group were conscious of a need to go on developing their subject competence they primarily wanted a course that would help them with the teaching side of their job, a view typified by this craft teacher when she explained what she wanted to get out of her Stage 2 course:

> . . . a great deal of knowledge. . . particularly with the techniques of teaching and the psychology of teaching. . . it wasn't the craft side of it that bothered me. . .

Teachers in this group were more concerned than others to develop the skills of putting over their subject and fulfilling the needs of their students, whether social or educational. Thus, a teacher who had done a Stage 3 course said that her course had changed her in the following way:

I think I look at things differently, a more enlightened approach, very often if you present things to people and they'll never have thought of them before. It does open up a lot of new doors.

A cookery teacher thought that the most important thing a teacher should do was to get "insight into your student group". The general impression given by teachers in this group is that they see their task as far more student centred than do teachers in the other groups.

A key to the motivation of the teachers in this group may be found in their reasons for joining a training course and becoming teachers. It is evident that this whole process provides considerable satisfaction. A woman who had recently completed Stage 3 explained what she had gained from the course:

I think self-satisfaction is a lot to do with it. . . satisfaction that you've been able to do it. Definitely a challenge.

From their comments, it is clear that adult education provides grounds for these teachers to feel that they have achieved something concrete — evidence of their competence in the field. A teacher said that after completing Stage 2, "I was quite proud when I got my bit of paper".

Teachers in this category are primarily committed to adult education in its broadest sense, rather than to teaching the subject *per se*. This group of teachers most readily appreciates the type of training offered by the Local Authority. It gives them status, confidence and develops their interest in people. The aims of the training scheme appear to match their expectations and they concur with the way they approach the task of teaching adults, possibly because they themselves have experienced adult education as students and they usually do not feel themselves to be subject experts.

SECTION 3: PART-TIME TEACHERS IN THEIR CENTRES

Adult Education Centres vary both with respect to their physical condition and the dedication and commitment of the staff running them; the experiences of part-time teachers differed according to the centre in which they taught. A typical experience was described thus:

As regards centres a lot depends on who is running them, I mean at Y we've got a very good relationship, there are no problems. Now I did a course at Z and I didn't feel I got much co-operation at all.

In the same way teachers found themselves working in widely differing environments from rooms that were little more than huts to relatively well equipped, purpose-built adult education centres. Some teachers worked in village halls with little contact with other adult education staff whereas others taught at centres where a number of adult education classes were being taken simultaneously. Teachers said that they needed support in two main ways in their centres. Firstly, they wanted an adequate supply of materials, resources and comfortable physical surroundings and secondly they required moral and professional support.

The existing situation in the Centres

Some teachers stated that their Centre Head was supportive, mentioning that they "feel free to drop in and see him." There were a few teachers who were glad that they received minimum interference from the Centre Head and there was evidence that at least some positively avoided contacting full-time adult education staff.

The only person I have contact with is the person who comes to collect fees and issues receipts at the beginning of term and who collects registers at the end of term. . . So I'm out on a limb which is nice and quiet, no people disturbing us.

They don't bother me and I don't bother them. They ask for my claim form and I supply it. Beyond that there is little contact.

Considerable disparity emerged in accounts of the amount of back-up of resources and facilities that teachers received. On the one hand some were very satisfied, while on the other there was a desire for more adequate provision. Generally those teaching 'exercise' subjects were the most dissatisfied with facilities. They mentioned that the rooms they were allocated were often not suitable because of the floor surface or perhaps because they were too noisy and lacked atmosphere, or that they had problems with pianos or record players. One Keep Fit teacher describing problems which made her job more difficult felt that she received "no co-operation whatsoever" from the centre.

Other teachers had problems that although minor in themselves proved to be aggravating and sufficient to make teaching a struggle. Such a situation was aptly described by a pottery teacher:

Things like getting locked in a building at night or lights switched off when you're still packing a kiln, little things no one understands.

The problem for part-time teachers was not only one of the availability of resources, but how to find time to use them effectively.

When you're only there two hours a week, just getting there and preparing it is one thing but borrowing films and equipment as well is such an extra process. . . there must be a whole lot of stuff in/or. . . that probably is available but I've never yet had the time to go.

Other problems of this kind were mentioned: poorly or overheated rooms, difficulties with caretakers, lack of access to duplicating facilities, absence of technical equipment such as tape-recorders, video or projectors, insufficient advertising about the courses or disagreement with the full-time staff of the institute at which the teacher worked, whether it be a school or further education college.

A commonly reported feeling among part-time tutors was a sense of isolation in their work expressed in terms of having no one to talk to about specific subject problems, feeling alone when actually going into a centre to teach and generally experiencing a sense of isolation within the centre often because there was an absence of "community spirit" among teachers. Such feelings were expressed in the following ways:

I don't feel there is enough contact between the teachers in the centre. I know it's very difficult when you're doing it on a part-time basis, the only time we ever meet is at the staff meeting before the term starts.

There's only one of you in your subject and you haven't the chance to exchange views.

I just go in every week and pick up my register, go up and take my class. I very rarely see anybody.

You are very isolated, you teach your class and then go away again. . . you never know what is going on, except for your bit.

This sense of isolation was expressed by teachers at all levels of training.

A notable feature that emerged from the accounts of the work of many trained teachers was that on the whole those who had undertaken adult education training were more likely to speak of a sense of isolation. Those who were subject trained or had no teacher training at all did not generally express such feelings. This is surprising at first sight, because it might be expected that experiencing a course of training would serve to break down the sense of isolation and give these teachers a sense of belonging to the wider body of adult education. However, it may reflect the trained teacher's ability to evaluate his own performance and to seek continued improvement through mutual aid and support. The untrained teacher may lack the confidence and ability for such self-assessment. Some difference may also be attributable to the role teachers perceive adult education playing in their lives. It may well be that a sense of isolation results from the teachers' own expectation and desires about their work in adult education rather than from the running of the centre. To the extent that training is intended to make teachers more aware of the wider social context of their teaching and to increase their expectations they are likely to expect more from centre staff and more adequate facilities.

The trainers were able to provide another perspective on the centres, in that many of them were Centre Heads and all had experience of visiting a variety of types of centres. It is clear from their accounts that there is considerable variation in the role of those who have to organise adult education and their usefulness to the teachers. In some cases individuals in charge of centres serve part-time; they perform primarily organisational duties but take very little interest in the more narrowly defined educational side of their duties. In others, Centre Heads are full-time, have specialist adult education qualifications, and usually many years of experience. They interpret their job in the widest sense to include organisation, administration, training, and educational and social functions. There clearly are difficulties when Centre Heads are involved in training, because they are very busy with administrative duties and they find it difficult to fit in tasks like staff support. One trainer commenting as a Centre Head noted that:

> I believe we talk about training but pay mainly lip service to it as professionals but it's a difficult role, it's not a role one can quickly get on with and identify and clear one's desk and say it's over and done with and we allow all sorts of arguments about other pressures in the service to get in the way.

Other trainers who were Centre Heads talked of their heavy work loads and stressed how difficult it was to find sufficient time to give their teachers as much support as they would like. Yet despite all these difficulties there was general agreement that the centres had a very important part to play in offering support to teachers and that this is especially vital whilst a training course is in progress.

The notion that training only begins on the training course and must continue in the centre was put forcefully by another trainer.

> Training is not just making a person available to teach a group of 20 people on a Friday night. It is more concerned with this support service. With the follow up and making of time to see people, getting to know what individuals are having to contend with in terms of their own teaching.

Some trainers had a higher opinion of the present provision of the support for part-time teachers than others. One trainer stated that for his county:

> I think that the whole way that they are inducted, co-ordinated in their centres leaves a lot to be desired. . . they see them once — there's your class, I want a report from you in 36 weeks time.

Yet another trainer who was also an adult education tutor described a far more encouraging situation:

> Really, they can knock on this door at any time of the day or in the evenings and discuss problems, which they do. . . So I think the support is on-going as far as it's possible to make it, without protecting the teacher to the point where they're almost frightened to move without seeking advice and help.

Despite this more optimistic view, in general, trainers tended to believe there was plenty of room for development and improvement in terms of training and support in the centres.

Another problem reported by trainers is that currently many Centre Heads are only part-time and may well not be professional adult educators. This means their supportive function is necessarily limited, mainly because of the continually increasing burden of organisational and clerical work. One trainer explained the situation in his county:

> They are appointed in the myth that they are doing an educational job, supporting the teachers professionally and monitoring standards — in practice this doesn't happen because those who are school teachers are unwilling to judge their peers and increasingly Centre Heads are not qualified teachers and are reluctant to involve themselves in this area, and spend their time on administration.

There was a gap between the role trainers believed Centre Heads should perform and the image the Centre Heads themselves had of their function. The difference between these two views was neatly summarised by a trainer who saw one of the weaknesses of his county's training system as "the support that people receive in the back-home situation". He described how many Centre personnel rely on attendance numbers as the only gauge of teacher effectiveness, explaining that in this circumstance:

> It's almost as if, they send them away to be trained by somebody else, they assume this magical transformation takes place on a training course and that people come back shining new and completely equipped. Training is somebody's job, running a centre is my job.

The lack of continued training/support in the centres was a fairly common complaint among trainers. Possible reasons for this were succinctly summarised by one trainer:

> — the Centre Heads aren't good enough. They are probably more resistant to our ideas then the tutors are.
>
> — they are not made to see that this is an essential part of their job, whereas they can see and have been made to see that administration is essential because it is on that basis that they get paid.
>
> — they do not get enough support in the centre so that they've not got time to do it.

So far as the teachers are concerned centres can either help or hinder their work depending on the degree of interest and support offered by the centre staff. To trainers the centres are one of the most important areas for training adult education tutors and seemingly the one where there is the greatest shortfall from the ideal. The next section will examine suggestions from teachers and trainers for improving this situation.

Centres and Centre Heads: improving training and support roles

Teachers were not very forthcoming when asked what additional training and support facilities they would like. They were rather conscious of the financial stringency under which adult education was operating and they tended to put forward ideas of limited scope which would certainly not call for a great deal of extra expenditure or organisation on the part of county authorities. The most frequent suggestion was that teachers would welcome the chance to meet with other part-time teachers of the same subject through the provision of subject-based training courses or conferences.

A few teachers wished that the authority would make more grants available for them to go on specialist subject courses. For instance in the craft area teachers might like to go on a course in general design, to provide them with ideas and stimulation or perhaps attend a course which would broaden their experience of different crafts. A number of teachers expressed a desire for one day courses, specialist weekends or refresher teacher training courses. Whereas there had been a fair number of these courses in the 1970s teachers understood (correctly) that they were now few and far between. Another area in which teachers felt they would like help was in the provision of and information about resources. Suggestions in this area were:

> Workshops to keep teachers up to date with new technology.
> Teachers' resource centre.
> A mailshop thing to keep you up to date with new things — publications or ideas.

One teacher clearly stated that the centre staff could play an important part in improving the service a teacher receives in respect of facilities and in helping him to make more use of them.

> I think it would be very helpful if whoever is running the centre in which you teach could get everyone together and show them what equipment is available, so that they know what they can use and show them how to use it. . . an efficient way of getting together and borrowing equipment and slides and perhaps a library at each centre.

Teachers believed that the sense of isolation they sometimes felt could be overcome, to some extent at least, by a more positive interest from the centre staff. The following sentiment was repeated in many interviews:

> It would be nice if someone now and again dropped in to see what you were doing and how the class is getting on and asked the students what they are getting out of the class.

Such visits were seen as part of training and one teacher felt that while he would not go on a training course he would welcome and profit from visits. As he said:

> . . . training in that way would be useful, because it wouldn't involve any further time.

It is highly desirable that there should be some responsibility on Centre Heads to provide this kind of support. In one county in the region, adult education has recently been reorganised and local Centre Heads have been removed and only staff in colleges remain. The trainers in this county regretted this action and the value they had seen in the role of these local Centre Heads was summed up by one who stated:

> Well I'd like to see Centre Heads back again. . . it's a great pity they've gone. . . the Centre Head had this professional role. The ones who were trained and who

understood adult education were excellent at it. Admittedly they all weren't, but this sort of pastoral on-going support not just during the training course but after the training course was marvellous.

The importance of the role performed by the Centre Head both in terms of general on-going support to teachers and specific help to those on a course was made clear. A useful summary of the general views held by trainers was provided by one of their number when he observed:

> First of all I think it's essential that the Centre Head knows that the tutor is doing a course and I do know of a couple of specific cases where they were given direct help as part of Stage 1. I'm amazed that some people have no idea whether or not their centre has a slide projector, film projector or overhead projector, I think every tutor should know that sort of thing, whether or not they are doing a Stage 1. I think every Centre Head should be expected to convey information of that kind of tutors. It's pointless for us to spend several hours talking to them about how to use handouts, overhead projectors etc., if the tutors don't know if those facilities are available at their centre. Centre Heads should inform them of materials and equipment available. I think Centre Heads should visit every new tutor at least once and I mean be there for a whole lesson.

An experienced adult educator who spent most of his time training, outlined the three ways in which he believed Centre Heads could help a teacher who was attending a training course: firstly, assuming that they were aware that a particular teacher was on a course they should show a positive interest in him:

> If they don't do any more than say to Mr. X or Mrs. Y every now and again, "How are you getting on, on your training course"? All that's saying is, I know you are on it, I'm pleased you are on it, I'm interested in your progress.

Secondly, they could offer more direct help with equipment or reading matter and make the teacher feel free 'to drop in' and discuss any problems she/he might be having with the course. Thirdly, the Centre Head could help the teacher in the transition from the idealised world of the training course to the realities of the centre. In one trainer's words:

> The 'back home', real life situation is often so totally different from that the Stage 1 and Stage 2 course try to train them for, there is conflict, there is a credibility gap.

Once the teacher has completed a course the Centre Head has a very valuable task to perform in ensuring that he/she continues to progress. The importance of this was underlined by the trainer who commented:

> Well, ideally they need encouragement from the Centre Head to continue with the ideas, because obviously they're going to try ideas that collapse and need to be regenerated and encouraged by follow-ups, visits and refresher days and tutorials.

As the present situation with regard to Centre Heads is far from ideal, attention should be paid to the suggestions made by trainers for improving the current situation. These were:

— Centre Heads should be involved in the training process
— Centre Heads should themselves undergo training, to make them aware of its relevance to their job

A clear message emerged from the trainers' interviews to the effect that they felt Centre Heads should have an active role in training.

Any full time Centre Head that's worth his salt sees a need to be involved in training.

The prime function of this was to give them an appreciation and understanding of the aims and objectives of training. That this can result from participation in training was demonstrated by a trainer who was a Centre Head and had just taken part in his first Stage 1. He said:

I wouldn't say that the experience has been a complete revelation but it has certainly opened my eyes, personally and I'm sure that if the Centre Head hasn't had that sort of experience then they can't conceive what should or could be done.

When asked if his involvement in training was of value to him as a Centre Head, he stated:

Yes, you so often forget what the purpose is in the medley of receipt books, in the minor details you forget what you are talking about, so it does focus you on to what the work is really about and I find it very helpful.

His opinion was confirmed by the comment of another trainer:

There is a big correlation in the county I suspect between the people who are used on training as tutors and those who run the best centres. It's not an accident, it's not coincidence. What I mean by that is, people who are interested in training are also interested in the quality of work that actually goes on in the classroom.

Currently Centre Heads are given very little training themselves and only minimal encouragement to be involved in training. They appear to get bogged down in organisational or secretarial detail and very few opportunities if any are given for them to develop their professional and supervisory roles. Trainers believed that special courses should be provided to help them. In the past, some counties have encouraged Centre Heads to attend 'Training The Trainers' courses, with the idea, according to one trainer, of getting:

Centre Heads more able to cope with developmental and training needs in their centres.

Apart from one local authority in the region, the reduction in expenditure on adult education seems to have stopped this. Countywide meetings of Centre Heads could encourage them to develop training in their centres but the following quotes demonstrate the more restricted use to which such meetings have usually been put.

Very, very occasionally, we have a county meeting of Centre Heads and I think once or twice it's come up in various forms, the idea of training, but it's never really been a major factor of these get togethers.

We don't get together nearly often enough. We've only had two meetings in $3\frac{1}{2}$ years, but we do have area Centre Head meetings, but again they are generally one a term and when we meet it's normally an occasion for administrative matters to be dealt with. We talk about publicity, we talk about fee rates, about new systems. We don't have meetings where we can devote time to tutor training.

A sense of isolation in their work extends to Centre Heads and it seems that provision of a forum for debating professional concerns might lead to more training in the centres.

Trainers clearly see the Centre Heads as important facilitators who could build on the foundations laid in formal training courses. Both trainers and teachers recognise that it is in the centre that problems of isolation and lack of confidence need to be overcome. It is quite apparent from these findings that training must involve a continuous, regenerative and friendly discussion between all adult education staff and moreover, that class visits are necessary adjuncts to formal training occasions. The general view suggests that the many Centre Heads who are not already so involved should be reminded that professional support for their part-time staff is an essential part of their job.

Specialist organisations

At this point it may be necessary to redress the picture that has emerged so far that the part-time teacher's position is not a particularly happy one. There are a number of ways in which teachers manage to overcome problems of isolation and of keeping up to date with their subject. A number of subject areas have developed their own specialist organisations that offer support and very frequently training. Some of the training schemes offered by these bodies are sophisticated and demand a considerable amount of time and effort from the teacher.

In the East Midlands 'exercise' organisations such as the Keep Fit Association and the Swing Into Shape Organisation offer well-developed training schemes to teachers. For instance, the Keep Fit Association offers training for three different groups of its members. Basic training for pianists is different in character from that for teachers. It is planned on the basis of two or three sessions of two hours of practical study with four or five weeks of observation and practice at Keep Fit Classes. Courses for those who wish to teach Keep Fit, exist at two levels. The first stage consists of one evening a week for two years; the second is also a two year course includes twelve Saturdays and a residential week. For those who have completed both stages of teacher-training and subsequently want to go on to train new teachers further training is required, extending over a total of four years. That is to say a two year course for potential trainers is held at regional level to be followed by another two years at national level. Refresher courses and courses on specific aspects of Keep Fit work, for example, work with the elderly, are also organised by the Association.

The value of this organisation to teachers, expecially in terms of maintaining morale and interest in the subject, was demonstrated by a teacher who was on the local committee of the KFA and described how with these committee meetings, training sessions and rallies she was involved in some activity every two or three weeks. Of the organisation she commented:

> Keep Fit teachers have the association to hang on to, other teachers might feel out on a limb, sometimes I think I would if I didn't have the KFA.

Though not strictly a specialist organisation, one association in the East Midlands offers a unique system of support to part-time tutors — The Northamptonshire Association of Part-time Teachers of Adults. This is an association initially created by a group of Stage 2 teachers at the end of their course because, in the words of one of them:

> We just felt that it shouldn't be the end of everything, we'd built up some close ties with each other.

This particular body serves as an interesting case study because it offers a practical solution to the problems of isolation faced by so many teachers.

Within the broad aim of "providing a stimulus for the exchange of ideas, experience and information" this group performs a double function. On the one hand it concerns itself with the continuing education of its members and on the other it carries out a political function. It does this by having representatives on the Regional Advisory Council and on appropriate committees of the Local Authority, ensuring that the voice of the part-time teacher is heard by policy makers within the county. The Association recognises the importance of the adult centre in the world of the part-time teacher and organises the meetings at different centres throughout the county. This serves the two-fold purpose of getting to know the Centre Head and extending the scope of the Association by inviting the part-time teachers teaching at that centre to come together under its aegis.

> We visit a Centre Head, we go off on a Friday evening to his centre and we get him to address us on a particular part that interests him and we have a wine and cheese party. . . and we ask him if he'd like to invite his tutors along as well so that we get to know them and they get to know us.

Because this Association is run entirely by practising part-time teachers it is particularly sensitive to their needs. Typical of its attitude is its involvement with the Local Authority in producing an Adult Education Tutor's Handbook which is intended to help teachers in their work. They also compile a register of members who are willing to go and see each other teach so that there can be a mutually beneficial exchange of ideas. As both these developments are innovations it is not yet possible fully to assess their usefulness but they certainly seem to fulfil some of the needs expressed by some of the teachers interviewed in this survey.

At present the Association is mainly restricted to post Stage 2 course members but it has been extended to include others (e.g. Stage 1 people) as associate members. In all there are about 80 members. It has the usual elected officers and a general committee, and each year organises two residential weekend meetings and arranges a programme of social and educational events throughout the year. The Local Authority in which it is based is very supportive and there is a close relationship between the Authority's officers and those of the Association. The Association sees itself as playing an important role in training. As a committee member said:

> I think it plays a big role in training. . . a very, very, very important role in helping to broaden people's attitudes to their role in adult education and. . . in a very informal way they can extend themselves.

He saw the Association as helping to build teachers' confidence and continuing the work begun on the training course.

> Stage 2 doesn't do everything; Stage 2 leaves you a little bit hanging on a string, you know, you're in mid air I feel, that's the way I felt and I think you can go on from there, it keeps you in touch with your colleagues, certainly there is a lot of informal exchange of ideas, it keeps tutors at one end of the county known to tutors at another. . . they do talk to each other on the telephone.

SECTION 4: THE CLASSROOM

The chief arena for the teacher is the classroom. Here interactions are private and it is difficult for outsiders to observe what takes place. The extent to which this problem could be overcome in the present project was limited and thus relevant information is inevitably second hand and has to be based on accounts from the teachers themselves and from the sample of students. The limitations of this research method are that the teacher is unlikely to be able to give an objective view of her/his own performance and students exhibited a loyalty towards their teachers and were reluctant to criticise them. Nevertheless these perspectives do give some idea of the activities and organisation of adult education classes in the East Midlands. This section will consider the following aspects of the adult education classroom: the perceived qualities of a good adult teacher; the problems faced in keeping up with the subject by the teacher; students' motivations and problems; the varying styles of teachers; and finally teachers' attitudes to training and the discernible effects that it has on their performance.

'Good' adult teaching

Earlier in this chapter, a distinction was drawn between some of the roles a teacher plays in the classroom, for example as a subject specialist and as a social enabler. Foremost is the role of educator, which subsumes both the other two, but is also distinctive in its own right. From the interviews it was evident that students and teachers were aware of these roles, and they were extremely sensitive to and articulate concerning the skills and qualities required to fulfil them successfully. We discuss below what students look for in adult teachers and what teachers regard as important in their own work. In passing it is interesting to note that when students were questioned as to the qualities of a good adult teacher, they were very likely to phrase an answer which reflected (favourably) on their own teacher.

Students and teachers were concerned that as a basic requirement teachers should be keenly interested in what they teach. This point was reiterated time and time again. Typical comments from teachers were:

> The first thing is you must know your subject inside out.

> A thorough knowledge of the subject they are teaching.

and from students:

> Well certainly the experience, knowing her stuff, I think that's for any teacher.

> Somebody like Mrs. X, she is good at her job, we know that she could write very fast shorthand, she had had all the experience.

The general impression is that subject knowledge was perceived as more important by the teachers than the students. It could be that students set store by other aspects of adult education or that they take their teachers' subject expertise for granted. Perhaps those teachers who see teaching as an extension of their hobby are most likely to be concerned with subject competence.

Many interviews leave little doubt that adult education fulfils important social needs. Teachers can play a very important part in facilitating social interaction, which for some students was crucial in determining how they learned in class. Consequently the ability of the teacher to facilitate relationships with students was rated highly by them; thus;

> Friendly. . . creates a good friendly group and mixes in. . .

> Interested in people, she wants to help them.

> Someone who gets on with everybody, treats everybody the same. . .

Teachers for their part appreciated that good adult educators should be aware of the social needs of their students. This was interpreted as creating an atmosphere in the classroom which was conducive to learning. Such attitudes are illustrated by comments from two different teachers:

72

A teacher needs to create a nice atmosphere in which they'll be prepared to learn and try new things.

I always tell them my christian name when they start, I've found that immediately makes an affinity. Things like that; we chat and have a look around at other people's work. Again I find that brings people out. It brings a friendly atmosphere.

In addition, creating the right atmosphere was seen as ensuring that students would be encouraged and made to feel that the teacher cared about them. In recognition of this obligation, one teacher listed the necessary qualities for a good adult teacher as "understanding, sympathy and caring". Part of this general attitude was to "be ready to listen to them and not just do all the talking". Obviously it relates to the teacher's perception of the student. Many teachers believed they should be "open minded towards people, taking them as they came". Such behaviour would in the view of one teacher make them feel "they've made a friend as well as a teacher". The purpose of being ready to listen and build up a personal relationship with students was seen as extending beyond strictly educational realms. Thus a teacher should be:

Somebody who is always prepared to listen to the people who come along, not just their problems with the work, but some of their other problems as well, personal problems.

Clearly, to perform this social function teachers need certain skills and these were referred to by some teachers during interview. There was a belief that teachers should be "outgoing", "be an approachable sort of person with a good knowledge of how people tick", be "approachable and friendly" and have "feeling for people whatever their age" and an "understanding of human nature", have a "sense of humour" and a "relaxed attitude". These criteria identified by both students and teachers portray the adult tutor's role as a socially demanding one that requires the teacher to be perceptive, friendly, sincere and responsive to other people.

The roles already discussed are important to the educational function of the teacher. As far as the student was concerned confidence in a teacher's knowledge of his subject and a perception of him/her as friendly and sympathetic, created a good climate for effective learning and teaching. Students were explicit about the educational practices they looked for in a good teacher, in particular that they should be treated as adults in the classroom. Consequently the qualities most important to them are a sensitivity to their learning needs and difficulties as adults and a sympathy with their feelings as adult learners. Evidence for this, emerges from a selection of their comments on this issue.

It's got to be somebody with real interest in what they are doing, able to put it over well but not on a level of like a school teacher with children.

Somebody who can talk to adults and appreciate that adults might know as much as they know. . . and not resent this.

I think it's the chap who sees a situation where somebody is obviously struggling, obviously doing something that could be done a bit better or a bit easier another way, being able to get that over to him, without necessarily giving him the impression that he's a bit of a fool.

Understanding that everyone is an individual; that people learn at different rates and are very different.

She is very patient and she explains over and over again, this makes quite a difference.

The students' evidence shows that they want to relax, feel at ease and enjoy themselves in class. In their minds, the ethos in the classroom was primarily determined by the teacher hence, it was important that he/she should be enthusiastic about student progress and achievements, as well as enjoying teaching. Two students who commented approvingly on their teachers illustrate these points well.

> She enjoys teaching us. . . that is the most important thing, enthusiasm.

> I suppose somebody who is pleased if we are pleased with the end results. If we have had a bad evening, well he's just as miserable about it as we were.

A professional attitude from their teachers was valued by a few students, particularly over things like preparation, concern for standards, setting work between meetings and making demands on people. So amongst other things students respected teachers who encouraged them to work.

> A friendly approach is necessary as is someone prepared to do some work in preparation. They have got to get to know peoople quickly, to know what they enjoy doing, because if you enjoy doing it, you are going to work harder at it. A teacher has to try and get the best out of pupils.

Finally this perceptive student summed up the difficulty in arriving at a set of qualities appropriate for good teachers:

> Honesty. . . when there isn't a set answer to a question, she'll say, "very well let's try it, we don't know, but we'll try it". But you appreciate that I don't know that there is a formula for a good teacher really.

It is worth noting that teachers echoed the qualities most valued by students. They were conscious that a good teacher should treat students as adults and that the best approach was one of teaching on 'equal terms'. For example one cookery teacher stressed the fundamental point of not talking down to people:

> You don't have to drill them with theory. You talk to them as one housewife talking to another housewife.

Often teachers stressed similar points and believed that a good teacher should feel:

> That you are exactly the same as people coming to the class and never set yourself up as anything else.

> Respect for them. I wouldn't dream of talking down to anybody.

> Able to talk to people without the lecturer being aloof and being above everybody.

They also thought that a good teacher should be "confident and flexible" and "willing to change ideas if they were not working" and as one teacher implied, self-critical and reflective. Several others spoke of the importance of having a professional approach to the job. Discussion of the qualities of the good adult teacher emphasises the demanding and diverse rôles they have to play.

Problems faced by teachers

The teachers who were interviewed were reluctant to admit to experiencing problems in their teaching other than those associated with equipment or facilities. Interestingly the few teachers who were willing to talk about problems were usually the ones who had undertaken adult education teacher training. This may reflect the fact that they were more confident in their work and more able to analyse the difficulties they faced, but just how teachers perceived problems in their teaching varied considerably even among the trained. Thus a woman who had done a Stage 2/730 joint course replied to a question about problems by saying:

I don't quite know what you mean by problems. I don't find any problems.

However, other trained adult teachers admitted that there were some. The most frequently mentioned problem was coping with the mixed ability range of adult students. A teacher of Spanish commented:

I think the worst is mixed ability in the class. You get several groups. In one of the classes at the moment I have three groups. So it's hard work, and they don't get as much time as if it were all one level.

and a craft teacher said:

With adults it might be anybody. Mixed ages and mixed backgrounds as well.

It was not only the individuals who were slower or less able than the majority who presented problems, but also those who were more able and knowledgeable. One experienced teacher who identified this problem explained how he saw and attempted to deal with it.

The only thing you've got to bear in mind, of course, is that with adults, with the adults' experience, there's always bound to be some part of the subject where somebody in your class will know more than you do, so you have to use them.

This is doubtless admirable advice but an insecure and inexperienced teacher might have difficulty in following it. The wide range of ability of people in adult education classes means that teachers have to find strategies for coping with them and with the different ways adults learn. The interviews reveal that this was a source of concern to many teachers and the difficulty as they saw it was not so much in identifying the problem as in knowing how to deal with it. Those of particular concern were:

— How to deal with the different learning rates of adults, especially the more elderly students.
— How to handle the 'awkward' person in a class.
— How to encourage students who lacked self-confidence.
— How to interest and motivate those who didn't appear keen to learn.

Adult teachers are usually employed on the basis of expertise and they are expected to be skilled and knowledgeable in their subject. Despite this the problem remains of keeping up to date with new developments and changing ideas in their field of competence. The previous section showed that teachers feel isolated in that they rarely, if ever, meet people teaching the same subject as themselves. It was also shown that certain subject organisations offer an effective back-up service to teachers offering both formal training and on-going support. Teachers who were not members of such organisations faced greater difficulties in keeping up to date. Some ways of overcoming this problem involve subscribing to relevant magazines, attending meetings or exhibitions (especially those teaching arts and crafts subjects), talking to friends who were also teachers or had the same interest, watching pertinent television programmes, attending refresher courses and developing an awareness of things in everyday life that might help them, (e.g. a needlework teacher may look at the fashions in the shops). Many of these activities cost time and money but quite a few part-time teachers appeared to be willing to spend both to keep up to date and in touch with current thinking in their subject area. The enthusiasm and commitment to widen their knowledge of their subject was high in the majority of teachers interviewed.

Student motivation

An important part of the regional scheme's training programme is directed at helping the teacher to understand the motivation and behaviour of their students. Students' reasons for attending an adult class affect their reaction to the teacher and their commitment to the subject; in part at least this will determine the approach the teacher needs to adopt in dealing with her/his class. Some students were vague when asked why they were attending classes. Typical explanations for attending a class were:

> From a personal point of view, learning a subject that I know nothing about.

> It's a hobby I took up around four years ago. . . I thought I'd better get into it a bit more. . . but you need some explanation on many things and I thought I'd get that advice and tuition from an evening class.

> I suppose purely to follow my own interest in something that I was interested in — a hobby of my own. And part social I suppose, you know, meeting people.

> I wanted to do something and the description of the class was well. . . it was slightly different. I had lost my father and I wanted something that had no connection at all. . . something entirely new.

> I'm looking for somewhere with facilities, somewhere warm, where I can spend two hours per week. The help is there if you want it. Others are using it because they have a requirement to learn something or a requirement to make something.

Most students attended classes in order to learn something new, to develop existing interests or for social reasons. A few attend for economic purposes. Teachers recognised that students have mixed motives for coming to their classes. Thus a bridge teacher said in analysing why people attended his class that he had:

> . . . those who want to learn bridge and. . . those who really just want an evening out, possibly for social discourse, rather than actual bridge.

Teachers were aware that many of their students were keen to learn more about a subject whereas a few came regardless of the topic. Hence the difficulty mentioned by a woman teaching pressed flower techniques, who in recognising some of the harsh realities of adult education, commented:

> One or two of my students said "we came to enrol for pottery, but it was full. . . "

Another teacher in a similar subject also recognised that students do not necessarily attend because they have chosen a specific subject offered in the prospectus.

> I think a lot might even see what night they're free and see what there is that night.

It is not surprising that the degree of student commitment differs. Some classes attract the 'not yet committed' or 'casual' student, other classes being more specialised may be less attractive particularly where they require expensive equipment and cater for the enthusiast. Machine knitting will only attract those who own a knitting machine and photography, primarily individuals with a camera and pre-existing interest in the subject. It was evident from the interviews that once in a lively, well taught class, the 'casual' student often turned into a highly motivated enthusiast. Yet judging from the teachers' accounts, a prime motive of this type of student for attendance at their classes was recreational and social.

Teachers made it clear that it was not only the casual student who came to classes for social reasons, for attendance might well fulfil needs other than strictly 'education/learning' ones. For instance adult education provides a convenient way for many women to get out of the home, especially young mothers who are housebound with children much of the time. Many teachers recognised the importance of this:

> Well I know that in the first place they come to meet other people, because a lot of them are young marrieds and have got young children at home. . . they make new friendships and then they meet them during the day as well and do other things together.

> A lot of them want to get away from their families. . .

Another group to whom adult education was recognised as important was those who had retired from work. Teachers frequently referred to the number of pensioners in their classes, as they did to people who were living on their own. The comments of two teachers point to the reasons why such people come to classes:

> I think more for the companionship, a lot of them live on their own and it's a way of getting out and meeting people.

> I've got some retired people, they also attend for company.

Several teachers mentioned that an important if small group they found regularly attending their class was the recently bereaved. For those people attendance at the class was one way of re-establishing a more normal pattern of life, as one French teacher put it:

> Most years there's someone who's recently been widowed and they find that they can meet other people again. They get into a small group of people that they get to know and they find that they're ready for a wider circle. I've noticed at least four or five of these have started a class in September, they've lost their partner during the summer or during the previous winter and they're just beginning to feel like moving into people again and then by about the spring, they've got confidence back and they've probably applied for a part-time job or something like that.

Finally, many teachers recognised, and strove to ensure that their classes were enjoyable and brought people a good deal of pleasure.

> It's a recreational thing. I think it's important they should enjoy it, as well as achieving something in it.

> They basically come because they want to have an enjoyable evening out. I hope they are actually achieving something.

> A sense of achievement at the end, friendship, and doing something they want to do and it turning out reasonably well at the end.

These and many other comments show that teachers clearly expected their students to achieve and to learn in their class but always to enjoy coming.

Teachers were asked what problems they found their students had in learning. There was a discernible difference in replies between those who had received formal teacher training and those who had not or had only subject-based training. Those who were untrained were far more likely to say their students had no problems or that their difficulties arose from their inability to cope with the demands of the subject. Typical comments from untrained teachers when asked about students' problems were:

> (from a cake decoration teacher) — No I don't think there are many, with my particular subject, it is mainly getting the right consistency, once they have that they are all right.

> (a wine making teacher) — I find that a lot of the ladies who come . . . they have an awful lot of problems with getting to grips with things like hydrometers and chemicals.

> (a squash teacher) — Their inability or lack of desire to move about the court. Secondly, basic racket-ball co-ordination, if they've not played a racket sport before.

Trained teachers were far more aware of why adults find it difficult to learn and the limits to their students' understanding of the subject. Teachers interviewed were able to put forward a number of reasons to explain some of the difficulties in adult learning, and the most commonly mentioned were, in paraphrase:

(a) — they come to a class after a day's work, and may not have much time to devote to the subject between class meetings:

> A lot of them don't do anything from week to week, then just come for the hour and say they haven't been able to do any work during the week.

(b) — students need to have confidence in themselves before they can progress. They may not have this confidence because they underestimate their ability, are self-conscious, are unrelaxed or have been out of touch with education for a number of years. Many teachers were conscious of these problems, as for example these who noted:

> Well the main thing is a lot of them are very stiff and getting them to relax, it's self consciousness really and tension.

> They lose confidence, when they hit a snag it then becomes difficult for them, sometimes, to keep going without them getting depressed or cheesed off.

> You find that if a person has not for some years done any actual learning of any kind they don't feel very confident.

(c) — some adult students have unrealistic expectations of their probable rate of progress:

> Well I think they want to jump ahead too quickly, run before they can walk.

> If they've never done it before and they're older, they have problems because they think that they should probably be able to pick it up a bit quicker.

(d) — the skills of learning may be in disrepair, an issue stressed by a typing teacher:

> Some, especially the older ones, say they can't think. So you have to encourage them. Concentration is a problem.

(e) — the progress of some students is affected by external factors that are not directly related to the class or the subject. One teacher who clearly identified this problem said:

There are other problems not concerned with class, for example, getting there. Other years we've had marriages breaking up, personal problems that came into the class.

Trained teachers seemed more able to appreciate the restrictions in students' comprehension of their subject. Untrained teachers were more likely to hope their students would simply acquire certain skills whereas those who had been trained went beyond this and hoped they would grasp a broader understanding of the subject. This is well illustrated by the comments some trained teachers made when asked about the effect they felt their subjects would have on their students and the sort of changes it might bring. Craft teachers for example expressed a hope that students would learn more than the purely manual skills of how to do a particular task. A good example of this came from a school teacher teaching silver-smithing — he hoped his students would get:

> Better awareness of how things are made. . . and metal working techniques and simply that people don't have a magic wand and they appear. . . they don't take processes and techniques for granted.

Along the same lines a pottery teacher said:

> I hope (they get) a lot of enjoyment, the ability to learn how to do something and to appreciate how something is done, they can now go to shops and understand how things are made.

This account very neatly sums up the teachers' dilemma — should they make students feel safe and secure or should they throw down the challenge at the risk of giving students a feeling of insecurity? This study suggests that trained teachers are more likely to do the latter. Nevertheless, many teachers spoke convincingly of the growth in personal confidence in their students. For example a Keep Fit teacher believed that at the end of the course her students would:

> Have more confidence. I've known one or two who came quite retiring and they're full of confidence at the end.

That same sort of change was noted by a dressmaking teacher:

> I think that some of the shy ones get quite confident at the end of their courses, they do, they change quite a lot and get more confident in what they do.

In a similar way, a cookery teacher felt attendance at adult classes could help women who have come to the end of of the child-rearing phase of their lives. She said of some of the women she taught:

> They'd been at home with families for some time and like myself when I came back to work, you feel that you haven't anything to offer at all and I think you increase your self assurance and feel you've got something to offer.

Other teachers saw their subject as having specific benefit for individuals in terms of helping them to cope with stress and strain.

A pottery teacher believed:

> Clay, actually pottery making, is very therapeutic, you know, it gets rid of a lot of tensions and inhibitions.

A Yoga teacher that:

> Often people come very tensed up and perhaps rather emotionally unstable and you certainly do notice a difference. They do learn to calm down.

Some perceived their work as carrying over into the family and the community. These teachers provided examples of those who felt quite strongly about having broad objectives for their work. Thus:

> I feel that I'm not only educating the person in that room, I'm educating the family because they take it home and then they try to change the family.

> I hope they get into a sort of community . . . and are prepared to work with other people.

Evidently students have mixed and wide ranging motives for attending adult education classes. The spectrum varies from totally subject based motives to those that are almost entirely social. Teachers are aware of this variety and appreciate that they have to serve the two-fold task of facilitating learning and helping to create a friendly and welcoming atmosphere in their class; one facilitates the other. Teachers' expectations of students' ability to be experimental and creative in their approach to the subject seem to vary according to whether or not the former are trained. This also seems to hold true for the teachers' understanding of the problems faced by students — trained teachers are most easily able to define these and to see them extending beyond the immediate confines of the class.

SECTION 5: TEACHING APPROACHES

Although this study did not set out to study teaching approaches, it emerged from the comments of teachers and students that these varied widely. Most appeared to fall into one of two categories: that of teachers who devoted most of their time to working with students individually and that of teachers who spent most of the time working with their students as a group. Some clearly combined these approaches, but little was said about them by our respondents. The following section indicates how these two distinctive approaches were perceived.

The 'Circular Tour' — individual teaching

This approach appeared to characterise most arts and craft classes and is used in some sports classes such as swimming and badminton. Typically the students arrived at their class and immediately got on with their own piece of work: the teacher then came to each individual in turn to answer queries or sort out any problems. The majority of teaching took place on a one to one basis and frequently the initiative for what a student did remained with each individual. Every student usually had a clear idea of his own project but this may have had little in common with the work being done by others. This method meant that there was no plan for the class as a whole and consequently there was very little teaching of the class as a group. Students described the method as follows:

> We all turn up and get on with our sewing and we call her if we have any problems. We can all sew a little bit and she is always on hand if you want her.

> People do things from carved chessmen to cupboards. Each person does his or her own project. . . we go in and do as much as we can and then yell for help. Mr X comes and has a look and gives us any assistance we need.

Generally students seemed satisfied with this state of affairs, the criticisms that were made tended to be concerned with the amount of attention individual students were given. It was evident that they kept a very close eye on how the teacher's time was distributed and were rather sensitive if they thought they had not received enough attention. This student left no doubt about her feelings:

> I think I ought to have got even more than I did. Some nights I just seemed to sit there.

This person was more phlegmatic about it:

> You might go one week and only see her for a fleeting few minutes. . . I mean she might attend to you for just a few moments because somebody else needed 10 or 15 minutes. . . and another time it'll level off when you need it.

Teachers using the 'circular tour' approach recognised this as one of their chief problems, as for example this dressmaker:

> You must get round everybody at least once during the session, if you don't do that you just lose your students; that is inevitable because you must give them some attention each time.

Both students and teachers had what were at times ingenious strategies to cope with the problem. Students aimed to arrive at the class early so that they could get the teacher's attention before the others arrived, as one student says:

> Everyone turns up and gets on with their own thing and you try and get there as early as you can.

Some teachers, appreciating that the 'first come, first served' method was not fair to those who could not arrive early, had developed methods that allowed them to distribute their time evenly. The following description is of a dressmaking teacher's method:

> I said to them you all always sit in the same place each time you come, so we have four corners of the room and one week I start at one corner and I work round this way and the next week I start at the other corner and I work so that the ones that I've seen the first one week are the last the next week.

From the evidence it appears that this approach can lead to student interaction. Because students were left more to their own devices, they found that they were able to learn from one another and the more able could help the slower or less experienced ones. Two students, one in photography and one in woodwork, described how this occurred in their classes:

> It starts off very quiet, but basically within two or three weeks, people are going around chatting. . . they'll ask "What is it you're making? What are you doing? And what sort of wood are you using"? And that sort of thing.

> And you learn equally as much perhaps from one another and their experiences as being taught it. You can get to know quite a lot from other people's mistakes and experiences.

The students appeared in general to be happy with the 'circular tour' method, and teachers had found that attempts to combine it with group teaching of points of general interest were often unpopular, perhaps where students were concerned with the production of an article rather than with the mastery of a craft.

I prefer this approach because two hours doesn't go very far, and if you had to stop, you might need that technique, but on the other hand, you might never need it, in which case it is better to get on with what you are doing.

'Class Teaching'

Teachers employing this approach usually taught academic subjects, or sports like Keep Fit, Circuit Training and so on. Typically, the teacher directed the operations of the students as a group, they worked in concert and communication was between the teacher and the group as a whole. Descriptions of what occurs in lessons based on this approach are given below.

We normally arrive and talk over the homework, which part of the homework we find difficult, we vary it each week, sometimes we do comprehension, sometimes it's summaries and then our homework is based really on our weakest part at that time.

We have a sort of warm-up period for twenty minutes, then go through a series of exercises, endurance exercises, then finish off with a game of football or badminton or something.

We go in, get changed and we do a routine to music and then exercises and then floor exercises.

Typically we go through the previous week's work which she has given to us. . . and then we do another one, and then we have some theory for perhaps half an hour.

In this context, teachers were able to plan in advance the content of the course week by week and the methods to be used. How far this was done was hard to assess since the syllabuses were not seen, but when teachers were following set courses like those provided in language by the BBC, much seemed to be predetermined. The evidence suggested that students taught in this way did not expect to be involved in planning the course beyond suggesting minor adjustments to what the teacher proposed.

He usually decides what we are doing. . . he knows better than we do.

She always decides for us. . . she seemed to cover everything that everyone wanted to do. So, you know, I think it's best that they suggest what they want you to do.

She decides, but I don't think she would be against a suggestion, but up to now everybody has been carried along by her own enthusiasm.

Joint effort seemed to promote group spirit and a number of students commented on the benefit derived from it:

I like doing things in a group — which is more fun than doing it by oneself.

As in the case of courses taught by the 'circular tour' method, students appeared to be uncritical about the 'class teacher' approach. It satisfied the needs of people who enjoyed working in a group and it also met the expectation of those who wanted to be taught by more 'formal' class methods, a viewpoint most clearly put by a language student when he said:

I prefer being taught and told what to do. . .

SECTION 6: ATTITUDES TO, AND EFFECTS OF TRAINING

There was a division evident among teachers over the issue of whether non-vocational adult education teachers should be trained. The teachers who had taken local authority training courses, came down heavily in favour of the view that training should be compulsory. They justified this view by the benefits they believed they had gained from training viz. increased confidence and a wider knowledge of teaching techniques and aids. Practically every teacher trained to S2/730 and Stage 3 believed training was important. Some suggested that everyone coming in to adult education should be trained specifically in adult teaching. Typical of this view was a Keep Fit teacher who believed:

> Even trained school teachers and subject trained teachers — I still think they ought to do an LEA course because it makes them see it from a different angle.

One Stage 3 trained woman had very definite views on why craft teachers needed to be trained; she remarked, that if this was the case, then:

> You might get away from this business of people bringing their work and thinking they're going to sit and do it for two hours.

In general it was suggested all new teachers should at least do Stage 1 and preferably Stage 2. Teachers tended to recommend the type and level of training they themselves had completed, with the exception of Stage 3 people who recognised that not everyone had the time and interest to undertake the commitment necessary to complete a Stage 3 course. At the same time a feeling was expressed by a few people with all levels of training that it would be a shame if a training requirement prohibited certain people from teaching; they inclined to the belief that some people could be effective teachers without formal training. A Stage 2 trained teacher, saw training as very important but:

> You occasionally find someone who's extremely gifted and it would be a sad thing to lose them.

Individuals who had received training from one of the subject agencies e.g. Bridge or Swimming, similarly believed training was important, envisaging this as being undertaken within the subject specialism. People who had not been trained to teach adults were less in favour of compulsory training. Some felt encouragement should be given but that it was preferable for people to decide themselves to take a course, as one teacher commented:

> If you have to, it always makes it so much more of a drudge than if you do it on your own initiative.

Others felt that whilst adult education training was necessary for teachers of academic subjects it was not so important for those teaching crafts. The perceived differences between untrained teachers and those who had taken a regional scheme or City and Guilds' course about the desirability of undergoing training suggests that there is a fundamental difference in attitude. Untrained teachers tend to see non-vocational adult education in terms of demonstrating or passing on a craft, skill or hobby, rather than as being part of a professional education service which provides a range of learning experiences for adults. Adult trained teachers are more likely to take this latter view.

Teachers who had been on adult teacher training courses were asked about the effect they believed training had had on their teaching. It was evident that they believed the major effect was one of changed attitude towards their students; many training courses generated a definite ethos about the way students should be treated. It was aimed primarily at making the students feel that their knowledge and opinions are valued and also to make them feel comfortable and unthreatened. An important theme, reiterated by teachers, was that the course had made them see students as equals who can be used as valuable resources in the classroom:

> I listen to the students, that way you're learning from them at the same time they're learning from you.

> There was a lot of emphasis laid on the fact that the tutor in adult education is not so much a teacher but rather one of a number who knows rather more about the subject than the others.

The other major change in attitude towards students was that teachers said they became more concerned with their students' learning difficulties and less with their own teaching problems. Thus one teacher described how she now encouraged students to learn through discovery:

> Now I let them finish what they're doing, then see what the overall effect is. When they stand back and look, they can point their own faults out. I wouldn't have thought of doing that at one time. I'd have been showing them rather than letting them find out for themselves.

Another teacher reported that the course had shown him the importance of ensuring effective learning.

> Well, before I was quite happy to stand in front of a class and talk to them not understanding whether they had learnt anything or not, I would be cross next week because they hadn't understood it. The first thing I realised on this course was that it was me who was the dummy for not checking as I went along during the lesson that they had learned what I was trying to tell them.

Teachers emphasised that their courses helped them to get the most out of their students. They were able to develop more fully the potential of their students than previously. This pottery teacher's account of how her course changed her in this respect is a good example:

> I have realised a lot about the students as well, I learned a lot about how to get the most from them, that was the most interesting thing. . . I hadn't realised how much I could get from the students by the way I taught or counselled them. You know, I used to be rather a silent teacher. I would give the information but I didn't really get much feed-back, I never thought, I didn't think I needed to. . . that came as an awful shock to realise how much feed-back I could get from the students.

A few teachers mentioned that they had also come to realise how individuals were affected by group influences and how the different types of interaction may occur in the classroom. In discussing this type of benefit one teacher said:

> Well I try to be more aware. . . one of the things they said when the tutor came over to watch me was that although you are talking to individuals, which you are quite a lot, you've got to be aware of what is going on in the class as a whole. I found that useful, you've got to sense the atmosphere and be aware of the problems on the other side of the room.

Most teachers benefited from their course by coming to appreciate the advantages of preparation and planning, especially the need for a syllabus and course and lesson planning. Many trainees on Stage 1 courses had not done much planning previously and found it increased both their confidence and the effectiveness of their lessons. Thus a teacher who had recently completed a Stage 1 said:

84

I try to think how can I get it across in a better way, rather than just lecturing, I've re-arranged the syllabus slightly and instead of plodding through in a straight-forward manner, I've tried to bring in subjects at a different stage to make it more interesting.

One inevitable result of teachers becoming more aware of the value of planning techniques was to spend more time on preparing for their teaching and to become more reflective about the whole process.

I put hours in before my class, you don't just go along and spout, come away again and that's it. You're thinking beforehand, you're thinking there and you're thinking afterwards, what they've done etc. It's changed my attitude in that, I go along well beforehand, so that I'm ready.

They impressed on us how important it was to be very, very well prepared, and I do prepare my work with much more time, whereas I only used to dedicate one hour or an hour and a half — I sort of think about it in much more detail.

Part of the business of preparation is to make decisions about how lessons can be made more interesting for students; training courses were particularly helpful to teachers in that they were enabled to see the value of using visual aids. If teachers were rather disillusioned with other aspects of the course they usually found the technical information about aids such as overhead projectors, slide projectors and duplicators valuable. This was especially helpful to those who had not come across such aids before, usually older teachers. One woman commented of her Stage 2 course:

The most useful bit, it sounds awfully banal, was the audio-visual stuff. . . feeling that this was a normal part of teaching.

Another benefit that most adult teachers derived from their courses was a development in confidence in their teaching ability. Part of this came from meeting other teachers on the course and seeing that they had to face similar problems and part of it came as a consequence of the course itself. Two teachers' comments illustrate this point:

Probably made me a bit more confident. Perhaps finding out that others were in the same boat.

Well I know exactly how to prepare my lesson, I know the methods to use, what communication, eye communication and all that sort of thing. . . I know things that perhaps beforehand I wouldn't have been aware of. It gave me more self-confidence in holding a class together.

Confident teachers usually give their students confidence which means that students become relaxed and find it easier to enjoy the class and to learn. A teacher described how the course she had been on had emphasised that the most important part of a class was the students and this in turn helped her to relate to her own situation.

I think this is a good attitude to put over to the students, because it gives them more confidence.

If a teacher's confidence increases, then he/she will feel more able to use the adult education system for the benefit of the students. This extends to publicising the course as well as getting improved facilities for the class. One woman described how increased confidence had affected her attitude:

It gave me confidence. I felt the student was the most important person in the building. For instance, I wanted to do a demonstration on a student and there were only little hard-backed chairs — so I marched out, went to the Principal's office and took his easy chair! They laughed, I said "No, you've paid your fees, you're the students, and you're having the right treatment". I fight for my students now, perhaps I didn't before.

An increase in confidence was very often reported as a result of attendance at a training course. However, in one extreme example a teacher who had been very dissatisfied with her performance on her Stage 2/730 course said:

I was so demoralised after mine that I had to do a correspondence course to get my confidence back.

Finally, training courses can affect teachers' perception of the overall nature of adult education. Several teachers said that the course had helped them to see their own teaching in a wider perspective and to see their place in this. They came to appreciate the nature and extent of adult education. Typical comments about how courses had affected awareness in this context were:

I was just an employee previously. I felt much more involved in the whole set-up after I'd done it.

We realised all the facts and things that can be gained from adult education. Because quite honestly until I started training I just thought adult education was someone going off to a local comprehensive school doing an evening class.

SECTION 7: THE UNTRAINED ADULT EDUCATION TEACHER

A major concern of many involved in adult education is the apparent reluctance of some teachers to undertake any form of adult education teacher training. It was not the intention of the project to look at this part of the teaching force in great detail but some data were collected on these teachers and it seems appropriate to present it under one heading.

Towards the end of the teachers' questionnaire, respondents were asked to indicate their intention to undertake adult education teacher training. Those teachers who had no previous adult education training and who answered 'NO' to this question were taken as unambiguously refusing adult education teacher training. There were 529 of them, some 34% of the total sample. There was first and foremost a marked sex difference within the sample. Men and women were near equally distributed in the 'NO training' group, 51%: 47% (272:251, with 6 non-respondents). However, when it is remembered that in the total sample there were twice as many women as men (64%: 35%, 993:544) it appears that whilst one in four of the women were refusing training, the rate for the men was one in two. This difference is the more striking when put against those who had undertaken adult education teacher training: women (390) far outnumbered the men (84) again. Thus it is quite clear that men teachers refuse training rather than women teachers, at least in this sample.

The differences in age between those teachers who refused adult education training and the remainder of the sample were much less clear. There is some suggestion that a slightly greater proportion of teachers in their twenties and thirties refused training than did older teachers. However, such a result cannot easily be separated from the effects of other variables such as qualifications and experience and any conclusions must at present remain merely speculative.

When teachers teaching within the four subject categories are considered differences can be observed. Teachers of Academic subjects were the most ready to say "NO" to training, 39% (107) of all those working within that subject area. This is also the group with the highest proportion of qualified school teachers and the lowest proportion of adult trained teachers. Arts/Crafts teachers were the least likely to refuse — 30% (139) of the total 464 — this group also had the highest proportion of adult trained teachers in its ranks. Teachers of both Skills and Sports/Exercises came mid-way at 34% and 35% respectively.

A comparison of the 'NO training' group with those who had undertaken adult education training as part of their years of teaching experience showed very similar distributions. There was an increased tendency for teachers to refuse training with increasing length of service.

The formal qualifications of teachers who refused adult training appeared markedly superior to those who had undertaken such training. Over 30% (156) of the refusers had degrees compared with only 5% (25) of the trained group. Only 5% (27) of the refusers had just GCE qualifications compared with 18% (86) of the trained, whilst those who apparently had none were 14% (72) and 24% (113) respectively. Though these examples are at the extremes it is clear that those who refused adult education teacher training were rather better academically qualified than those who undertook such training. Not surprisingly, those who already have undertaken other forms of teacher training are much more likely to refuse adult training then those who do not. Some 52% (277) of those saying 'NO' were qualified school teachers and a further 17% (88) had subject training qualifications. Only 30% (160) had no teacher training of any sort. The comparable figures within the adult trained group exemplify this finding: little more than 5% (23) were qualified school teachers though about the same proportion had subject training, 18% (87). Apart from their adult training, however, 75% (354) of the adult trained sample had no other teacher training.

It must be stressed that the figures given here are derived from frequency tables and do not represent any analytical statistical comparisons. It is likely that such analyses would modify to some degree what is outlined in the previous paragraphs. Nevertheless the descriptions we have given, speculative though they are, suggest that teachers who are reluctant to undertake adult education teacher training are likely to be male, younger rather than older, and to teach academic subjects rather than art and craft. Their tendency to resist training will grow with length of service and it is probable that they will have formal qualifications resulting from higher education and as likely as not to be qualified school teachers.

Of the total sample of 63 teachers interviewed, 24% (15) were untrained teachers with a further 9% (6) qualified school teachers. Part of the interview schedule concerned their reasons for not undertaking training and an account of their responses is given here. One reason given was 'pressure of time' though it was not offered as frequently as might have been expected, and it was usually given supported by other reasons. Thus one inexperienced teacher said that he would go if he had the time and admitted that it would help his use of visual aids. Another young teacher said she was quite happy with the way her course was going:

> I don't feel that with the sort of course I have been doing it would be of any great benefit. I feel that my job has helped me pick up the necessary techniques.

Some of the qualified school teachers spoke of the time problem though they recognised the value of training:

> I didn't know of any courses for adults, which seems awful — you just assume that you can teach adults. Now I have learnt a lot, but at first when I started a couple of years

ago, I found it quite difficult, but it is easier now because I have learnt to cope with the problems that you get with adults.

I'm not sure how good a teacher of adults I am. I think that if someone came in and assessed me and said "you could improve this and that by doing certain things" I'd say it would be beneficial. I think it would be better had I had some form of course before I was thrown into the deep end because I've learnt by making mistakes. If I started a new course then I would approach it in a completely different manner.

The reason one teacher gave was that he had not attended because of the lack of time yet he recognised that training was "broadening" and if he were to attend he would be:

Learning whether I am teaching properly. Whether I am getting the subject across. (Also). . . as much as anything talking to other teachers and realising that any problems I have I'm not the only one with those problems. . . how to deal with awkward students. . .

Nevertheless, if training were to be made compulsory he would go into private teaching altogether, some of which he did already.

A number of teachers either did not know what a training course involved or were unaware that they were available. Thus, one inexperienced teacher would have liked to have gone on a course but said:

I don't know what would be involved. I think it would be useful to have resources to go to get ideas how to teach, how to get ideas across. I feel a right beginner — it's just my confidence in knowing the subject overall that has got me through.

She had in fact been told it was better to go on a training course after she had got some teaching experience but nothing had happened and she was waiting for "them" to tell her. Another more experienced teacher gave a similar answer but in her case she had never been asked though she presumably knew about training. She was in this respect unlike the teacher who said that she would have liked to go on a course but she did not know of any.

I've certainly no objection to being taught the basic principles of teaching along with people who are doing other subjects.

There was also a rather older man who felt that a course might be interesting but clearly did not fancy working with young teachers, nevertheless he said that he was unaware of any course that he might attend.

The belief that with knowledge of the subject and experience teachers really do not need formal training was expressed by some individuals though rather mutedly. One retired school teacher was quite definite and maintained that there was little difference between teaching children and adults, except for 'discipline' and consequently saw no need for training.

The principles that guided me through teaching children still guide me through teaching adults. . . I have found no reason to alter anything.

Another experienced AE teacher also said that as far as she was concerned there was little point undertaking training after having taught for some years, yet she went on to say:

I would have preferred to have done it at the beginning before I started to teach and got it over with. I'm not criticising teacher training, I'm sure I would learn a lot and I would like to have done it, but I also think that I am learning this way, the practical way.

In like vein an inexperienced teacher said that she felt that training would not be very useful to her 'for she knew her subject'. Yet she admitted that she might possibly learn something about the approach to teaching from a general course. In her case it had been suggested to her that she should go for training and it would seem that with a little encouragement she would go. A full-time training officer decided that he would not get much out of a training course but that without the experience and knowledge from his full time work he would not "have dared do it".

It is necessary to recognise that the sample of teachers available to us were self-selected in that they had offered themselves for interview; they were clearly aware of the project's major interest in training of AE teachers. It is reasonable to suppose that they would be unlikely to hold strong feelings against training; from their responses they were not antipathetic towards training. They seem to be ill-informed and unaware rather than prejudiced against. There are some who hold to the tenet of 'training though experience' but this is appealed to far less than popular AE belief would indicate. It cannot be doubted that pressure of time is a real problem for many and to hold down a full-time job and to teach a part-time class as well does not allow a great deal of freedom to take on the added burden of a training course. Bearing in mind some of the comments made by teachers actually on training courses it may be that the excuse of time is given as the more ostensible reason and masks those of apprehension and uncertainty about training. It seems that poor communication underlies at least some of the apparent resistance to training though this does not excuse one experienced woman teacher who felt that she ought to undergo training, yet had not:

> Just to make sure that I've done the right thing — that I'm giving the students the best I can. There might be something that you could learn to help get your students going more, just the way you speak, things like that. . .

She clearly knew about training courses. Similarly, another experienced teacher who said that people should be trained in AE, because courses are generally important for stimulating new ideas had singularly failed herself to attend such a course. It must be recognised that teachers who have other forms of teacher training are those most likely to refuse adult education teacher training. Presumably they believe that it has little to teach them.

SECTION 8: OVERVIEW

Who are these part-time teachers of adults and what is their world? Often informally recruited, these people are attracted by the enjoyment that can be derived from teaching, by the sharing of their skills and knowledge with others, and by the satisfaction of watching students grow and develop. They come into adult education as individuals from a wide range of backgrounds and they embrace a comprehensive and diverse range of subjects. They are frequently skilled and exhibit great expertise in the subjects that they teach. The part-time teaching force is not a homogeneous group; there is little evidence of stereotyping and views are highly individualistic. Nevertheless some crude classification of teachers can be made on the basis of their reported attitudes and behaviour. They may be described as the (qualified) School Teachers, the Subject Enthusiasts, the Professionals, and the Apprentices. Membership of each category has implications for adult teacher training; the qualified School Teacher is unlikely to undertake adult education training whilst the Enthusiast appears to prefer subject-based teacher training. The Professional, by virtue of his subject qualifications, sees himself adequately prepared to teach his subject and does not favour adult teacher training. Only the Apprentice is particularly likely to have received AE training or is indeed likely to seek such training. This last group of teachers is the one more likely to perceive adult education as playing an important part in their lives. They have a very real sense of pride and achievement in their work with adults. For many in this category training courses provide not only a means of acquiring teaching skills but open up an avenue for personal growth and self development. In this sense training is regarded as second chance education.

The way that teachers describe their work makes it clear that they have certain expectations about the centre in which they teach. They expect to receive whatever advice, counselling, support and training they feel they need and even more fundamentally expect to be given some feed-back on the work they do. It is clear that many teachers experience a lack of professional contact with full-time staff. They feel unsure about their status and the quality expected of their teaching; they report feelings of real isolation. The role of Centre Head to whom teachers are immediately responsible was perceived rather differently by teachers, trainers and Centre Heads themselves. The major tension lay between the organising function and the staff development/supportive function, with the latter seen by practically all teachers as the important one as far as they were concerned. There was also recognition that whilst the current financial climate led to a marked diminution in the provision of formal training it should not prevent a more positive approach being made to part-time teachers by the full time AE staff. Personal interest in, and visits to, a teacher in her classroom were identified by many as a vital and achievable activity on the part of such staff. Teachers also expect to have the physical resources of the centre at their disposal. Typically, those involved in movement and exercise subjects felt most keenly where resources were poor and accommodation was unsuitable for their work.

There was a good match in teachers' and students' expectations with regard to the general qualitites of good adult teaching. Within the classroom the teacher was seen by teachers and students as a subject specialist and as a 'social enabler'. Teachers were seen to need knowledge of their subject coupled with the social skills necessary for working equitably with adults — sympathy, interest, friendliness and responsiveness. Students spoke of the need to feel relaxed and to be at ease in their classes, they implied that how this occurred was primarily determined by the teacher. In their view a good teacher should ideally be a person enthusiastic about student progress and achievement as well as someone who enjoyed teaching.

Teachers themselves did not easily recount the problems they met though the difficulties associated with teaching mixed ability groups were typically cited, as were the more individual problems of handling 'the awkward student', and those who lacked self-confidence and/or appeared less than keen to learn. Students spoke of their reasons for going to classes: to learn a new subject, to continue a hobby, to develop an interest. They also went for rather more socially defined reasons not least because "it's Tuesday". The expectations of both teachers and students is that learning will take place in a pleasant atmosphere, and will lead to the development of a level of personal achievement beyond the original starting point. Some teachers go further as if they possess some kind of social idealism. They want students to enrich their own lives and they see adult education as a means to this end.

Teachers clearly work hard and are committed, even devoted, to their subject. They anticipate that their students will achieve high standards of skill and efficiency in what they learn and hope this will take place in a friendly environment. Teachers expect to act in a social role as well as an educative one, actively caring for their students' welfare; not unreasonably they expect to receive some similar concern themselves. Many teachers seem to have learned to cope to some extent with professional isolation and the variety of difficulties and problems of the classroom. They appear on the surface at least to have become self-sufficient and self-reliant.

> I find a lack of help (though). . . I find myself running my classes myself. . . I have got used to plodding on myself and I do it myself and keep it going.

There is the realisation amongst a not insignificant number of teachers that training could ameliorate some of the urgent problems they have to face.

There was some division of opinion about the benefits that are derived from adult teacher training and attitudes about such training showed a broad distinction. Typically, the trained adult teachers saw adult education training as both necessary and desirable. The untrained teachers on the other hand were much less convinced about the need for training. They tended to see non-vocational work as simply a matter of the transmission of skill, and did not share the perceptions of the trained teachers who saw their teaching in a wider professional framework. A major outcome of training recognised by many teachers was a change in their attitudes towards students. Not only was there the requirement to make each class member feel valued and unthreatened but there was also the realisation that student learning was of greater importance than teaching performance. Teachers spoke of developing a more professional approach to their work and most importantly this seems to lead to an increase in general confidence levels both inside and outside the classroom. Whilst some of those who refused adult education training did so with clear reason, both implicitly and explicitly stated, it was apparent that there is less awareness of the availability (and benefit) of training amongst teachers than might be expected.

CHAPTER 4

The Trainers

This chapter is based upon the interviews of trainers who were currently teaching on Regional Training Scheme courses during the 1980/81 period. Stage 1, Stage 2 and joint Stage 2/City & Guild 730 courses are represented. Beginning with a short description of the training personnel the chapter is set out in nine sections with a final overview. They are:-

Who are the Trainers?
Training the Trainers
Teachers' needs as learners
The Regional Training Scheme
Course Content and Approaches
Applying the Course in Practice
Evaluating Training
Some questions about benefits
Overview

In common with both the preceding and the following Chapters, the information reported and discussed seeks to reflect the perceptions and opinions of respondents rather than to be an objective analysis.

SECTION 1: WHO ARE THE TRAINERS?

The 'trainers' in 1980—81 were all full-time professional staff in Adult or Further Education. The wealth and diversity of experience that they had does not lend itself to the type of statistical treatment accorded to the data derived from the teachers and the trainees. What can be done, however, is to indicate the breadth of this experience.

The vast majority of the twenty-three trainers for whom data is available were employed as full-time adult education staff, typically as Centre Heads, Heads of AE Departments, Area Tutors or Area Principals. A minority described their posts as 'Staff Tutor' or 'FE Lecturer'. There were four women in the group; age was equally distributed across the thirties and forties though four were over fifty.

All trainers had been involved in education for most of their working lives. All had taught in the maintained school sector with the exception of two who had only FE experience. Slightly under half of the group had also worked in FE colleges, typically for ten years. Full-time adult education experience was common to fourteen, some of whom also had part-time non-vocational experience; in both cases this was typically 8–10 years. Several trainers were currently teaching part-time adult classes, four being within the non-vocational category. A number of trainers also noted other experience, for example Teacher Training and H.M. Forces.

As for qualifications, twelve trainers were graduates and nine were holders of the Diploma of Adult Education. Only two of the whole sample did not hold a Qualified Teacher's Certificate of Education, two being Further Education Certificates. There was a variety of other qualifications, for example, Diplomas in Physical Education or those connected with the Institute of Management.

Experience as a trainer on adult education training courses varied. One man who was currently teaching both a Stage 1 and a Stage 2 course had previously taught four S1's, four S2's and two Stage 3 courses. One woman, also teaching at two levels, had similar experience except that she had not taught at S3 level. More typically, those who were teaching on S1 courses had previous experience of two or three first level courses and often one at the second level; current S2 trainers had nearly always taught before at that level. Rather fewer training activities of other kinds were specifically noted, though there was mention of 'informal gatherings', 'induction courses' and 'class visits' as well as subject-based sessions and weekends. There seemed to have been few newcomers to training in the last three or four years, with the exception of one county where there was a policy of introducing new people into training teams, and another which had recently given all area tutors responsibility for training which resulted in several new faces.

The group as a whole may be described as being made up of people engaged in full-time educational employment with considerable teaching experience, a large proportion of which was in the FE/AE sectors. Practically all held Qualified Teacher's Certificates of Education and over half of them were graduates in addition; almost a half had specialist advanced qualifications in adult education. Most were experienced trainers of part-time teachers of adults, though their formal training for this role was rather varied. Half the group stated that training was specifically part of their job description but no overall picture of the proportions of their time that involved training was obtained. The general picture within the region was one of trainers working in teams of two or three, either together, or planning together and running courses separately with joint residential weekends.

In the interviews, some time was spent discussing what people felt they got out of their involvement in training, and how they felt it related to the rest of their work. Most trainers were primarily adult education organisers and teachers, either as area organisers based in adult education centres or people doing similar work through adult education departments in further education colleges. Five were lecturers in further or higher education, but of these, two had special responsibility for various forms of teacher education and one had originally been appointed as a training officer for adult education and youth work. The counties vary in the extent to which they make clear whether full-time staff in adult education are expected to be involved in training. Only one county specifies this in contracts of area organisers. Their counterparts in two other counties take on adult teacher training in addition to the rest of their work and receive supplementary payments. Nevertheless, the adult education organisers interviewed tended to see training, both formally (through courses) and informally (through contact with teachers) as an integral part of their work.

There is nothing written in our job description requiring us to do training. Consequently, at the moment any of us that get involved in training in the S1 course get additional remuneration for doing it.

I don't believe you can be responsible for standards in a service without being responsible for training. You'd have a training role even if one wasn't doing formal courses.

Where trainers were based in further education colleges they allocated their time to training through a combination of personal choice and interest, negotiation with Heads of Department and College Principals and custom and practice in the department.

It's not in my job specification. What we are expected to do now we're under further education, is teach. But I've always taught on training courses anyway, so it's just a matter of carrying on what I've been doing by custom and practice. . . They don't pay

93

extra, but it is included as teaching on a timetable. . . it's not included as training, it could be any sort of teaching, in that sense there is time allowed for it, but no payment, nothing extra for weekends.

It's part of my normal duties. I'd expect that.

The whole job here is as a lecturer, of which part of the time is allocated to teacher training.

People we spoke to seem to accept training as an integral part of their work as full-time staff in adult education; however, we did not speak to any Centre Heads or area organisers who had chosen not to become involved in training. Only one person interviewed raised the question of whether adult education organisers have the qualities of trainers:

There is again a tradition, and it's probably a bad tradition, that any full-time member of staff involved in adult education automatically adopts a training role. As though, magically, by becoming an organiser in adult education you have the wherewithal to teach others to teach which I don't think is true at all.

Training was seen to complement the role of full-time adult education organisers. One important way in which it helped their work was to provide a means by which they could control the quality of teachers working in their area — they could 'talent spot' for new people to work in their centres, and they had an opportunity to work with teachers in a formative way.

I get to know a wider circle of potential tutors. . . it enables you to do a sort of selection process without having to give them a try on your patch.

I think it fundamentally important that we keep renewing our stock of teachers. We have to find them from somewhere rather than put an advertisement in the paper and take one of any who will apply, or — which is more prevalent, I think, in Adult Education — social contacts, friends of friends, "How would you like to come and do a course on. . . ?" There's too much of that. I would like to have a far more systematic and formal entry into teaching in further education and adult education, which means that one should if possible put people through a course of part-time teacher training, such as 730/Stage 2 and thus I am contributing directly to the quality of education by ensuring that the teachers themselves are given a minimal set of skills.

As Adult Education Area tutor it does let me keep tracks on the people. . . it enables me to try to ensure that no-one is teaching without some form of training.

Training enabled adult education organisers to develop a close, understanding relationship with their tutors and kept them in touch with the kind of problems the part-time tutor and the person teaching for the first time faced. It allowed them to get to know their tutors better and this helped to reduce isolation.

It just refreshes me. I find that I'm just more able to break away from the administrative shackles, as it were. I can talk to teachers, I feel more like an educator in the sense that I can talk to teachers about the job, listen to what they say, I feel fresh, I can do different things with them, rather than just giving them a register and saying "Cheerio, off you go to your class".

You meet your new members of staff, or members of staff who are teetering on the brink and not quite sure whether or not they can cope with a class — they're not very certain of themselves, or of you perhaps. You get to know them much better than you would if you were just dropping in three or four times a term. I think the sort of things you do in class give you the backup and the authority, or the excuse perhaps, to go and visit a class and advise and help. It makes it easier, because if you haven't trained somebody or if you don't know them too well, it's more difficult to go in as a helper or an enabler, because they see you as 'the person in charge' and think you're criticising them. If they've been on a training course, they're much more inclined to say, "I'd welcome some help on this" and take what you're saying as part of their on-going training partly because of the sort of atmosphere that's established on courses.

As well as increasing their sensitivity to and awareness of teachers' difficulties and problems, trainers claimed that involvement in training broadened their own outlook in other ways. For example, preparing the work for the course stimulated their thinking and made them look again at their own work and the courses brought them into contact with new ideas and alternative ways of thinking. The following comments are a selection of trainers' views on this issue:

> The rest of my work in adult education definitely benefits, there's no doubt about that. Obviously my own work on S1, the preparation, thinking that I've had to put into it reflects on my own course planning, my own selection of tutors, my own attitude towards tutors.

> It's given me an opportunity to meet tutors from other centres, who are working in a centre that's organised differently. That helps, finding out about other systems of organisation and whether I can change things here for the better.

> What I like is the two-way process, because they have such a lot to contribute in terms of things they've tried that have worked, and that haven't worked and they're so willing to share experiences. With me I'm their fellow student.

The trainers interviewed were practically all experienced teachers before they became organisers and administrators, and many of them clearly valued the opportunity to teach.

> It's probably about the only consistent form of tutoring that one is able to do as an adult education organiser.

This teaching role gave trainers a great deal of personal satisfaction — they enjoyed teaching, mixing with teachers and being able to help them in their work.

> The enjoyment comes through creating groups for training, these individuals forming the group are no longer in isolation. I think one of the real benefits of training is to create groups of part-time teachers who for the first time come together and can discuss their difficulties.

> I find it quite uplifting. . . my wife always says "If you've had a session with your tutors you come back quite animated and it's done you good. . . ".

Some were also very honest about their influence over teachers.

> I suppose I enjoy watching new tutors come round to my way of thinking about how adults should be treated and taught and how they should be helped to learn.

> I think you've got to say part of it is an ego-trip if you're not careful. . . if you could get people to come clean about teaching and training, you do get a lot of job satisfaction out of, in a sense, being in a position where you know and other people don't. I think all the teachers, if they were honest, do get that. But I think that's just a fact of life. I think you've got to say, well that's how it is and for heaven's sake hope that it

doesn't get a stranglehold on you!. . .

On this particular course I've had a sense of control and power, which I've never had before. . . I've never honestly realised how much power I have over people, or one could have in an imposed role, so it's given me an insight, I don't know if it's been of help to me personally. . . simple things, I simply said, "Don't you think we ought to go and have coffee?" and everybody jumped up. . . from then on I realised every time I moved my eyes, I smiled, everything, afterwards I found out that it was having an effect on people. . . I tried to be as non-directive and non-dominating as I could be, but still people look for things.

The main problem for trainers in combining training with the rest of their work was that of time. Both those who did training as part of their normal work load and those who took it on in addition found they had to balance the various demands on their time though inevitably they sometimes felt other things suffered:

I'm quite happy when I leave the centre at night. . . I leave it in charge of X, but this is the danger that if you get carried overboard with a lot of enthusiasm for training you need to be in other people's centres working with other people's tutors and you neglect your own.

It's extra hours. Basically what happens is that it comes out of my normal working time, because I work pretty well all through the week in the centre, so I just take time off to do the training. . . I've thought about this really honestly and I don't know whether I would do the training courses if I didn't get paid quite frankly. I'd be sad not to do it but I'd find something else to do. . . I'd improve what I did with my centre, training for staff development, that sort of thing.

These comments show the commitment of trainers who are willing to make time for training and the importance of ensuring that training does not become "an extra chore and burden you could well do without".

SECTION 2: TRAINING THE TRAINERS

The help and support which people felt had proved most useful to them in their work as trainers fell into five broad categories: courses aimed specifically at trainers of adult education teachers; help from and contact with others involved in training; their training experience especially in the field; a wide variety of courses they had taken, not specifically for trainers and self-help, self-education.

Courses

'Training the Trainers' courses have been offered in the region under the sponsorship of the Regional Advisory Council through the ATO/DES and the DES/ Regional Schemes and by two LEAs. Most recently an adult education trainers' course was held in Northamptonshire, forming part of the county's training programme. Fourteen of the trainers in the sample had taken part in these courses. Many felt that with the cutbacks in adult education LEAs would be more reluctant to finance attendance on such courses. Some of those who had been on courses commented on what they had got out of it:

I suppose the 'Training the Trainers' course helped me structure the ideas I already had and introduced me to a whole lot of new ideas.

It was quite good for somebody new to the game. I wasn't brand new, but it was good in that as well as teaching me something about training, or teaching me to be a better trainer, it also meant that I established a number of friendships and got to know people around the region, which is important too.

Contact with colleagues

Trainers mentioned two kinds of support they received from other people involved in training. Several had profited from more experienced trainers who had made a special effort to help them when they first became involved in training. Most trainers spoke of a range of committees, course teams and other more informal groups and contacts where issues and ideas had been discussed which had helped their thinking on training. This highlighted a whole range of individuals, committees and organisations who have a potential role in supporting trainers (e.g. the Regional Advisory Council, City and Guilds, EMRIAE, HMI, Moderators and Assessors). The importance in learning from other colleagues is highlighted in the following comments:

> I got thrown in at the deep-end. "You will do a Stage 1 course and you're in charge this year" — it was my first year in adult education. Having said that, I must admit that I got a lot of help from my senior colleague. He launched me on the right path and I got all sorts of resources.

> Probably the most valuable experience I had was doing the Stage 2 last year. . . because there I was on a par with two other tutors. . . working with two chaps with whom I sympathised, who had feelings for adult education and they are few and far between, Centre Heads who I feel, really feel for, working in that particular sector of education. There's still a spin off from that particular course. . . We support each other really.

> Areas undertook their own training, and the officer for my area got us together and we talked our way through training days, training evenings. It was very much a case of 'I sat by Nellie.' He is a gifted teacher of adults and you know one learnt a lot from him. One sets oneself up as an expert on very flimsy evidence.

> Having done moderation you have got around seeing various people at work and you discuss things, and you bring the whole thing out. So in a way, I have been very fortunate in the way I have had the region behind me. But if I hadn't — and some of my colleagues hadn't — the county's attitude is 'well you're the experts, get on with it!' You either sink or swim. . . It is just that I have been lucky in that I have got together with other people who are in the same kind of work, and in a way we've trained each other . . . I have found out that several of the HMIs were very good in assisting this process.

> I gain an awful lot from looking at courses in other counties and from attending moderators' meetings with reports of all the courses relevant to me. Probably, if I'd been just doing my own courses, Stage 1 & 2, all the time with nothing else, I'd have probably got very stale.

These comments indicate the way in which co-operation within and between LEAs and via RAC Committees, meetings and trainers courses, and the reciprocity involved in moderation, created a regional team spirit among trainers as the scheme envisaged right from the start.

Experience

One way of learning is through doing the job, for people tend to improve their expertise through experience. In addition a number of trainers used their experience of training gained in other fields such as the Services, the Youth Service and the training of literacy tutors. Two examples serve to make this point:

> I think you have to make the assumption that a lot of training for trainers will be done *in situ,* and will be done, probably like most effective training is done, by the seat of your pants, by experience, by learning on the job. . . I was the one who sat in on the Stage 1 and listened to what went on and made some sort of inane contribution for the first time and then gradually made more sensible contributions, and gradually became prepared to take a block of work — to see a group of students through a particular piece of work. And it builds up.

> I would probably upset a lot of people by saying that the adult education 'Training the Trainers' course was the least helpful of the training that I've undertaken. I certainly found the Youth Service training course I did much more useful and much more exciting even. I did a three month training course as an instructor for the Army Education Corps. I believe that three months training course taught me a lot more about teaching, particularly teaching adults, than any of the subsequent training I've done.

Other courses

As well as 'Training the Trainers' courses, which are aimed specifically at questions related to training, the people interviewed mentioned a wide range of other courses they had attended which had helped them as trainers. These included higher degree courses, University Diplomas in Adult Education, teacher training courses and specialised courses, for example on audio-visual aids. Although not intended specifically for adult education trainers these courses appeared to have been helpful in a general way.

> I'm a sort of study lunatic! I did seven years with the Open University, studying all the educational courses that they produce; add to that three years on the MSc. . . The educational courses with the Open University have been a very valuable back-up for training teachers, without a doubt.

> Any post-initial training that a teacher has, he will get most of it by his own volition, and his own initiative. . . I did the 730 course myself ten years ago. I did an in-service Cert Ed, seven years ago. I am currently doing an M Ed, . . . I have also followed several, probably it must be running into double figures now, short courses which have been deliberately designed to enhance my capabilities as a trainer.

> I tended to go back to my university diploma days — although there wasn't at that time a training element in the diploma course as such, there was a comparison of a few training schemes available. I tended to lift out of those and put together something for my own course.

Self-help, self-education

A number of trainers had clearly put a lot of energy into finding ways of equipping themselves for their task, partly out of personal interest, partly out of a sense of survival. Some were self-taught whilst others had attended courses which they believed would equip them better for their work.

The following comments illustrate the importance of self-help and what trainers gained from the process:

> It was a case of 'you've got this job of training to do; find out as much as you can off your own bat'. . . I really didn't have much help and I really didn't think about any help. It seemed to be one of the entrepreneurial things you do in adult education, just get on with it!

> I've taken opportunities because I'm the sort of person who ferrets things out and goes and finds them. Its mainly because I don't like to be alone in the job I'm doing. I am very conscious that trainers. . . can be very isolated and devoid of support, so in order to be confident of doing a fair job I like to find out what others are doing and share experiences and perhaps also there's some career advancement in it for me.

It is clear from what trainers say that they draw upon their whole range of relevant experience; that all opportunities to meet colleagues and to discuss issues relating to adult education and training are of potential value; that trainers can receive support from a range of other people — more experienced trainers, moderators, HMI and that 'self-education' is also an important part of their training. 'Training the Trainers' courses seem to figure most frequently in the answers from the trainers who have been involved since the early days of the scheme. There is now wider scope for an 'apprenticeship', a more gradual introduction to training.

Asked about their future training needs, trainers views were divided as to who could offer further 'training for trainers'. Some trainers believed that validation by a university, or some other nationally recognised body, would lend more professionalism and greater status and recognition to adult education training.

> If it were provided by the DES, at least you would be assured of some sort of national level, a national aim, objective and so on.

> In our case we're lucky, because the University has got an established reputation and its people in adult education are in adult education for real. They're not theorists, they know what we're talking about at ground level. . . Of course, I think if you're going to ask people to do training, to spend time and energy doing things perhaps a University validated diploma or certificate is a good motivator. I'm not saying the county couldn't do it. But. . . if training is important, perhaps you need to get it as high up as you possibly can in terms of the hierarchy, so it's valued.

However, more usual was a concern that training for trainers should be in the hands of people with considerable experience in LEA adult education and respondents questioned whether University staff had the necessary experience.

> The problem on the 'Training the Trainers' was that their practical experience of adult education was in the University or WEA, which I believe is vastly different to the LEA situation. There is a world of difference between sitting down and conducting a ten week course in dressmaking or woodwork or badminton. The situation is very, very different and I believe one of the weaknesses of adult education as it exists at the moment is that a lot of the training at the higher level is done by people who have not got the LEA experience.

> Part of the team should be working in direct contact with the S1/S2 people in the field — I think this is vital, people who are coming face to face with their problems should be part of the team. I don't think it should be hived off to the Universities entirely, or

the Poly., or County Hall, because I don't think those people are in contact with the people in the field and their problems.

These comments seem to be working towards a scheme where trainers are in 'control' of their own training. They suggest that to be successful, a training scheme should facilitate the exchange and sharing of ideas and experience, it should have a stong emphasis on local needs and conditions; make use of people with considerable experience of adult education and training, it should draw in new ideas by making contact with trainers in other areas and other regions and use 'experts' with credibility amongst adult educators to contribute on particular issues. These were some of the prime intentions of the regional scheme. The trainers' courses were run to build basic resources and momentum. There was an expectation that thereafter the 'team' would renew itself from its own resources and bring in new members.

Evidence from one or two trainers suggests that they did not feel themselves to be members of a regional network, and that perhaps weaknesses have developed in the regional scheme.

Some counties seem to be more advanced in this work than others. I don't know if there is any liaison between the counties, this would seem to me to be very profitable — an exchange of ideas could help all round.

I really feel there's much more scope for meetings with tutors of other courses in the area.

SECTION 3: TEACHERS' NEEDS AS LEARNERS

It is official policy in the counties studied that all part-time teachers in non-vocational adult education ought to follow a Stage 1 course. Various categories of teachers are often exempt however: school teachers with qualified teacher status or other teaching qualifications, people who had considerable teaching experience before the introduction of the training scheme, people teaching short courses and people teaching subjects in which there is a shortage of teachers. The typical teacher aimed at in Stage 1 courses is a person recognised as proficient in the subject which they wish to teach but who is not qualified to teach. In two of the counties, the courses are only for people actually teaching in adult education. At Stage 2 level, adult education teachers follow Stage 2 courses whilst people teaching adults in FE tend to take City and Guilds 730. The two other counties are more open in their recruitment policy — for example, courses included people involved in teaching or training in the youth service, industry, the Forces, hospitals, prisons, St. John's Ambulance Brigade and further education. Only one Stage 1 trainer in these counties spoke against this policy because he believed there was not enough common ground between such teachers. However, most trainers felt there were benefits in including people with varied experience: they further pointed out that this practice helped to maintain the viability of courses when numbers were low either because of declining recruitment into adult education or because of travelling distances in rural areas. In both these counties Stage 2 courses are run jointly with City and Guilds 730 courses; the nature of the 730 course encourages a wider recruitment.

In the interviews, trainers focused on a number of general expectations they believed teachers have when they come on courses. Their perceptions of these expectations are formed from the experience of working with teachers; some trainers made a point of asking teachers on the course to say what they hoped to get out of it. On the whole, hopes and expectations seemed to be broadly in line with trainers' intentions for the course.

They are of four main kinds:

— teachers expect to finish their course more confident about approaching their work.

— they hope to become better teachers, to enhance their skills and knowledge about teaching.

— they hope for 'self-development'

— they expect to improve their chances of employment

Trainers in addition laid special emphasis upon the following:

— they hope teachers will come to look at their work through the eyes of their students.

— an emphasis on how adults learn, rather than on teacher performance.

— they hope teachers will be able to look at their work in a more questioning and objective way.

— they hope to broaden teachers' views of teaching and adult education and they hope to trigger off an on-going process of development in the teachers.

It would seem that the way trainers choose to emphasise different aspects gives each course its particular character.

Confidence

This was emphasised particularly by Stage 1 trainers. They felt teachers were hoping:

— to have their ability as teachers confirmed:

The ones we have almost invariably would hope to have a greater confidence, a greater understanding of their students and a greater repertoire of ways of getting their material across to the students. They come to us basically from a position of wanting to do this sort of work, without really knowing whether they are ideally suited to it. . . it's really a confidence booster, I think.

— to have some feedback on their work, to be reassured they are 'doing it right':

I think they want to enhance their range of skills and techniques and I think they want to build their confidence. They might be coping, but they are in a pretty isolated position. I don't suppose the Centre Head's paid many visits to them and they probably had very little contact with any other teachers of the same subject. . . so perhaps they are needing the reassurance that they are not alone. They are needing some feedback as to whether or not they are doing it right.

— for some to be 'measured' against an external test or assessment:

It's mainly people who find themselves thrust into the situation and they want to improve their teaching skills. They want to come to see whether or not they've got the makings of a teacher. They come to improve teaching skills and I think they come to be assessed by someone who's more experienced than they are.

There's a question of status. I'm conscious of this — every now and again it's quite important to test yourself against somebody else's yardstick. Can I take this course? Can I get this piece of paper? Am I as good as I think I am? Am I as good as the bloke next door? So if you come on a course like this, in a sense you are putting a challenge to yourself (Stage 2 trainer).

Trainers considered that these points were especially relevant to untrained teachers who did not possess specialist subject qualifications.

Teaching skills

Stage 1 trainers spoke in particular of teachers' hopes for 'golden rules', 'do's and don'ts of teaching', or 'lifesaver courses' which would help them cope with the first few class meetings. Thus those new to teaching expected to be given a series of 'tips' about how to do the job and to be provided with the answers to many of their problems. Comments from two trainers illustrate these expectations:

> Basically teachers themselves say they need what you might call a survival pack. They need to be able to survive the first few weeks of contact. It's a frightening experience in some respects and they need to be able to get through the first few classes.

> A kind of life-line or footing, a way, a basis from which to analyse their experiences. What we've got to do is to give them that equipment. It's very difficult if you've never taught before to know what kinds of problems you might meet. . . just the very basic stuff. . . how do you cope in the classroom. Those are the things that worry them.

Many trainers were aware that a number of teachers hoped that training courses would help them improve their teaching skills and acquire new approaches and techniques, reflecting a more positive approach to their work than the first group. Some trainers were rather imprecise:

> You can ask them why they come and I think the stock answer you'll get is that I want to be a better teacher. That is simple in the sense it's almost trivial, but that is what is in their minds — I want to be a better teacher.

Though others were clearer and more specific about the things that they thought teachers looked for to improve their teaching. As one experienced trainer said:

> They come along wanting to know how to use a blackboard, should I use a blackboard, can I shove the furniture around, what's the best way to do it, what is an overhead projector, and how do you use it? That's the sort of thing they seem to be asking. . . they've plenty of confidence in their subject, but what they're not confident about is getting their subject across to a group of adults.

Trainers also recognised that some teachers, particularly those without subject qualifications wanted to be better teachers by improving their subject competence as well as their teaching skills thus posing a dilemma for course organisation in terms of meeting these expectations.

Self-development

This was more often mentioned by Stage 2 trainers. Having been through Stage 1, teachers hoped Stage 2 would lead to a continuation of the process of learning and development of their thinking. For some teacher training had become a way to further their own education.

> You get the old pat answers like "I want to make my teaching better" or "I want to be good at my job". Not very neat, tidy, articulate answers. But obviously what is shining through is that they are interested in their own development and are interested in making a contribution as well.

I think they're saying, in some mysterious way, that if I come on this course, I can only be a better teacher. But I think you've got to look below that. . . they presumably found Stage 1 interesting enough to want to go on and do something else. And they just tend to be interested in adult education. One of them said to me. . . "I think that (self development) is what I'm getting and will get out of the Stage 2 training course — in the sense that I know it will probably make me a better teacher, but I'm enjoying the course because it's making me a better person".

If it wasn't teacher training, I suspect with many of these people it could be something else. Because they're the sort of people who need to be stimulated and developing themselves and challenging themselves. Now I'm delighted that this need for stimulation and challenge can be channelled into something like teacher training. . . but I think that's quite an important motivator.

Improving job prospects

New teachers of adult education within the region are now expected to follow a Stage 1 course. There is an element of compulsion about taking the course and many Stage 1 trainers were aware of the difficulties this could cause for them. The following example is typical of how many trainers saw this problem:

Some people come because they are forced to. If the subject is very popular and we've got plenty of teachers, we can say to them 'we can't give you a job unless you come on the course'. They are rather unwilling participants to start with, although one can usually win them round and they see the benefits of it.

The same problems are not true of Stage 2, where teachers are aware that it can improve their job prospects. Trainers on Stage 2/730 courses gave most weight to the career possibilities resulting from taking the course, perhaps because City and Guilds 730 is a nationally recognised course with wider currency than Stage 2. This comment from one trainer illustrates not only that he recognised why the students were attending but also that he was aware of the realities of obtaining teaching work:

I think they're expecting to get a job out of it. . . in the end. Maybe part-time work. This is perceived as a bit of paper which, if not a passport into a job, is something which can be very useful. . . equally connected with getting a job, certainly very early in the course they perceive that the teaching practice that they have to do is a very important contact point — if they are seen to be doing a good job on teaching practice, that they can then be offered something. . . (it will) give them contacts.

Concern for student learning

There was a common feeling amongst trainers that the course should shift teachers' concern from their own performance to a greater consciousness of how their students react and learn.

I think what *they* expect is a sort of 'tips for teachers' course. . . what I think they need — more often than not — is that they have to reverse their perception of what is going on and think of students rather than teachers. We spend a lot of time at the beginning of courses, saying that this is not about you standing in front giving information out, it's about students, wanting to learn something and you being able to manage the situation so they can learn.

I say to them I can't teach you how to teach. I always say, now we are going to give you a deeper insight into how students think, how students learn and so on, and then bearing all that in mind, let's consider how your teaching can be more effective.

A more objective view of teaching

By helping teachers look at their work in detached and critical ways, trainers hoped teachers would be better able to understand and cope with new problems and new situations which arise, and that they would be willing and able to reassess and improve their teaching. These two comments illustrate the attitudes of many trainers:

> What we can do is to get people to be objective about their own performance. . . not to go to pieces after a rotten night.

> I feel the most important ingredient of any course is to enable them to understand themselves and their own motivation and to begin to learn about group dynamics and individual dynamics and begin to learn how people behave in situations so they can use that to their advantage.

A number of trainers perceived that their work was much more complex and wide-ranging than simply helping teachers to acquire a set of basic skills and techniques. They believed that they should broaden teachers' attitudes by helping them to understand the general context of adult education, especially the functions and structures of the organisations in which they were employed. They gave a number of examples of ways in which they considered their courses could do this:

— by making them look again at their subject, its potential for development, its purposes in the adult education curriculum and its relationships to other subjects.

— by making them more aware of the context in which they worked and of how adult education relates to the rest of the education system. Part of the reason for this emerges from this comment:

> I would like them to feel. . . they are part of a structure, a set up, at the moment I don't feel that they do. Although they go once a week to a centre, in a lot of cases they don't feel part of that centre. . . So they are not really involved with, shall we say, the curriculum in the broadest sense, or the service that the centre offers. And part of their expertise I think would be useful to the development of the centres.

— that through an understanding of the adult education system, teachers would develop their own philosophy in their approach to their work and adult education, a view which becomes apparent here:

> What they're getting is something that's much more slow to show itself. A deeper view of teaching, a much more 'thinking-person's' approach to teaching. . . I think they're better adult educators, know more about adult education and teaching in adult education. What you've opened up to them is a vast area to consider which, having analysed it, they've got. . . to synthesize and produce their own approach to teaching.

This process of synthesizing that the course has introduced continues long after the end of the course. It is difficult to separate it from the ideas of self-development and critical awareness discussed earlier. It is a process which can have impact on a person far beyond his work as a teacher which first brought him to the course. Its importance was raised by many trainers:

They have seen the training course as an adult education class. They had enjoyed it as a class, rather than seeing it as a training session for themselves and they have come to expect it as a kind of intellectual stimulus. . . their evening out. And many of them do go on to other things, University or Stage 2, or some of them go back to college and get 'O' and 'A' levels in an attempt to perhaps go on and get on a full-time teacher training course or whatever. . . This is probably why I like doing it, I rather enjoy awakening this kind of extra dimension in people.

SECTION 4: THE REGIONAL TRAINING SCHEME

Trainers tended to mention the same range of aims and expectations whether they were involved in Stage 1 or Stage 2 courses. Both seem to cover the same broad areas of content. Certain questions persist, however: in what ways do the courses differ, how do trainers see the two stages relating to each other, and what is the relationship to the more advanced Stage 3 course?

Stage 1 is a very short course and trainers hoped that teachers would progress onto the longer Stage 2 course. However, in planning Stage 1 they had to accept that many teachers do not, and Stage 1 must therefore not only lead into and relate to Stage 2, but also be a self-contained course. Because Stage 1 is only 36 hours long trainers had to make choices about where to put their emphases. Most saw it as essential that it should be a practical course which helps teachers to cope in the immediate situation they face and introduces them to new ideas and ways of thinking. Some trainers then saw Stage 2 as going over the same ground in greater depth with the introduction of more background reading and more theory. Trainers' perceptions of some of the differences between first and second level courses emerge from these comments:

> It is important for us to gear the course to the fundamental, practical level, certainly with not too much of an academic input, so they can see the relevance of what we are doing.

> I tend to relate all they talk about down to real classroom experience and get away from generalised theory, which can appear on the Stage 2 course.

> I think Stage 1 is necessary and needs to be done as soon as possible after someone has started teaching. But they do need to be told that it is only an introduction. There is something called S2 and S3 and they've only scratched the surface — they've been given a survival kit by S1 and if they really want to delve into philosophy, sociology and psychology of teaching and they want to get to grips with the more complex side of teaching techniques, then they need to go on to Stage 2.

> Now I reckon Stage 2, in actual façt, drags them back and now invites them, instead of saying "do what I said, or do what I suggest on Stage 1, can we now start to analyse all these things you are now practising, all the rules we said it would be useful to follow on the Stage 1 course. Can we go right back to the beginning, look at them in some depth and analyse them." And can you at the end of the course — and this is what I don't know about — can you come out with some new synthesis of all this analysis which gives you a new starting point, if you like , a philosophy, a mode of working, a set of beliefs, a set of skills.

These quotations mainly focus upon the relationship between Stage 1 and Stage 2 content — a move from a practical introduction to a more considered study of the same areas. They hint at some discontinuities in approach, a shift from 'how'? to 'why'?, from a very supportive course to the adoption of a challenging and questioning approach. Some trainers accepted that they must work within the constraints of a short course and recognised that teachers who were on Stage 1 were likely to be tentative about their teaching and training. This kind of discontinuity was questioned by others:

> I think it's an on-going process. I think we can certainly ask things of our students at Stage 2 that you can't ask at Stage 1 but I think the whole process is the same.

> One of the other Stage 1 tutors and myself disagree. . . he thinks that he should tell them, lay it down clearly for them to see. My own feeling is that they should writhe a little bit, have a little bit of anxiety about things, because it prepares them for the rigours of being on their own again and also going on to further training. I've clearly stated to them that this is preparation for further training. . . although it's a good compact course, they come out better teachers, no question about that, they don't need to get complacent. I don't like them getting complacent and my own feeling is that they should be ready for Stage 2 at the end of it. Ready for the rigours of Stage 2 which really strips things apart and tears learning down into its basic components and gets them to question everything they do.

Because of the autonomy allowed them, the Stage 1 courses run by individual trainers inevitably differed in their style and content. One trainer pointed out the difficulties this could create for Stage 2 courses which drew teachers from a number of Stage 1s.

> There were certain Stage 1s that, because the trainers had knowledge and they were party to a Stage 2, they could therefore keep the Stage 1 as it was originally envisaged, as a feed through into Stage 2. . . It wasn't as easy for some people to come off Stage 1 on to Stage 2 and it was more easy for others, as the Stage 1's became different . . . the topics covered, the depth to which these were covered.

Most trainers saw Stage 1 and Stage 2 as closely related, with a much greater gap between Stages 2 and 3. Stage 3 was different from the other two lower stages in that it demanded much more academic work from those taking the course and this could be a difficult transition for some trainers. As one trainer said:

> I see it as very much a spiral curriculum process, definitely Stage 1 and Stage 2. Stage 2 is a greater depth of the same areas. A 30/40 hour Stage 1 can hardly do anything but introduce the thing. Stage 2 gives a reasonable analysis of them. Stage 3 should require greater depth analysis, but it's at Stage 3. . . where the wider reading and the understanding of philosophy comes into it. That's where the substantial jump comes.

SECTION 5: COURSE CONTENT AND APPROACHES

The last section described some of the general aims of Stage 1 and 2 courses and some of the hopes and expectations trainers and teachers might have of the course. It suggested that although most trainers would agree with these aims, they seemed to differ in the emphasis which individual tutors gave to them. This difference is manifested through the choices trainers have to make about course content and approach. Trainers tend to argue that teachers learn as much, if not more, from involvement in the activities, experiences and processes of which a course is composed as from the direct 'messages' that trainers put across. This section looks at some of the experiences through which trainers hope teachers will learn.

The content of courses

Course 'content' denotes the topics or areas to be studied as laid down in the course syllabus. There is now a fairly standard list of topics covered by most training courses in the region, and the list is similar for Stage 1 and Stage 2 courses reflecting the view that Stage 1 introduces ideas and areas which are developed and considered in greater depth in Stage 2. The selection of topics has been influenced by county training proposals, Regional Advisory Council recommendations and the requirements of City and Guilds (in Stage 2/730 courses) as well as by trainers' own choice and judgement. The ACSTT proposals on training for part-time, non-vocational teachers of adults seemed to have had little direct influence on trainers' decisions as they were made after the emergence of the regional scheme, and they are less than explicit in their proposals for course content. When training courses have been running for some time, newer trainers naturally take into account the patterns of course content developed by their predecessors:

> The City and Guilds' document is far more specific and prescriptive in what it requires — (than the Regional Advisory Council's). . . but there is no conflict so I take as my bench mark that there's certain compulsory City and Guilds stuff.

> We try to stick to the regional thing, that RAC thing. . . I scratched out the bit about the knowledge of its history, because we thought that was not quite relevant.

Several trainers were struck by the common agreement on course content and by the similarities between the content of their own course and those they had seen in other areas and counties.

> Before we met (as a training team) we all did some homework and we all jotted down what we thought might go in the course, and there was very little difference.

> To a degree they're pre-selected by the syllabus that is set. You can expand your syllabus. It's quite amazing when I meet course tutors elsewhere — you think you have got a wide choice when you start devising a scheme, and in the end, we all put in the same things. Perhaps that's a bad thing; perhaps it's a good thing, that it reassures us.

Course outlines typically covered the followed broad areas:

— Adults as students: their needs, motivations, expectations; how they learn; learning difficulties.
— the role of the teacher
— methods of teaching
— teaching/learning aids and resources
— planning for learning; planning a course; planning a lesson
— the teacher's subject: the learning opportunities it may offer
— assessment in adult education
— the teaching environment; creating the right environment; the adult education centre
— adult education in its broader context: its history, other providers of adult education, its relationship to other sectors of education.

Aims and objectives

One way of expressing the rationale behind the choice of course content and approach is to formulate a series of aims or objectives which the course is designed to achieve. All the trainers interviewed were able to refer to a statement of aims and objectives for training, whether these were drawn up in the Regional Advisory Council's outline for the regional scheme, by City and Guilds, at county level, or by the trainers themselves. In most cases, there were broad aims for the course as a whole rather than specific behavioural objectives for each session. However, trainers used the terms 'aims' and 'objectives' interchangeably and they were divided in their views on the usefulness of this approach to course planning. Objectives do not seem to be in the forefront of some trainers' minds; rather they seem to be implicit in the way these trainers think about and organise their work. A state of affairs illustrated by this trainer's comment:

> I don't usually write them down, I have them in my head.

Trainers felt that objectives, like course content, were fairly standard — they became familiar and obvious:

> The objectives of a Stage 1 are so obvious to me that having them cleverly formulated and set down simply doesn't provide any practical help. I suppose for any course you need to state objectives at the beginning and I suppose these have to be formulated, but they've been of no practical value to me.

The two quotations which follow, suggest the possibility that rather than sharpening and focusing a trainer's thinking, aims or objectives can become so general that they could apply to most courses without giving any indication of where the differences between them lay.

> Objectives can be stated in the most general terms, and, therefore, they don't indicate very much of what happens with the actual content.

> I think (the 730 and Stage 2 objectives are) fairly wide-ranging, they do cover a lot. It's like a good policy statement, it's all things to all people. . . I think you select from them, and put an emphasis on some rather than others.

This trainer found it was not always easy to express some of his own hopes for the course in the form of objectives:

> The things that don't appear, of course, on a formal piece of paper like this are the things that you personally believe in, and they're difficult to put down. You know, I think 'an interest in and an enthusiasm for the subject', looks foolish on paper but it's a hidden part of what you want to put across.

Other trainers were more positive about the usefulness of written course objectives. This approach can be particularly useful to a new tutor coming into a training team:

> When you've got a new tutor, you have to give him some kind of mental basis on which to organise his thinking.

or, for a trainer planning his first training course:

> I don't think you could design a course without knowing what you expect students to know at the end of it. So obviously, in terms of deciding what areas we are going to cover, we had to decide what those teachers would be able to do at the end of the course.

Trainers who personally found objectives valuable mentioned a number of other ways they could be used. Several said they gave them to teachers as a basis for discussing the course with them; they were useful in helping trainers and teachers reflect upon the course and to decide whether it had achieved what it set out to do.

> It helps the students to know where they're going. And, as with any objective in any field, it gives you a point of comparison, to know whether you've succeeded or you haven't — and for students themselves.

> We're using behavioural objectives, and the course structure now is presented in objective format, so there's been a tremendous amount of spadework done at the beginning to try to make sure we're on the right track. . . Each student on the course gets a copy of the syllabus, which is in objective format. They can clearly see the route along which we're travelling. So when a particular area of work has been taught, I've told them they can tick it as they go.

Trainers were conscious that they had to retain some flexibility, and to ensure that the course was responsive to teachers' needs.

> Obviously you come across specific teachers with specific problems, which you perhaps hadn't accounted for when you designed the course, but if you know a teacher finds terrible difficulty with. . . your objectives then have to be adjusted.

The formulation of aims and objectives is an approach to course planning which Stage 2 courses, and some Stage 1s, presented to teachers. Indeed, some Stage 2 courses were insistent that teachers should make use of this approach. Whilst it can be said that all trainers had aims implicit in the way they operated their courses, not all found it very useful to formalise these as the framework for planning, describing and evaluating their course.

Learning through experience as a student

When teachers go on a course, their role is suddenly reversed; they find themselves at the other end of the teacher—student relationship. Most teachers probably learn a great deal just from experiencing this change, some trainers take active steps to develop and explore this opportunity. Perhaps the most immediate and powerful effect of this experience is to generate in teachers a degree of empathy — helping them to understand their own students' feelings and reactions. As a trainer said:

> By trying to prove to them or at least demonstrate to them that the Stage 1 course is a course in adult education and much the same as theirs. We are dealing with training as tutors, but the problems they have as trainees are many of the same problems as the students in their class. They will have difficulty in understanding what is being demonstrated and they will have the personal crisis of deciding whether to be brave enough to admit their ignorance or to cover it up. We try to show them that their situation is identical to the one their students are in and their problems are the students' problems and my problems are their problems.

As well as becoming aware of their reactions as students, one trainer hoped that he would be able to get teachers to look more objectively at what had been happening on the course:

> I reckon probably one of the most valuable things is that they see events in two ways . . . as an emotional, interactional thing, and as a cognitive fact . . . also to be able to stand back and look at those events for what they are, they are only things that are passing . . . I really think that I try to start this process off by saying, "Lets live in the here and now. O.K. lets react to things, to people, as they affect us — but also to

be able to stand back in our heads as it were and view, from a sort of viewing room, events". And if they can start to do that, to live things and also view things from afar, then they're going to be a lot better teachers, because they can then stand back and say "Well, what did actually happen there"? "Why was I sharp with that person"? I think that's important, that they see themselves in a group being taught — how they're behaving and so on. But that's only very tentative. They do it more on Stage 2 . . . and from what I've heard about Stage 3, it's quite a central issue.

There are other ways in which trainers felt teachers could learn from the experience of being on a course. For example, a Stage 2 trainer described how group interaction was an important factor in modifying teachers' attitudes:

> If you find somebody who's intolerant, what can you do? You may say it's not a good attitude for a teacher, but you can't have a lesson on intolerance. . . If people on a training course show themselves intolerant in a group or if people are brow-beating or bombastic or hog the scene. . . by and large the group will shoot them down. They don't 'see the light', what they do is a very selfish reaction — "being in this group is painful to me, if I'm intolerant, or if I say too much".

though he went on to say:

> I don't know if it's a racial thing, but I find British groups so flipping tolerant they'll put up with awkward individuals for so long that sometimes the 100 hours of the course isn't long enough for the group to deal with problems. . . for example, if somebody is hogging the discussion, you can wait for ever for the group to do something — you as the tutor may well have to tell that person to shut up. . . the group's being so tolerant or hasn't got the confidence to sort it out themselves. So part of the tutor's job may be accelerating group processes. . .

The most frequently mentioned way that trainers used teachers' experience of being on a course as students was to introduce them to new methods of teaching, actually using them on the course and giving them the experience of learners.

> In a sense we've got to practise what we preach. We can't stand up there and say "We are here to tell you how to teach", and get them to accept that. So they've got to discover this for themselves and we, effectively, in the very first few lessons put them through a whole range of learning experiences themselves. They have to do a case study and they have to do a role play. . . and they have to do all the other student centred techniques. . . and they have to look back and analyse what's been going on. And the basic attitude is that everything that has happened to them is a learning experience. . . so the basic strategy is the one we hope that they will adopt when they go out and teach a class of adults.

> We go through the whole range, the idea being that we want to show these teachers these techniques in use so that if they feel they'd be useful, they've had experience of them and how to manage them, from watching how we handle them.

These two comments lean towards the idea of the course providing a 'model' which teachers can relate to their own work.

The course as a model of good practice

Trainers never actually used the phrase 'a model of good practice', but many were very con-

110

scious that they ought to be seen to 'practise what they preach'. There seems to have been two main reasons for this. Firstly, it gave them credibility with teachers, a credibility which involved not only how they conducted the training course but also demonstrated their experience as teachers. Indeed, they based their advice and made their judgement upon this.

> Well, this may sound trifling, but we try to use the whole lot (of teaching methods), because we are conscious of the charge that teacher trainers preach but don't practise . . . I would say the right sort of person to be a teacher trainer is somebody who is from a teaching situation where he has had the necessity and the chance to try all the methods . . . Again, I think it's very incumbent in terms of credibility, we've got to use videos. I remember whilst on my Cert Ed, being lectured about video equipment and we never saw the thing.

Secondly, trainers felt they should be offering an example from which teachers could learn:

> Presumably your own teaching methods will teach them how to do things.

> It would be nice if the technician could set things up half an hour before I go there. In a College of Technology you could do that. But on the other hand, it would be totally unrealistic. None of my teachers could do that. A certain amount of teaching and learning on a Stage 2 course must be by example. If they see I'm usually there first arranging things . . . they see a teacher has to do these things so it's realistic. However, they tended not to discuss how teachers might actually learn from observing them at work. It is undeniable that the skill and professionalism of some trainers could intimidate a number of teachers, unless trainers are prepared to take the risk of revealing their own uncertainties and problems as teachers.

Some courses invited experienced teachers along to give demonstration lessons:

> On the residential weekend, two experienced teachers came — one a teacher of macramé and another of Spanish — both using different teaching techniques to show them what could be done.

City and Guilds includes observation of other teachers as part of the 730 course requirements. The Regional Advisory Council Scheme does as well; observation is intended to be part of Stage 1 and Stage 2 courses and should be a structured element in the training process. Evidence from trainers suggests that some courses were failing in this respect. A few trainers did try to provide such opportunities in order to widen teachers' experience of different approaches, particularly at Stage 2 level. Two Stage 2/730 tutors described what was involved:

> The teachers within the College are very receptive to having students in for observations. . . They are able to see not just teachers in their own sphere — in fact I try to discourage that — I let them see at least one or two, but they must go and see what teachers in other subjects do.

> They have to observe at least two other classes in their own subject, they have to write a report of not less than 2000 words. That is difficult for them — to write an objective, fairly lucid, accurate report. Not a criticism, a report.

This Stage 1 trainer's comment suggests rather less compulsion:

> We encourage them to (go and see other teachers in their subject). It's an informal part

of the course. I should think about 50% do something or other, even if it is somebody else on the course that they hitch up with and go and visit.

Shared ideas and experiences

So far, this section has illustrated how trainers used professional teacher experiences on the training course as a kind of content. This is in line with the 'principle' of adult education that adults bring a wealth of experience to any class. The trainers were very much aware that teachers on the course brought with them a considerable experience of teaching, of being students, of work, of life, all of which had potential use on the course — to illustrate points; to analyse and draw out particular ideas; to compare with others' experiences; to support or challenge ideas, theories and viewpoints. Every trainer mentioned ways in which the course was able to draw upon and use this experience to get across points they wanted teachers to grasp. They created opportunities for teachers to discuss and share their views and ideas — for example, they set group tasks or got trainees to introduce a discussion and then draw generalisations or points out of what emerged.

> We decided at the beginning that we would consider it a failure if we did all the talking. . . what I've tried to do is to get them to talk and then try to draw together what they've said into some kind of pattern and make it relevant to the point we began.

> You notice the difference from Stage 1, where people have so little experience. On a Stage 2 course, you can set problems knowing the pooled knowledge of any group of Stage 2 students is likely to be able to produce an answer to it. . . They can all draw analogies and find examples of things that have happened to them.

> Tonight, for instance, I asked two of them to give me a class profile of the class they are teaching. I then ask the rest to tell me what problems would be evident in a class like this and check to see if they were evident — and then talk in terms of how you'd deal with it. . . I know the points I want to get home, but I don't know how I'm going to do it in that I'm dependent on what they say about their class. That's the general approach — start with one person's experience and try to draw out generalisations, rather than starting things by saying, "This is what you should do" and then getting them to try and relate it.

On Stage 2 courses, particularly, trainers used teachers' own experiences when they discussed a theory. This helped teachers to assess the theory's relevance and to look more selectively and analytically at their teaching.

> I think it's true to say, in teacher training we don't just pay lip service to the fact that we are one amongst equals in terms of experience and background — we do actively encourage discussion and everything else, to bring out what individuals feel their experience brings to bear on whatever topic. And too, whilst being as academic as possible in the nice sense of being accurate and specific, to personalise experience without being anecdotal, to personalise theory and say how they have brought it to bear in their experience, how it has worked for them.

An important aim in many courses was to give teachers help with the problems they faced in their teaching and this was another area where trainers encouraged teachers to share their experiences. They realised that they were not alone in the problems they faced and by identifying the problems more clearly were able to work towards a solution.

> Those who have taught before are eventually quite happy to talk about the problems

they have had. Once one starts. . . they'll all chip in. It's a matter of getting the first one to say "This class isn't going too well". . . which I encourage by talking about my problems as well. I've had control problems — and I'm quite happy to talk about it. Not setting ourselves up as the perfect teacher.

They come together with very differing backgrounds and differing subjects, they can not only put a new light on particular topics of general interest, but they can draw on the experience of their own practical teaching situations, which are similar or even dissimilar in solving a specific problem of another tutor.

We now encourage them to keep a diary of what they experience in each class that they teach. One hopes that the discussion that we usually work in to each training session again allows them to bring to the top of their minds some of the problems that are puzzling them. And the fact they've written them down. . . in that way one finds out.

Sometimes there were people on the course who had a particular expertise or knowledge which trainers could use more directly.

On this course, we have a chap who teaches painting but works in a training department, he is involved in working with overhead projectors and knows them inside out. That's unusual. But in general, they've got all sorts of experiences that are valuable and we can make use of them — from their professional backgrounds and previous teaching experience.

They are individuals and they've got points of view, they've got interests etc., on a wide variety of aspects of life . . . (one) is a school secretary and we've spent time listening to her telling us about the organisation in her school, because I feel it's important for these people to have knowledge of what goes on in school, other than what they remember.

These comments suggest a variety of ways in which trainers used teachers' experiences. The process of openly sharing and discussing problems, ideas and points of view was seen as part of the general atmosphere they hoped to encourage on the course. Teachers became free to raise questions and problems and in sharing experiences expected their colleagues to question and criticise when appropriate. If this kind of atmosphere can be created teachers will be more likely to learn from one another informally as well as through the course:

They bring a grave apprehension about their ability and they fulfil all the adult syndrome there, in that fear of exposing themselves to ridicule by the peer group. That is another area in which I feel I can try and develop the appropriate attitude, which is to expect criticism. I will jump on somebody very quickly if they were saying that it was rubbish — I would want to know why and also I think I would suggest that's probably not the language to use.

On Stage 2 there is more questioning of you, and of each other, which is good. A lot more cross-fire between students — establishment of inter-relationships in learning. On Stage 1, it often tends to be the teacher talking to each individual student. . . I know towards the end of Stage 1 you've got good group feeling, but they still haven't got the necessary experience to enable them to make very fundamental exchanges with each other or the tutor.

Learning from teaching

Stage 1 and 2 courses are first and foremost courses to help people in their work as teachers.

An important part of most courses involved giving teachers opportunities to translate into practice all they had learned and to work out the implications for their teaching. During the course, most people had two kinds of opportunity to teach; firstly in the sheltered environment of the course itself where they were given the chance to try out their ideas in comparative safety through peer group teaching and micro-teaching; secondly with their own classes at their place of work.

All Stage 2 courses and almost all Stage 1 courses included some micro-teaching or peer-group teaching and according to trainers many teachers were video-recorded at least once. They had the chance actually to watch themselves at work. Trainers were enthusiastic about this kind of exercise and obviously enjoyed using closed circuit television.

Trainers recognised that this part of the course makes teachers very anxious. However, by overcoming the fear of getting up in front of the group they felt teachers gained a tremendous sense of achievement and boosted their confidence. In the eyes of most trainers the rise in confidence justified asking teachers to micro-teach.

> I can't remember any one occasion where I have forced everyone on the Stage 1 course to do some micro-teaching but there are always in a group of a dozen or more, three, four or five that have got that extra bit of confidence.

Even at Stage 2, teachers found micro-teaching an awesome experience. This trainer explained how using it early as a participative course set the tone and helped to establish a supportive group atmosphere:

> The idea is that as soon as possible these people have got to get up and do something — which concentrates their mind and they become very rapidly aware that it's that type of course and not just sitting with folded arms. . . They learnt a lot there . They start off by being scared to death of it, but when they've done it, they realise that they're all in the same boat and it helps the group cohesion. They appreciate that the mistake that one (person) makes one week, they may make the next week and they're very supportive towards one another. By the end of three or four weeks we have a good group.

Sessions varied from a five minute presentation, using a particular teaching aid, to a much longer lesson in which teachers had to concentrate on using one particular teaching method.

> We do peer group teaching exercises in which all the input, all the activities in the course are summarised. . . this is a half hour lesson which is enough to give them a chance to teach a bit; for students to do some practical work; some sort of evaluation, some sort of assessment of students learning and so on, all within that half hour period. It's a good exercise, they've got to be concise, they've got to get it all organised to the minute.

> We're looking at method particularly, and subject secondly — although you can never divorce the two. So they are almost forced to look at method — five or so particular methods - exposition, discovery, discussion, demonstration, simulation, role play etc. They don't know which method they will be asked to teach until something like three weeks before the time. I give them a full Friday evening when they can discuss it, plan it. . . it's done at a weekend session. Before that time, when they're told what they're going to be expected to do, we have two or three nights when we're talking about teaching method. So it focuses their attention on what I'm saying because they might very well be asked to participate in one of these particular approaches. It's a mean

device if you like, to make my lectures more effective.

Most trainers were enthusiastic about this kind of practical teaching exercise and raised no major problems with its use. One person who no longer used micro-teaching on his Stage 1 course gave two reasons why:

— The group was so supportive it was unbelievable, (they would not criticise). Their turn was going to come so it was no use getting the knives out.

— You always had such a large element of artificiality — "Well I wouldn't have done that really" and how much you could assume the students know or didn't know. We always tended to get teaching at the basic level.

Groups may become uncritical in discussing each other's teaching. This raises problems for this kind of exercise: does it stimulate or inhibit objective, analytical thinking about each other's teaching? When teachers get to know each other well they may hesitate to be critical, especially as they share the same apprehension and anxieties. They may be more objective and critical privately — and learn from watching each other's mistakes — though they don't show this in open class.

The second reason for abandoning micro-teaching was the artificiality of the situation. The situation had arisen in a peer group session where a typing teacher faced a genuine mixed ability group. The question at issue was whether to use role-play with beginner students or whether the teacher should teach them as a mixed ability group.

I put a fair bit of emphasis on teaching it in the here and now. . . from experience, I know that they pretend that they're teaching an evening class of people. . . We have this game playing going on continuously. "If you were a teacher on a typing course, you teach Linda not Mrs. X or Mrs. Y, you teach Linda typing. Now if it so happens that Linda is already a typist, then that's your problem. You've got to deal with it, because that's the way things happen in adult classes." I made an awful song and dance about this and it frightened the life out of some of them. . . because they seem to be afraid of breaking out of this mould of using a set syllabus. . . They have to learn that training courses are artificial, yes, but they are good excuses to get to grips with real life situations and not to shelve them.

Class visits

All the courses (except one Stage 1) arranged that someone would visit each teacher during the course, to observe them teaching their class. On Stage 2 and City and Guilds 730 courses this is part of the assessment. On Stage 1, the visit usually counted towards a trainer's more informal assessment of the teacher. It was not always clear exactly what the purposes of the visit was — some were seen as 'pastoral' whilst others clearly formed part of a formal assessment. Trainers recognised that visits were rather uncomfortable for most teachers and sometimes for themselves. One way trainers tried to alleviate the anxiety was to delay their visit until they had got to know the teacher on a personal basis.

The obvious problem is that they are nervous and conscious of the fact that they are being observed. I do my best to put them at their ease to alleviate any worries about being observed. I try to impress on them that it's not an assessment. ... Before I go on the visit, I try to get to know them as much as possible, so that we've got a good relationship between the two of us.

I give them time to get into their own course and to know me. I hope when I go there they recognise me as a friend rather than a person in authority.

People are so worried about their teaching anyway that if you go and sit in on the lesson right at the beginning of their Stage 1 course they're biting their nails, they can't give a good lesson, they don't really know what they're doing or what you want from them and it frightens them to death. That could work against their achieving. . . more confidence.

Trainers who used observation of teaching as part of their assessment procedures had to decide whether it was helpful to inform teachers of the criteria by which they would be assessed.

I always talk to them about the criteria of good teaching, there's a whole stint on that. Then I give them a handout — I call it 'ideals to be aimed at', and it goes through the various stages of preparation and planning, method and presentation, teacher/student relationships, appearance and voice production, and approach to the class, then a few details as to what I'm hoping that they can achieve during that lesson. I've only used this in the past few years. . . but I've found it's a lot more productive if I give them guidelines as to what I'm looking for, even though I don't give them the assessment schedule as such. They generally become more confident and more successful.

(Stage 1 trainer)

I prepare them, as much as possible, by discussing the criteria we will be observing. They are given, at a very early stage, the assessment sheet to try and encourage their objective analysis and their self-critical analysis of what constitutes good teaching.

(Stage 2/730 trainer)

Observing teaching was a task which trainers approached cautiously in view of the constraints within which they had to operate. They knew from experience that the lesson they observed might not be representative of the teacher's performance and were fully aware that their presence in the class affected what they saw — both the teacher's behaviour and the students' reactions. Moreover these effects were not constant between classes — some teachers were much more self-conscious than others when being watched. These factors are unavoidable and probably do not matter when the main purpose of the visit is to offer help and support but it makes assessment difficult, especially when the assessment is graded and the trainer is limited as to how many visits he is able to make. Trainers avoided the problems of grading observation of teaching; the impression given was that people very rarely failed on this element alone and the trainer used his observations to confirm his knowledge of the teacher's performance on the rest of the course. Amongst most trainers, the emphasis was to use class visits to offer support and help, rather than to assess teachers.

There's almost a pre-emptory requirement for Stage 2 that they've made for themselves — that they can teach, that they can be successful, that they've lived in this game long enough to survive. They're not going to get thrown out of teaching jobs because they're terrible at it — they wouldn't bother coming. Essentially you're talking about improvement and help.

The question arises as to whether or not it is helpful to combine an opportunity for teachers to learn and receive help with a visit that is used for assessment. Obviously, a teacher who is being assessed will want to be seen at his best; one who is offered a chance to be helped in his work may prefer to be seen when he is in trouble. Whatever the purpose of the visit, it seems teachers are likely to be anxious. How then did trainers feel teachers benefited from this ordeal? Trainers believed that visiting classes enabled them to get to know the teachers better and as a consequence to support and guide them more effectively.

> If I can spend something like 6—8 hours with this badminton tutor, I will get to know him very well. He will probably. . . realise that I've got something to offer him other than as an authority. . . I would also make it clear to him, he has something to offer us and to offer me. The relationship will hopefully change. I see that as a very important part of teacher training.

To understand the teacher and the particular conditions he was working under made it possible for the trainer to help the teacher as an individual.

> First of all, I want to get to know the environment he's working in if I am to help him more effectively — just as in one sense, we're trying to get them to understand our more academic, theoretical environment. If he thinks, "this guy does at least know what I'm about" then he's maybe more able to accept what we're saying or what we're trying to guide them towards than he might be otherwise.

Trainers mentioned how, by making simple observations and offering another perspective on the situation they could help teachers avoid obvious pitfalls.

> I think quite often when you are a teacher you miss things — you miss opportunities, you miss student reaction, you miss your own reaction, you may not be aware of how the room's organised — a whole host of things like that. Somebody going in from the outside can be aware of these things and can point them out.

Teaching observation offers trainers the opportunity to assess a teacher's performance in class and to initiate a discussion about the teacher's work. The teacher is helped to think more clearly about what is happening in the class. Trainers each had their own ways of offering feedback to teachers and there were some interesting differences in approach. Most trainers saw it as a two-way process, a dialogue. They were very much aware that teachers hoped for some feedback and expected some judgement on whether things had gone well:

> . . . inviting them to discuss the work that has been done and they don't really need an invitation. They're only too happy to talk about it, to see whether or not it has gone well.

Trainers offered their impressions with differing degrees of formality, ranging from a written report, with an assessment grade, to a chat over a cup of coffee. In fact most trainers seemed to make a point of talking briefly to the teacher immediately after the session, just to assure him. In such ways did trainers seek to help teachers through the medium of the visit. Although they varied in style they all seemed to emphasise an exchange between trainer and teacher initiated by the trainer. One trainer described how he based his observations on a list of criteria drawn up by the teachers themselves:

> What we did last time and have done this time, is to prepare a check-off list, so that when they sit and watch these good teachers they've got some notion of what to look for. And then, I'm afraid with my group I throw that back on them and say I'll be using the check list when I come to look at you. So it's a check list they've helped to contribute to that I use to observe them. I have the list and do a carbon copy to give them and we discuss it on the first course day following that visit. I don't do it on the spot.
>
> Sometimes it helps to write down comments, . . . but mainly I just talk to them over a cup of coffee — at most a week later, because if you leave it longer than that they've

probably forgotten — or I'll have forgotten.

> . . . the next day, I usually write them a letter. It is a letter, not a report on a form with ticks or crosses. . . it's part of my make-up that I hate making snap judgements. I'd rather go home and mull it over. . . Obviously I write and say "if there's anything you want to talk over, grab me at the next meeting."

Other trainers encouraged teachers to give their own reactions and tried to get them to analyse events for themselves and to identify why things went well or badly. Again, there was an emphasis on the process being supportive and positive. One trainer did feel it was his responsibility in extreme cases to let a teacher know about a fault he considered serious in a teacher of adults.

> They're not learning from my visit, they're learning from their own performance, from their own students. All my visit might well do is act as a catalyst for certain processes of self-assessment or whatever. What I might do is direct some of their thinking, or self-criticism, along certain lines.

> I try to get them to tell me what they thought. . . It must be supportive. . . it's really them bouncing off me. . . I should make very positive suggestions. . . It does bother me that I find it difficult to be highly critical of poor classroom performances. . . I can cue on the good bits.

> In the past I've written quite long spiels, and I thought it was a bit impersonal. So I said, "Look I'm going to ask questions, I'm not going to tell you you're a lousy teacher. I'm going to ask you. . . how you felt it went, was there any need. . . for any particular change". That sort of thing.

When trainers visit a teacher's class, they have to decide what role to adopt, dependent on the type of subject and to a large extent on what makes the teacher and the students feel most comfortable. From the trainers' descriptions of what they did when they visited teachers, it is evident that they employed a variety of observation techniques ranging from the formal to the participative. With the former, the trainer sat at the back of the room and did not become involved in any form of class activity. This seems to have worked effectively in sports classes. The comment from this person describes the hallmarks of this approach:

> I just try to make myself invisible — I sit in the corner and don't intrude in the class. And with a bit of luck, after a while, they'll forget I'm there.

On the other hand a large number of trainers preferred to be more directly involved in the classroom, particularly when observing subjects like languages or crafts. The most common approach was to take part in the lesson as a member of the class group. This trainer had adopted a more novel approach by sharing the teaching with the person being observed:

> I'm going along next week to see one of my group and I'm going to participate, because I want to go more than once. That's not very easy, but I don't want to go and sit there with my note pad, which is the worst possible thing. Possibly one of the better ways to do it is to go in and join. The first one I'm going to see is a badminton class and it is one of my games so I can go in there and I can actually help the tutor, and we'll do a bit of mixed teaching.

Between these alternatives lies a method which combines something of both; the observer participates by moving round the group and talking to people individually but does not become involved in the central content of the class.

Classes such as Ladies Keep Fit and Yoga seem to have been especially difficult to observe — for female as well as male trainers. It may be worthwhile looking for alternative ways of helping these teachers. Perhaps there is a case for using only teachers experienced in these subjects.

> I don't know about a ladies' keep fit class — the problems outweigh the advantages. . .
> I'm not comfortable.   (male trainer)

> I think one of the problems is her subject — Yoga — and it's difficult to observe without intruding on it. So I have watched her, but I've listened more to what she says about what she does. I'm satisfied that she's doing very nicely.

Perhaps it matters less which approach the trainer adopts if teachers are not being assessed — it is more important that teacher, trainer and students should feel as comfortable as possible with whatever is arranged. If teachers are to be graded by observation of their teaching, then the method adopted could make a significant difference to the trainer's perceptions of what is happening in a class. As with micro-teaching, trainers seemed to accept the difficulties involved in going to watch teachers at work, but felt that they were more than outweighed by the opportunities to help and support.

> I'm uncomfortable in the sense I may be disturbing the class and the students . . . That is permanent and unavoidable. But I don't feel uncomfortable now about my relationship, because I know in my heart of hearts why I'm there and what my relationship is. And although it may be a question of assessment and saying somebody is or isn't a good teacher, that's fairly low down on my list. I'm really going to say "Is there anything I can do?" to be helpful. . .

The major problem trainers found in observing teachers in their classes seems to have been one of time. Many trainers pointed out that it took up many hours and was difficult to organise. They were seldom able to see each teacher as much as they would like.

> If you're going to do the job properly, it needs a hell of a lot of time. . . I know full well that I'm going to put in twice as many hours as I will ever get recognition for on a time-table. I could go along for 10 minutes and probably get away with it. But you'd lose a lot of credibility. . . And if you are looking at your own staff development there's only one way of doing it — otherwise you're not happy about the way you've involved yourself. It's a long term thing, it doesn't just end when the course ends. You've got to build up that relationship with your teachers.

Some trainers had tried to involve Centre Heads by asking them to go and observe teachers for them but none had met with much success. All the trainers who discussed this interestingly enough were, or had been, Centre Heads themselves. They clearly saw this as a natural part of the role of a Centre Head and a way of involving Centre Heads in training. One person said he sometimes found it 'politically expedient' — as a Centre Head himself — not to intrude into another's area. Although Centre Heads did not seem openly hostile to the idea, neither did they seem exactly eager either. Trainers felt this was either because of time or because they felt uncomfortable about doing it and were unsure what to look for.

> That bothers me in that it doesn't work as efficiently as it should — because the Centre Head is too busy or because he doesn't see the importance or relevance of it. Out of eight trainees I haven't received one report from a Centre Head.

They only visited after considerable pressure and reminders and reminders. . . Some others we felt did it so perfunctorily that it wasn't worth doing.

They should be able to do it. . . I think to a certain extent it is practice and I don't think they have a lot of this and unless I tell them what to look for, I get the impression that they really wouldn't know what to look for.

One trainer suggested supplying some guidance to Centre Heads if they take on this kind of activity, but clearly it is a sensitive area and relates back to the question of whether supervision is, or should be, an integral part of a Centre Head's work. Certainly this kind of involvement has potential as one way of narrowing the gap between those who are and those who are not involved in training, thus drawing more people into training teams.

These are the tutors that have never done any training before and this is a very good way of training some of these area tutors as part of the county team.

Course work and individual study

Trainers made suprisingly little mention of writing as an activity through which teachers might learn to articulate their ideas. All trainees on Stage 2 courses were expected to do written work for assessment. On Stage 1 courses, minimal demands of this kind seem to have been made. Trainers were conscious that teachers varied quite a bit both in actually doing written work and in their willingness to do it. There appeared to be some reluctance to demand a lot of written work from them, especially amongst Stage 1 trainers:

Just a little. We do set them inter-sessional tasks, often it's as much thinking about something as actually producing written work. There seemed to be a feeling among the students that they came along to the meetings, but felt that they didn't want to do the work in between. Especially the trained school teachers who feel it isn't relevant to them.

Where written work was demanded trainers were aware that it presented many students with difficulties:

The written work presents a problem in that there's tremendous variation. . . Some of them haven't had the experience, ever, or for a long time, of putting pen to paper in a coherent lengthy piece of writing.

Several trainers on Stage 1 courses got teachers to keep logs or diaries of the course itself, or of their work with their class as an alternative to formal essay writing. One trainer described how he used a course log in such a way that it gave rise to various benefits and purposes without it becoming too onerous a task:

I do ask them to keep a log, and each week I ask a different person to read it out to me — I tell them that it is really for my benefit, I don't keep notes, but if we get sidetracked and go on a particularly interesting topic, I like to have a record of that. . . Sometimes I spring it on them as they arrive, "those logs that you've done I would like to take them in and have a look at them to see if we've covered all that we should have done". I also tell them to put in the logs any interesting cuttings that they find. . . I also expect them to keep all the handouts that I give them. . . The log serves several purposes. . . as an assessment of the way they are progressing, it serves as a help to me. . . if I see things missing, either I haven't concentrated on that, or that particular aspect of the course isn't relevant anyway, and should I leave it out next time round?

Also, of course, it is very helpful to other students. . . if somebody is away. . . it is without knowing it, an account of their own development.

At Stage 2 level, trainers did expect written work, partly because of the nature of the assessments and also because they felt teachers coming on the course ought to be willing to tackle this kind of work.

Two Stage 2 trainers described how written assignments could be used in such a way that teachers produced work which would be of use to them later:

> What we try to do is make sure that everything they do is going to be useful afterwards. When they make visual aids up, the idea is that they make up ones that they are actually going to use. . . If they do a scheme of work, it should be one which, given a bit of chance, they can actually use next year and plan for next year's course.

Trainers generally tended to be wary of insisting that teachers did a lot of reading during the course. They were conscious of the time required and that teachers might be unfamiliar with this way of working. They all tended to mention the same books and journals — Teaching Adults, Adult Education, Adults in Education, Adults Learning. Several Stage 1 trainers said they did not recommend that teachers read these during the course, but they did photocopy extracts from books and journals, produced their own handouts and gave very selective reading lists.

> Handouts are very helpful, because you can put on what you want. You can structure them according to the needs of the students themselves. . . Textbooks, there are so few that are any good, I use two — BBC's Adults in Education and Jennifer Rogers. I don't tell them about these books. Firstly, I don't want them reading ahead and secondly I think they are very useful for them to look back on when I have done the course.

> (The College Library) will produce a book box if you ask them. On Stage 1, I tend not to do that, because I like them to have just one or two books, with specific chapters to refer to on specific topics. That gives them a narrow basis, admittedly, but a fairly directed one. Because you find on Stage 1, it's not an academic course, they're not academic people and they like to be directed in their study and it helps them to begin to learn to read and write in terms of assignments and so on. Its good preparation for Stage 2, where there's a much broader reading list and a full scale book box.

While Stage 2 trainers did expect teachers to do more reading, they were still careful not to overburden them. This trainer tended to reorganise and summarise written material into handouts, but recognised that this would be difficult for trainers with less time to spend on their courses:

> The biggest source is the standard textbooks. If you get people to draw up a book list for an adult education training course, they very often come up with the same books. There's a classic core now of books you use. A lot of things I do, I tend to extract, précis, put into other words, writing papers on certain things. I have a theory that people at Stage 2 level won't tend to read as much as, say, the average University student. You can't rely on them reading all the books you'd like them to because they haven't got time and it's not a way of working that they're used to. So I think part of the tutor's job is to be highly selective and to produce simplified shortened forms of a lot of the material that's available. Over the years, because of my job, I can spend time doing this. Other people obviously don't have the same time. I'd get journals and copy

121

them or extract the meat and put it into a paper of my own.

Reading and written work are parts of the course where teachers work alone, outside course time. Some trainers saw the strength of this kind of individual course work in the opportunity it offers to teachers to work on something related to their own particular subject or interests — giving them a chance to fill in some of the gaps there may be in the course for them personally. Also reading is a way of learning which teachers can continue to use after a course has finished. Only one Stage 2/730 tutor explicitly said he hoped the course would broaden teachers' reading, indicating that he tried to introduce them to different kinds of relevant materials — adult education journals, subject—specialist books and periodicals and more general books on education.

Residential weekend

Three of the four counties in the region provide funds to enable courses to include a residential weekend; many trainers considered this a very important and significant part of the course. Why is this such an essential component of Stage 1 and Stage 2 courses?

There were a number of practical reasons why trainers liked to include a weekend. If a Stage 2 course, of 100 hours, is going to be run in one year it requires some tight planning to fit in the hours. A residential weekend of twelve hours or more eases this problem. Furthermore bringing two or more courses together for a joint residential weekend enabled trainers to introduce new methods of teaching or group activities that would be impracticable for a small group alone and it made it easier to give groups access to resources, hardware, and other facilities they may not have had in their usual meeting place. Trainers mentioned a whole range of different methods that they could use with larger groups — for example, films, games, simulations, demonstration lessons and video equipment. Also the weekend allowed time for larger projects which otherwise would have had to have been stretched over several weeks. Possibly the exercise could be done more cheaply in non-residential day sessions. Why then did most trainers feel so strongly that a residential session offers much more? The two main arguments were that a weekend allowed teachers to get away from their families and everyday responsibilities and freed them to concentrate on their training course; secondly the weekend allowed much more scope for informal and social contact amongst teachers. Both results can be highly beneficial. One trainer, no longer able to have a residential weekend, clearly found a non-residential weekend very much second best:

> On a residential weekend, the facilities are available for short free time breaks — whether they go for a swim or get together over a cup of coffee — with time to chat over meals, time to go out in the evening and still talk shop, they always do. But now, you feel that you've got to cram everything into a shorter time, keep them occupied to make it worthwhile. Because it's so concentrated, I think you lose some of the teaching time, because they get tired — you can't have such a large break to let them recover, get their second wind. You lose the social element and the sense of group identity and the whole thing is broken up by them going home and coming back. Having experienced both, every time I would come down in favour of a residential weekend.

This person also saw the informal aspects of the weekend as the most important element:

> You ask yourself, 'what can be done in residence that you cannot do elsewhere'? And generally it's nothing to do with educational objectives. . . they're social objectives and social education really, in the sense that it's an opportunity for people to meet

together and talk and share problems, see that other people have the same weaknesses, deficiencies and strengths that you have and this in a way is comforting, gives you confidence etc.

Spending time together on the weekend clearly helped the members of a group to get to know one another: as one trainer put it "When we came back they were a much better group than before they went". This might have implications for the actual timing of the weekend — it would be a pity for a course to conclude just when the group feels they are getting to know one another.

Subject teaching

The previous section mentioned that trainers were aware of teachers' hopes that the courses would offer help in the teaching of their particular subject. Unfortunately trainers admitted that they were unable to give much assistance here and their comments on the whole issue were hedged with uncertainty. Any help they could offer tended to start from the basis that teachers had no problems with the subject itself, only with the teaching of it. Indeed the Regional Scheme works on the assumption that exercises, projects, etc., all give opportunity for trainers to teach work within their own subjects. Within the limitations of Stage 1 and Stage 2 courses, trainers found a number of ways to help trainees apply general teaching principles to the subjects they taught. Course work and assignments were often done with special reference to the teacher's own subject, as for example:

I always try and make sure that when we do any exercise, e.g. "Draw up a checklist for how you would proceed on the first night of a class", that it is done in the subject context.

Specialist subjects — this comes in when they come to prepare a scheme of work and assessment scheme in their own area. But in addition, I make them do an assignment on assessing — the cake decorator sometimes has to assess the woodwork. They start off by saying no-one can assess anything other than their subject. I think that's wrong, because as course tutors we sit in judgement in a variety of subject areas. Why shouldn't the teachers we are training have an awareness of the wide range of activities and how they can be assessed?

We don't really offer them much subject help on training courses. . . Contact with other people who are doing the same kind of job, that's one very powerful force. We try to get them to meet other teachers and to visit other centres. I say "if you want to see another teacher teaching cake decorating, we'll try and find a centre where there is a course".

These comments indicate that the reality fell short of the ideal and not much cross-fertilisation of the sort referred to appears to have taken place on the courses we studied.

One trainer tackled the problem by recommending books, journals and subject associations and he saw it as part of a teacher's professional responsibility to keep himself in touch through these means:

They should be familiar with any specific subject teaching techniques — subject teaching resource books that are available. So every student that I have, I identify as near as I can what subject specialist books there are. . . There is a subject teaching association for most subjects and I tell them the name and address of this centre and I encourage them all to write to it. . . Equally, there are so many periodicals published that there is virtually certainly going to be one they can read and as professionals they should be taking that magazine. But if they are not, I (nudge) them towards it.

This is an interesting way of coping with the situation and one which would clearly benefit from a sharing of knowledge and resources — trainers, subject specialist teachers and subject organisations could all have a role in helping teachers in this way.

Two other trainers who were themselves language teachers discussed how this might influence their work with language teachers on their courses and raised the question of whether or not a trainer should give subject-teaching help when he is able.

> Obviously every Stage 2 tutor has his own particular interest. This time I've got a couple of language teachers — when I go to see them teach, I suspect I look at them with a slightly different eye because I'm a language teacher. They go more under the microscope. . . I think they would regard it as possibly being helpful.

> To a certain extent, I am able to do a little bit because my own subjects are such that I can talk about. . . but I feel in a way that I am giving these people who share the same subject as me an unfair advantage, so I tend not to do it because as you know, you must treat everybody fairly.

Another possibility might be to run separate modules for particular subjects as suggested in the second ACSTT report. Some counties have offered such specialist courses in the past, but they have not been related to the Regional Training Scheme. At present there is no provision of 'subject modules' at Stage 2 level in the East Midlands Region. Taken together, the evidence suggests that although trainers do recognise the principle of helping trainees relate course content to the teaching of their own subjects, this remains an element of course design which is relatively weak.

Being taught

So far, this section has emphasised the various ways in which trainers believed teachers learn from being on the course. This reflects the emphasis of trainers themselves, who tended to discuss the course in terms of what they believed teachers got out of it and why, rather than in terms of their own rôle as facilitators or managers of these opportunities for learning. During the interviews, trainers were asked directly about the teaching methods they used on the course. Their answers give a clearer impression of how they guided teachers' learning and controlled some of the ideas and material that they wanted to get across to them.

Most trainers claimed that they used as wide a range of teaching methods as possible and they said that they used lectures, discussion, case study, role play, games, simulation, projects, group tasks etc. They indicated that they saw these methods as opportunities for teachers to experience different ways of learning and felt them to be necessary in terms of their own credibility since they were advocating that teachers use as wide a range of methods as possible with their classes. When asked about the methods they personally favoured, almost all trainers mentioned discussion:

> I like case study and discussion . . . Discussion, as a method on Stage 1, gives people the confidence to speak among peers and compare notes and also to put forward a reasoned case and that comes in on Stage 2 when they've got to write a reasoned case. . . also I think it's a much more adult way of exchanging information than perhaps any other.

> You tend to end up using discussion rather more than anything else, because that is

the one area where you can ensure that everybody is making a contribution or getting involved. It's involvement that's essential more than anything else.

After discussion, case studies and lectures were the most popular teaching methods. Trainers did seem to face something of a dilemma when talking about teaching methods for as earlier parts of this section have shown they were committed to student-centred learning with students actively involved in analysing and learning from their own ideas and experiences. The position remained however that they had certain ground they hoped to cover, certain ideas they wanted to get over to teachers and a limited time available. Trainers, therefore, described how they tried to guide teachers' discussion and analysis along the lines they considered most fruitful and used case studies designed to bring out certain things. Many trainers used lectures to get over basic points and information before teachers discussed the issues involved. The quotations below illustrate the mixed feelings trainers had about lectures; some appeared almost guilty at saying they used this method, whilst others believed that they could save teachers a lot of time this way.

> There are certain times when you have to give them a straight lecture. . . One can then turn it into a discussion afterwards, but there are certain subjects where a lecture is the only way to do it, unless you are going to spend far more time than we have got available.

> 'Lecturing' is a dirty word in some places. But to encourage people to find out for themselves is sometimes such a long process it's hardly worth doing. We don't all have to discover the wheel.

Other trainers said they did not use lectures but the following observations show how trainers used open-ended teaching methods.

> We analyse together why certain things happen. I'm afraid, while they're analysing I suspect I'm in a sense falsifying the analysis. I would like the analysis to be honest, but I would like to point that analysis in certain ways which I regard as being well-proven enough to be profitable. . . It's a bit like discovery learning when the teacher decides what they're going to discover. . . If they want to analyse other things, we're always prepared to explore highways and by-ways, we get off the main road if they want to. But I think it's part of a tutor's job. . . if he's professionally competent, to make some decisions about the content of the course, where you are going. And I would regard this analysis, or discovery, as being only a method that you would use to teach certain content items, upon which you've already decided. And if that's cheating, I'm sorry!

Quotations from experienced trainers show that these dilemmas about teaching methods and styles are never totally resolved. This trainer seemed to have settled for covering less ground in a way he felt had most impact on teachers:

> I started off by using the formal approach, but I find the students learn much more if the tutor just acts as a catalyst and gets them to do the work. It is hard work for the tutor, it takes a long time. It would be so much easier to say at the beginning, blank, blank and blank, but they don't get anything out of it. So although it takes time to do a case study etc., and to get them to tease out the crucial points, it comes to the same thing in the end and they remember far more. So that's why I use it, plus the fact that I don't like being too serious, because people remember through laughter. . .

How a person teaches can change over time and it is important that the method matches not only the material being covered and the needs of students, but also the trainer's own preferences, personality and experience.

> I find as each course goes on, for some reason or another the trainees bring more. Probably because I can use it more. I've calmed down a lot now. I used to be a great believer that I knew the message and that they had to have the message and then we could talk it around. I tend now to throw less messages out, but just odd ones, and this group in particular seems to pick up the cues and come back to us.

> You've got to adapt teaching methods to circumstances and content. That's the basic lesson really! So I wouldn't favour one more than the other. But I'm quite convinced certain people, me included, have certain methods in which they're more at home — style, personality etc. Perhaps you could go so far as to say to some people "until you get better at a certain technique perhaps you oughtn't to try it too often. . . because you're less effective." I think you balance the method the content suggests to you against that which you feel confident with. I think you can only build up a range of techniques yourself, I've got better over the years at certain things I wasn't very good at before.

SECTION 6: APPLYING THE COURSE IN PRACTICE

Stage 1 and 2 courses are intended to make an impact on the way in which teachers approach their work. Trainers were asked how they helped teachers to relate the course to their teaching, and whether they found teachers had any problems in doing this.

Many were clearly concerned to offer a degree of flexibility in their courses in order to respond to teachers' specific needs and interests. This kind of flexibility offers a degree of freedom to students, to choose which areas they wish to concentrate on in their own work and a degree of participation as a group to influence the direction of the course itself.

Trainers enunciated a number of problems in making a course responsive to the needs of the group. Firstly, teachers find it hard to say what they want the course to cover.

> I think their views on what to expect are so nebulous that they are perfectly prepared to go along with what we have to offer, provided. . . they can see it as being useful, and valuable.

Secondly, trainers themselves had strong ideas about what they would like to cover. On Stage 1 in particular, there is little room to deviate from the course as planned apart from minor shifts of emphasis, or finding more time to go over problem areas. This comment summarises the difficulties that would be raised for planning and for the trainer personally if teachers were given more say in the running of the course.

> I sometimes wonder if I personally allow enough participation in the sense of their making decisions about what should be done on the course. I don't think I do, actually. Some people lay great store by this — that at any time, the course can change its direction a bit, or even quite substantially. Now I've never felt under pressure from students to change the course. That may be because I'm cheating, because I've never allowed them to! I suppose I always think I know best about what they should be doing. I think it's very difficult to get students to participate in deciding the course content, because you never get them until the course. You could say you take the first

week or so deciding what they would want to do, but I've never been brave enough to do that. I know one Stage 2 course that more or less lets the course build itself — which frightened me, frankly, in the sense I like things a bit tighter than that. It's just my own security I think.

I also think the tutors of the same Stage 2 course found that although they let the course go certain ways they'd got certain things they were going to insist on being in anyway, whether or not they arose from the students' wishes. . . they were prepared to say "this has gone far enough", "if you don't suggest we do this, we're going to do it anyway!" I think it would be quite necessary to have a course team if you did that. I think I would feel very exposed as a single tutor/director. I think I'd want to be able to go away and talk to people, to colleagues.

Although no trainers gave teachers a major say on how the course was run, many did give examples of how they were able to give individuals some scope to follow their particular interests. This was done mainly through course work and reading, both flexible enough to allow each teacher to relate his course work to his own subject, or to look at an area that interests him. Some tutorials were offered though these were demanding upon time. Trainers seemed to accept the need to help teachers relate the course to their work as part of their responsibility and that it was an integral part of the course, pervading all its activities. Trainers believed that when teachers try to change the way they teach they encounter problems concerning their own willingness to change, within their students and their expectations and in the environment in which they all have to work.

Trainers were conscious of the fact that many experienced teachers are set in their ways because they have learnt to conform to traditional models of teaching. These teachers do not find it easy to accept fresh ideas and new approaches and they tend to reject concepts which do not seem readily to apply to them. It may well be easier for them not to try to change; it requires effort, it suggests a need for improvement and can be threatening because it increases the risk of the unpredicted happening. As two trainers separately pointed out:

I think change is painful, because it involves work — it's easier not to change, you don't use any energy in not changing. And if you're invited to change and you accept that invitation you're saying something about your status, you're saying up to now, what you've been doing is not necessarily wrong, but certainly not the best.

I suppose they find their own present style comfortable. We are talking about people who are doing this as a spare-time occupation, it's not their livelihood. . . If they were pressurised to change too much, I think next year they would say, "thanks very much but I shan't be working for you."

Only one trainer warned of the danger that training courses might pressure people into change for the worse. Courses tend to put a lot of emphasis on trying new methods of teaching and this could in some cases destroy a teacher's natural spontaneity.

There is a danger of, on the course, being introduced to alternatives in presentation etc., and that native ability being totally destroyed.

Sometimes, it is not the teacher who finds difficulty in changing but their students. Teachers have to choose whether to risk trying new ways of teaching that may prove less effective or whether to meet their students' expectations.

I've always been of the opinion that you can't go back to a course today, having finished yesterday, and start stamping around with new ideas. But it is possible to start incorporating new ideas carefully and gradually into a course — or if you like, to say I don't want to start now, I'll wait until the next session starts. The only people then who will interfere are the Centre Heads and the teacher's own fear of stretching their students further than they have done in the past. . . you've got to bear in mind you've got, in the main, fee paying students at the other end and you can't jeopardise their learning by playing about with various ideas that some silly person on a teacher training course says you've got to look at. So there's always this compromise.

The final category of problems that trainers felt teachers met in implementing ideas from the course were those related to the facilities available at the centres where they teach. This raised the question for trainers of whether they ought to be training teachers for an actual or an ideal working situation. They preferred the latter hoping that teachers would put pressure on their Centre Head to provide better facilities and conditions. The dilemma for the trainers emerges from this quotation:

The back-home, real-life situation is often so totally different from that the Stage 1 and 2 Courses try to train them for, that there is a conflict, there is a credibility gap, almost. . . At a very practical level, some of the things we're suggesting tend to be a bit idealistic, in the sense you could probably do them in the best centres. . . I know that lays me open immediately to the accusation that 'What good is a course that doesn't match the back-home situation', but generally I would be prepared to say that I would rather the back-home situation changed, than the course changed. Because I think that what we're trying to do on the course is probably better for adult education than trying to make the course fit some not very good back-home situations.

In effect many evaded the question and this is one of the reasons why some specialist and voluntary organisations find LEA training unsatisfactory. It is rather unrealistic even to hope for radical improvements in the physical conditions and educational equipment of church halls and WI huts. It may well be that more courses need to prepare teachers for a greater variety of conditions and to seek help from outside the public system of education in the process. They need encouragement to keep trying new ideas and to help them cope with the new problems these inevitably bring.

SECTION 7: EVALUATING TRAINING

This section looks at three approaches to evaluation which were discussed with trainers.

Evaluating the course itself. Trainers were asked how they approached course evaluation and what they had learned from the exercise.

Assessing a teacher's performance. How it is decided whether or not teachers should be awarded a certificate.

The benefits from training. This takes a broader look at how trainers see the benefits from training courses.

128

Evaluating the course

As teachers and trainers are the two groups directly participating in training courses it is not surprising that trainers should have concentrated on the ways in which the two groups formed and presented their judgements. To do so they drew upon their own perceptions of the course — how things seemed to go and how teachers reacted to them. In fact, this constitutes an important element in their evaluation of the course, described by trainers as 'a gut reaction'. In addition to their own feelings as participants, trainers spoke of other evidence they used to evaluate courses. Most of this related to teachers' performance and behaviour on the course, their assignments, and their teaching.

> Attendance, participation — do they participate more or less as the course goes on? Do they become more or less articulate? Think more? Get used to the idea they have to defend what they say? Do they think more about what they say?

Course work was another useful indicator to trainers of what teachers had learned from the course. One tutor who asked teachers to keep a log of what had been covered each session found this gave him valuable feedback on which areas of course content had impact or relevance for teachers.

> The course work is designed very tightly to cover all the objectives, and thus we have a continuous feedback.
>
> (Stage 2/730 trainer)

> How/whether they do assignments. These are elementary, in so far as they're designed to test that which has been taught...They are very much part of the teaching, a recapitulation of things we've discussed and worked on together. So assignments are a useful test of effectiveness, of teaching and learning.
>
> (Stage 2 trainer)

> They keep a log...if I see things missing, either I haven't concentrated on that, or that particular aspect of the course isn't relevant anyway, and should I leave it out next time round?

Trainers mentioned how watching teachers actually teach on the course, in micro-teaching or peer group teaching sessions, or in their classrooms, gave feedback on how the course had influenced them. However, as this trainer pointed out, it was not always easy to see change or progress.

> Usually, on two visits I don't see very much difference. Most are good teachers anyway — the syndrome being I'm a good teacher, I'm interested, I like training.
>
> (Stage 2 trainer)

In addition, most trainers described how they shared and discussed their detailed impressions when they met as a tutorial team.

> The team meets regularly, at least once a week, to discuss how it's going...it means we're monitoring student progress, and our own progress on the course, and the direction we're going.

> We get together when the dust has settled and mull over how the course has gone.

As well as formulating their own judgements on how the course was going, trainers discussed the various ways in which they got feedback from the teachers. Inevitably, they received it informally throughout the course — depending on the extent to which teachers felt free to discuss their reactions openly and spontaneously. Some trainers made a point of asking teachers' views throughout the course.

> I suppose I do (evaluate the course) in a sense. I think it's a continuing thing...I can evaluate it with my students, which I would do, but I suspect not in any highly structured way.

> I don't do it at the end of a course, I do it throughout the course. At the end of each tutorial we positively think about what we've done, and try to identify it's value to each of the members of the group...It's an on-going thing.

Most trainers said that they had a session towards the end of the course which they devoted to asking teacher's views. One advantage of having some retrospective impressions was that reactions change with the passage of time.

> They very often don't like things that make them think...that make them have to write...that make them have to participate. But usually afterwards, when it's all happened and it's all gone, then I think they're in a position to give me a more balanced judgement.

> You get reaction on a week to week basis, but...students are so keen to assimilate and make use of what you tell them, you can easily get the impression that the course is going better than it is.

Many trainers used this kind of discussion session, sometimes at the end of the course as their main or only evaluation method.

> There is an interim evaluation at the end of the Stage 1 weekend where we just ask for gut reactions, and then the whole of the last afternoon we sit down and really sort out what's gone on here, and talk it through, first of all with the group, and then with the three course tutors.

> What I do is to shut all the tutors up, so that they can't argue back, or justify anything, and just let the students have a free for all discussion. I lead it — I find it needs to be just led with questions, to spark them off, more than anything else. Usually, I ask one of the students to take notes, so that they've got a record for themselves, which we can then circulate...

These rather unstructured, informal, methods of evaluation predominated; only two trainers described a more structured approach — one using a questionnaire, the other requesting teachers to use the course objectives to assess the course's success. One trainer said he had used a questionnaire and subsequently reverted to more informal methods:

> We have devised a questionnaire in the past and wondered if we learnt any more from them than from the gut reaction.

Course evaluation is an area that many trainers spoke about as though they felt they could be doing more, as though there might be better ways of doing it. In particular, they pointed out the subjectivity of the approaches that were used. The following point was made by a number of trainers:

> It's been fairly subjective, the reaction and response of the students and tutors on the course.

Though this frank comment summed up what was implicit in many trainers' views:

> I think this is the thing we do worst, the checking back on the effectiveness of the course.

Few trainers mentioned people outside the course who could contribute by offering a more detached view to complement their own judgements. Two specifically mentioned the moderator and assessor on Stage 2 and City and Guilds courses:

> In my case, I value the moderator a lot. The opportunities to talk to them, and for them to say what they think is happening on the course, and to suggest ideas or modifications.

Stage 1 trainers have no moderator whose views they can seek; one such trainer felt the advisory team in his LEA could play a bigger role in evaluation. Being outside the system, they may be "more ruthless" in their comments. It is significant to note that few trainers commented upon the lack of evaluation of the outcomes of training i.e. what does it do to subsequent teaching behaviour.

Perhaps less important than the actual methods used to evaluate a course is the spirit in which the evaluation is conducted, itself in part a measure of the atmosphere and relationships which have been established. Above all, it seems important that teachers should be free to say what they really think and not feel inhibited in criticising when and where they feel it to be necessary. Trainers should be open-minded and receptive to teachers' views. It seems desirable that there should be a large element in course evaluation which takes advantage of the perceptions, experience and imagination of all participants.

Whatever is said about the course and whatever criticisms or suggestions were made, the trainer had to use his own judgement in deciding whether and how to act upon them in future.

> I think what you have to do is to take into account what they say and then equate it against what you think is right, and come to some kind of compromise...It's a three cornered compromise between what the students say, what we believe, and what we are able to do.

> When it comes to a tutors' meeting, we can sit down and have a look at it, see what was justified and what wasn't, and how we can improve the next one...You have to be a bit careful. Sometimes you alter it in the light of what they've said, and the following course, they say the opposite.

The kinds of changes trainers said they had made as a result of evaluation tended not to involve major rethinking of the approach taken:

> It's changed I think, but in essence it's the same kind of course as it always was. There's always been the elements it's got in it now.

By and large the changes made were in teaching methods and style (for example, using more micro teaching or fewer lectures), a move to a more practical, less theoretical course; alterations in timing and sequence of topics, changes in emphasis and reductions in the amount of material covered. These changes also suggest a growing skill, expertise and confidence amongst the trainers concerned.

131

Evaluating a teacher's performance

Requirements for certification vary between courses. Stage 1 certificates are awarded by local education authorities, and there seem to be considerable variations in the criteria by which they are awarded. There is a general expectation that teachers will attend about 80% of the course. Additional criteria for Stage 1 ranged from "we just have to say that they've presented a satisfactory effort", to courses where classroom teaching and course work were more systematically taken into account. There appeared to be no agreed criteria, consequently it is difficult from trainers' comments to understand what the regional standards are. Stage 2 Certificates are awarded by the Regional Advisory Council, and there is rather more consistency in that three elements — attendance, teaching and course work — are always taken into account. Where Stage 2 courses were combined with City and Guilds 730, formal assessment seems to have been given most weight. These joint courses used as many as 20 assessed tasks and an assessment of classroom teaching: teachers were graded on a scale of pass, credit and distinction for the City and Guilds 730 award.

Despite these variations, it is very rare in practice for teachers to fail. If teachers stay until the end of the course and complete the required work they are almost certain to get a certificate whatever the methods of assessment. Although trainers said they would be prepared to fail people if necessary, only one person actually spoke of doing it:

> I had the unpalatable task of telling her that she had not met the requirements...the credibility of the qualification requires it.
>
> (Stage 2/730 trainer)

A number of reasons were given why the issue of failure rarely arises. There is an initial process of self-selection, particularly for the Stage 2 course which is an optional one. Trainers argued that if teachers were interested enough in their work to take the trouble to come on courses they probably had the qualities of a good teacher. Having been told something about their course, they had a chance to opt out if they felt they could not fulfil the requirements.

> The fact that they'd applied for Stage 1 and were prepared to give up the amount of time it demands, reflects that they are concerned about their teaching, and not confident that their teaching is 100% efficient, that they want to improve, that they do want to learn something and make changes in their teaching.

> There's a certain amount of self-selection which goes on...they get a fair amount of information about the course before it starts, and they're either interviewed or come to a pre-course meeting, at which I try as carefully as I can to let them know what they're letting themselves in for. I won't say I lay it on a bit thick, but I certainly don't let them get an impression that it's something they ought to undertake lightly.

In addition some trainers did say they would intervene if they felt people were not ready for Stage 2 or would be very likely to fail if they took the course.

> Some of them just aren't ready for it. Yes, they've done Stage 1, they can survive in a classroom without making a complete hash, but they're not up to Stage 2 yet...They need to get some experience.

> I would intervene...if I had personal knowledge of somebody who's applying for a Stage 2 course, for whom I thought it would be too risky...I'm a great believer in not letting people embark upon things where they can fail — that doesn't mean to say that you don't let people try and reach for something which is just a bit beyond their

capabilities. But if you anticipate that it's so far beyond, that what they're doing is putting themselves in a vulnerable position, and can only fail, I would counsel them out of it.

Trainers spoke of how teachers having started on the course tended to drop out if they saw themselves to be in danger of failing. The Stage 1 trainers who spoke of this came from a county where Stage 1 is not compulsory. They did not say whether teachers who dropped out of training also tended to drop out of teaching. As this next quotation illustrates, trainers seemed somewhat relieved to see these potential 'failures' leave:

> Luckily, on these courses, somehow the failures disappear within the course, as if the mental message gets to them, that they know they're not going to make it. This saves a tremendously embarrassing situation for the person in charge of the course.

Only one explicitly mentioned what counselling and support were offered. This must be important in helping teachers view this experience positively with an emphasis on self-awareness rather than admission of failure.

When trainers were asked about the assessment methods used on their course, they immediately referred to those factors taken into account in making decisions whether or not to award the certificate, and in the case of City and Guilds, what grade teachers should be given. This process of sorting or grading teachers did raise problems. Trainers discussed the general issue of whether assessment ought to be based on teachers' achievements and abilities at the end of the course, or on the progress they had made during the course. They pointed out that teachers start from very different points, for example in their case at expressing themselves orally and in writing, in their experience of teaching, in what they have read. In their comments there seems to be an implicit belief that it would be unfair to judge everyone by the same standards. Even during a course, trainers may have to alter their standards. This trainer on a Stage 2/730 described how the question arose when he spread assessments over the course rather than concentrating them towards the end:

> This has meant accepting a lower standard on some of the course work e.g. an analytical case study can be given in the first week or the last week, and you'll get a totally different quality of answer. But a continuous assessment course has to be that, and it means you adopt a different standard of criteria at the beginning, and in the middle and the end.

Trainers recognised that although it may seem fairer to consider achievements in terms of progress, it would be very difficult to implement especially on a rather short Stage 1 course.

The quotation below summarises the attitude of trainers in the regional scheme towards problems of assessing and grading the work of teachers:

> It's very difficult. You've got to be moving individuals forward. They're all at different starting points, and maybe you've got to move them forward even to different finishing points — provided you know those finishing points are all above a certain level...If people get above that, it just becomes a bonus.

City and Guilds demands a rather stricter approach to assessment:

> We have to accept, I think, that if you're awarding some sort of certificate, certainly with national standards, then you have got to ask for some evidence of certain understanding at a certain level. You can do that subjectively through discussion or

observation, or you can do it totally objectively through a piece of written work, or an examination. But I think we have allowed ourselves a certain freedom of interpretation of written work, which can, if you like, better benefit the person who is not as able to express themselves in writing. But if ever you dilute too much this process of objective evidence, you can run the risk of saying that the course is fairly meaningless. In a sense, the students themselves need to be reassured that they are giving that evidence. We live in something of an academic world, in terms of qualification, and I think we have got to accept that.

This discussion of assessment has emphasised the purpose uppermost in trainers' minds. They speak of assessment as a process of sorting or grading people into those who do or do not qualify for an award. In keeping with trainers' own views of a course as a part of a continuous process of teacher development the regional scheme only passes (or in rare cases, fails) teachers, it does not grade them. Given that grading is not really very significant as most people pass anyway, it is noticeable that trainers did not lay much emphasis on other purposes that assessment might serve. Only one or two hinted at the possibility that it might have diagnostic value. If the trainer receives feedback on what teachers know or understand, presumably this could serve two purposes — it could highlight areas where his own teaching could be improved, and it could diagnose areas where teachers need further help. They did not explicitly talk about using assessment in this way. Feedback to teachers was stressed by trainers when discussing how they followed up visits to their classes though it was not mentioned in the context of written work.

Evaluating the benefits of training

There is no doubt that trainers thought training was beneficial. During the interviews, trainers were asked about the kinds of benefits they could see, and their answers can be grouped in six broad categories, listed in order of the frequency with which they were mentioned:

(a) Teachers' increase in confidence

(b) They become more open-minded and self-critical

(c) They use a wider range of teaching methods

(d) They show a greater awareness of students' needs and of the situation in whch they are teaching

(e) They benefit in ways which may be described as personal growth or self-development

(f) Teachers come to see their class and themselves within a broader context of adult education

It is quite striking how closely these benefits reflect the purposes of the course as seen by trainers, and form a cluster of related and mutually reinforcing developments.

(a) An increase in confidence: Trainers were quite certain that they saw teachers become more confident as the course progresses though it was difficult to define or measure this kind of change.

I think that's a sort of gut feeling. I think you can tell, but how on earth you describe a change of confidence, I don't know.

One possibility is that successfully completing the course in itself increases self-esteem:

I find it mostly gives people a lot more confidence. It gives them a bit of status in their own eyes to have got their certificate.

Or they benefit by simply having survived it unscathed:

> They're very tentative about how they approach Stage 1. They come in and they're as frightened as anybody going to an adult class very often. It gives them confidence to see that it's not a destructive thing, they won't be destroyed as people — some of them fear that they will be put in an embarrassing position, which we try not to do.

(b) An open-minded and self-critical approach: In most cases, a training course exposes people to a lot of new ideas and new perspectives both from the course tutors, and from fellow teachers. Initially, this must be threatening, because it brings a teacher's own ideas and practices into question in a way that many part-time teachers, because of their isolation in their work, are unaccustomed to. In fact trainers saw teachers become less defensive about their own ideas, more willing to criticise their work and to accept that there are other ways of looking at teaching.

> Perhaps a more humble attitude, because through their ignorance perhaps they were able to reassure themselves, maybe subconsciously, that they were doing a fair job. But when one presents such a range of alternatives, matching up to that standard means they're not doing such a good job, and there is perhaps an initial period of insecurity caused by the realisation that there's so much more they could be doing, and then the frustration of not being able to do it all at once, because of the time it takes to adopt new skills. That's one of the major things, to make them self-critical.

> They become more confident...an openness to try new ideas...they will flirt with new ideas less self-consciously...people are able to look a little more dispassionately at their own teaching...and they feel freer to experiment with what they are doing.

(c) A wider range of teaching methods: Of all the benefits trainers mentioned this is the one they felt would be most easily observed when watching a teacher in the classroom. From their own observations, and from teachers' discussion of their work, trainers saw an increasing awareness of the range of possible teaching methods and learning aids, and a greater willingness to experiment with and use these.

> They do tend to use more methods and certainly take advantage of learning aids...that's where you really can see a change.

> They are far more experimental, they use a wider range.

> I think it's an attitude of mind, and an attitude of confidence that you see in the change. And the willingness on their part to present their material in a much wider variety of ways.

A Stage 2 trainer felt this change was particularly noticeable amongst teachers experiencing their first training course, and in their first encounter with a wider range of teaching methods. It may be harder to see further changes in classroom behaviour during subsequent training:

> When I see them teaching, I'm not as impressed by their progress in teaching, they don't change as much as on a Stage 1 course, where they start from nothing. On Stage 1, if they only start to use a blackboard, or visual aids, you can see a quick change. I

don't think people change in their actual classroom behaviour all that much on a Stage 2 course.

(d) Awareness of students' needs: Many trainers said that they had noticed an increasing awareness and understanding of classroom processes in teachers. In particular, teachers became more sensitive to students' reactions and to their needs and came to see them as people in their own right:

> They certainly develop an awareness...for the students that they teach...they come to realise that they are individual people rather than a set of students who have come to do upholstery, or whatever.

> I believe that the majority of them, by the end of the course, have readjusted their views of themselves in relation to their students, so that at the end of the course they are recognising that the important factor is the students and their requirements, rather than their own personal performance.

> Most seem to be looking at their students less as the 'opposition'.

(e) Self development: Trainers mentioned a lot of changes which might broadly be described as 'self development'. These are benefits of training which have implications for them as people as well as teachers. Whilst this is true of the other benefits which have been discussed trainers put more emphasis on how teachers had developed and changed as individuals. Again, this development is not always easy to describe, but it was noted by a number of people:

> I would guess their teaching must have improved on the way, but the way they've improved as people has been much more observable.

A key element in this change seems to have been the experience of working together in a group which was supportive and was involved in sharing ideas and experiences. Trainers saw teachers' contributions grow, in part through an increasing ability to formulate and express their ideas and opinions. There was also a greater willingness to engage in the co-operative process of sharing and thinking together, and a greater willingness to listen and respond to the contributions of others.

> They arrive as 20 individuals who don't know each other — and they draw ideas from each other and help each other, and use it in their teaching.

> A greater willingness to trust, to contribute to the discussion, a realisation that other people have something interesting to say.

Training offered teachers an experience of education which many enjoyed in its own right, and which whetted their appetite for more:

> For some people, training is a benefit in its own right, even if it never produces any benefit for the people in a classroom. It is an educational experience which they've valued.

> They see their personal development as being more important than...when they came on the course. Their own development, personal, educational development. What can I do after this?

> There is a degree of need for...some educational guidance.

Finally, training also 'refreshed' teachers. They left the courses more enthusiastic about their work and therefore more likely to enjoy it and to do it better:

> I don't expect the students will see much difference, they won't know whether a person is trained or not. But a teacher, certainly whilst on a training course, and soon after, may have had a bit of a lift, a brightening of their eyes, and that challenge that will help their class be a better one. How long it lasts for I don't know.

> This is a difficult one. I think at the end of the course, if I am getting teachers who are clearly motivated to a higher degree than they were before, and they are coming forward with ideas, suggestions, enthusiasm for the future, then I think that's the way I would evaluate it.

(f) An awareness of the broader context of Adult Education: This includes all the ways that trainers felt teachers came to see their teaching and themselves as part of a large whole. They believed for example that training breaks the isolation of the part-time teacher, and gives a sense of belonging to a larger professional group:

> Also you can feel that they are much happier about belonging to an organisation, however diffuse and ill-defined; they feel after Stage 1 they're part of a group not just single, isolated teachers. They have the first stirrings of a feeling of being involved in a professional or semi-professional task with other people.

> One is isolated when teaching adults and any system which brings people together to share experiences must be beneficial. Whether it changes teaching style as such is more open to question. But it does build confidence and gives people a feeling of being associated with something a bit larger than what you see on a Monday night in the village school.

Teachers also become more aware of resources and support that should be available, and are likely to be active and involved in the centres where they work; a viewpoint summed up by this Centre Head:

> I never cease to be impressed by what happens on a Stage 1. They come out as almost new people, they really do. They're more aware about what's going on around them...on the audio-visual section for instance, they have to go and see what's in their centre, and they find out that they've got a little bit of purchasing power, they've got a bit of push, they can say to a Centre Head, "Look, I want an over-head projector, it's up to you to get it".

Beyond this, teachers were thought to come to have a wider view of adult education, and take this into all aspects of their lives.

> By the end of the course, they recognise that there's much more to adult education and recognise to a much greater extent the social value of what is being done as well as the educational.

> We encourage them to see adult education as a service offering a whole range of spectrum...they can, I think give to the community a much better, broader knowledge, a greater appreciation of adult education. So there's a spin-off for adult education in the community in which they live. I mean, many of the teachers are members of the W.I., Townswomen's Guild, other women's or men's groups, and they take their experience there.

SECTION 8: SOME QUESTIONS ABOUT BENEFITS

Throughout their comments on the benefits of training, questions were raised by the trainers themselves about the difficulties of evaluating change. This is not to say they were unconvinced that there are benefits. But because trainers believed that teachers can only be assessed subjectively by someone who comes to know them well and watches them change and develop, trainers were very much aware that they were unable to give a detached view. Most of them had considerable experience of training, their judgements based on years of watching teachers on these courses. yet at the same time a number of experienced trainers also believed that there is an element of hope or faith that teachers in some way do benefit from their training.

> Much of what we do is an act of faith, and I'd be hard pushed to really prove the benefits of what we do.

The following quotation raises an important point; that to ask only about 'end-products' may in part ask the wrong question about the benefits of an educative process. Training may be an act of faith, but not of blind faith:

> I think you may well be talking about something as naive and yet as valuable as saying, "we don't know about the end product, but we're able to observe the process, and from our observation of the process we think it's extremely likely that there must be a beneficial end product" . . "; so much of our observation and our judgement is concerned with process, because either we can't or we won't, or we haven't the resources to monitor the end product. I've had enough reassurance and support from people around the county, and people who manage the purse strings for me to be saying, 'well, at least they recognise that the process is alright".

Trainers themselves pointed out that there were ways in which their views of benefits might be biased or coloured by their own involvement. It was difficult to approach the task without any preconceptions of what kinds of changes may be possible: it was particularly difficult for trainers who had very definite ideas of the changes that they hoped to see.

> (for) in many ways the attitudes we see changing are the ones that we want to see changing.

Some of the changes trainers saw may not be the result of training alone; they may be the product of added experience of teaching and/or of teachers getting to know trainers better so that they felt more at ease and more able to be themselves. Another problem raised was the possibility that some teachers just acted in the way expected of them on the course. This explanation was given by a trainer when asked why some teachers may remain unaffected by a training course:

> Most probably because I, as their tutor, have not been able to hit the right button. I've not been able to hit the right wavelength for influencing them or their thought patterns, or their attitudes or opinions. This probably happens more often than we know about. Adults tend to be quite good at adopting attitudes that they think are required.

Are these changes to be seen in all teachers or do some people remain unaffected? Several State 1 trainers made the point that their course only lasts 36 hours and this was not very long to influence anyone who was resistant to change. Even in the 100 hours of a Stage 2 course they recognised the limits to what may be attempted:

138

I think in 100 hours, when you're talking about adults, change in attitudes is the most difficult thing you can attempt...you don't change the attitude, but you may change the way in which that attitude is expressed. You may say "is it wise"? "Is this the best you can do"?...or "Is there something else you could do"? It's a different way of responding or behaving, springing from the same belief.

When trainers spoke of people who seemed unaffected by the course, some felt the reasons lay within the person — his personality, his age. Others felt that there were other reasons; ineffectual approaches by trainers, failure to establish sound relationships with the course tutors and other students even the fact that he might have been coerced into attending.

A few trainers did question whether anyone can remain wholly unaffected. At least teachers must be aware of new ideas even if they choose not to act on them.

Their attitudes must be affected, even if it (only) makes them more aware of the alternative possibilities in any situation. One of my things is to impress upon them that even if they do stick to discussion methods or lecturing or whatever they prefer, they're aware of the alternatives. The criterion of a good teacher is knowing the variety of possibilities.

Obviously some people are changed more than others:

Some are affected more than others, but I deny anybody to be unaffected by a teacher training course. Even my teacher of 17 years vintage. It's a slower job and it's a harder nut to crack, but he's been affected.

We have to go forward on the assumption that we can change some of the people some of the time.

This trainer raised the possibility that sometimes teachers may appear unaffected, but may change much later:

I don't really say...they are completely unaffected by the course. They may seem to be, but I think that if they stuck to the end of the course, they got something out of it, but it may not come out until 2 to 4 years later.

There was the additional concern that the effects of training may not last; teachers may revert to their previous way of working. Trainers tended to lose contact with teachers after the course unless the teacher worked in their centre or they met on further training courses. Otherwise, trainers had to hope the teacher's Centre Head will provide continuing support and guidance.

They were aware of the difficulties of sustaining the effects of training back in the 'isolated' world of the part-time teacher and they knew that more should be done to follow up training.

They were disappointed that they might not have any contact after the end of the course...but in practice, there's no reason why we shouldn't keep in touch. I shall certainly make this clear to my group, that I'm always available to go and see them and have a chat. They've had an invitation right from the beginning of my course to come into this centre to see my tutors and how my centre works. Hopefully most of them will go on to Stage 2.

On the whole trainers described ways their courses affected teachers as people, rather than how the courses affected the way they behaved in the classroom. The most visible change in

139

their actual teaching was the use of a wider range of methods. Trainers themselves pointed out that they could not really judge how teaching changes on the basis of two or three visits to a class. Do the effects of training stop at the teachers or do these changes have an impact on how they function; do they benefit their students? These are questions teachers themselves may be better able to answer. It is difficult to imagine that the kinds of changes trainers describe would not affect how teachers relate to and work with their students. This particular trainer was certainly clear on this point:

> If people devalue, or don't value an educational experience, I think it has very few results in terms of their behaviour, and what they do. But if people appear to have benefited personally, they will value it, and what they value will tend to come out in their work.

Training is a mater of changing and improving individual teachers though it cannot be assumed that all trained teachers are better than untrained teachers; there is no accepted model of good teaching, or of students' needs or preferences. The problem of isolating the impact of training on students is complex. In the end, those few trainers who did suggest criteria they could use only pointed to simple questions like 'Do teachers keep classes'? 'Are they still employed'? 'Do their students want more'?

Teachers and students are not the only beneficiaries of the training process; trainers themselves felt they gained from involvement. It has already been suggested that teachers may derive benefit in several aspects of their lives as well as for the organisations and activities in which they are involved. Trainers felt that the LEAs who finance these courses gained by the resulting enhancement of the quality, status and reputation of the service they exist to provide.

> I suppose a certain amount of kudos comes up somewhere or other for them (the LEA)...I suppose if your teachers are more effective, they get more students and, therefore, more money comes in. I can't think of another reason, apart from the notion, if you get good classes in the Centres, then the authorities get a better name.

It was believed that training could put adult education on a more professional footing, even though as this first comment suggests it might be for less altruistic purposes:

> Helps with politicians, and hopefully lays to rest the picture of a set of amateurs doing a fairly indifferent job with a large amount of social element.

Though as this trainer said:

> I think if they look at the 'long distance' value, if they could see that they're getting some rattling good teachers from the students through the system, who are going to put back into the county what they've had out of it.

SECTION 9: OVERVIEW

In the East Midlands, the training of part-time teachers of adults has been carried out on the whole by full-time staff in adult education. There has been a practice of training by people with direct experience and knowledge of the world in which these teachers are working, rather than by staff from Colleges of Education or Universities. This seems to work well. There is a strong feeling of enthusiasm, commitment and concern for the work amongst trainers and a strong expectation that training courses themselves will be an example of good adult education.

Most of the current trainers have a long involvement in this work; there is not a rapid turnover. However, new people are required to keep training courses alive and changing. Most newcomers are full-time adult education staff though little was said about the possibility of in-service training of experienced part-time teachers or how they might contribute to training teams and courses. Several trainers invite teachers to give demonstration lessons or arrange for trainees to visit their classes and this role could be extended, especially as the courses place such emphasis on sharing ideas and experiences.

Trainers find their work in training complements the rest of their job. It seems to them to be a natural extension of their duties as Centre Heads and adult education organisers. Time is a major constraint; given the very full work load of full-time staff some see different aspects of their job as more important. Those interviewed were by definition the ones who see training as an important part of the work of every Centre Head and organiser.

When talking about their own training for the work, it is quite obvious that trainers bring all their experience and education to bear; courses designed specifically to help, such as 'Training the Trainers' courses, form a relatively small part of their preparation. The most important continuous need of these trainers is for opportunities to share their problems, ideas and experiences with other trainers both within the regional scheme and from other regions. This kind of contact could take many forms — both formal and informal — but many trainers now feel they are in a position to define their own training needs, and to say where they need further 'expert' guidance or help and to know whom they would consider best able to provide this. The training needs may be rather different for newcomers to this field. People describe how courses in the earlier stages of their involvement in training helped to clear their thinking on adult education and training and gave them confidence to do the job. There are now opportunities for an 'apprenticeship model' where new trainers join an experienced team and can gradually increase their contribution as they gain confidence and experience. On the other hand there is evidence from the research and from RAC moderators' reports that the need for information and methodological expertise among such new recruits is not always met.

This chapter has looked at how trainers see the purposes of training courses, the kinds of learning they think take place, and the benefits they feel training brings. It is striking how closely the kinds of benefits they describe reflect the purposes of the course. The benefits they describe are inter-related and mutually reinforcing. They tend to reflect changes in the teachers' awareness of the issues surrounding their work, of different ways of approaching it, their ability to look at these new ideas more openmindedly and to be more self-critical about their own work. Trainers say much less about changes in teachers' knowledge — but presumably they would see these as pre-requisites of a willingness to assess the relevance of new knowledge and ideas most usefully. Trainers do not seem overly worried by the lack of observable change in the classroom, because they believe the kinds of changes they see in the teachers as people will inevitably benefit their students.

Trainers admit these benefits are difficult to observe or identify. There is a discrepancy between the benefits they describe and the things the course is able to assess. Yet trainers described how micro-teaching often gives teachers a tremendous boost of confidence and can provide them with an opportunity to experiment with new approaches. The experience of being a student makes a teacher more aware of his own students' needs and of how it feels to be on the receiving end of various methods. The experience of meeting other teachers and sharing ideas, problems and solutions was also felt to be a vital part of the learning process; it is a process which gives teachers confidence because they find they are not alone in their difficulties. If the atmosphere in the group is right it gives status and consideration to everyone's opinions and experience, whilst encouraging teachers to see alternative ways of looking at things and thus to become more critical of their own views. Trainers believe that many such benefits cannot be directly 'measured'; they cannot attach numbers to changes in confidence, attitudes to students, ability to analyse problems and questioning self-critical approaches. Written work can touch directly on some of these things but this is usually not its emphasis. Written work is only one way of communicating and although it might be argued that all teachers ought to be able to use this medium at least at a basic level, it is more difficult to claim that this ought to dominate the assessment of teachers. Trainers believe that the most important assessment of a teacher is his work with his own students. Despite all the problems of assessing teaching, they feel that this is where the important factors ultimately reveal themselves.

This chapter illustrates the range of views expressed on particular issues, rather than contrasting the approaches of different courses or reflecting the very individual style and approach of each course. The courses differ in the emphasis given to stated objectives, they differ in the balance of approaches to learning they use and therefore they presumably differ in the balance of benefits they encourage. The content of training courses has become fairly standard; the main differences now seem to be in how this content is handled. Trainers are very concerned that their courses should be 'good adult education practice' and they make use of the reactions of teachers to their experience of being students in order to help them understand the feelings of their own students. All trainers are very much aware that as part of the adult education 'deal' a course should make use of the knowledge and experience of the people on it. A minority of trainers are interested in developing these ideas further, and use the course process itself as an opportunity for experiential learning. They discuss and analyse the processes of teaching and learning as they happen on the course, and analyse the interactions between trainer and teachers and amongst teachers themselves. Several trainers point out the similarities between their training course and an ordinary adult education class though it is for each trainer to answer for himself whether he and the teachers on the course will be able to benefit from this approach.

The type of approach to be used is one of the many choices facing trainers. Some seem more willing than others to discuss the problems and decisions that face them in running a training course. For example, how far should they be directive in their teaching and how far should they allow teachers to draw their own conclusions? How much room is there for experiments in approach and how do they handle the risk that things will turn out unexpectedly? How far should trainers make their course responsive to teachers' demands and how far should they insist on covering certain areas? Trainers clearly feel very responsible to their trainees when they consider questions like these: they see part of this responsibility as the control of the content of the course, the methods and approaches used, the outcomes and the 'messages' that are put over. It would be unfair to imply that trainers are restricting the course by guiding the learning of the teachers on it — in some cases it may be quite the opposite. Trainers describe how teachers often hope to be 'told' and given the 'golden rules'. The issue then becomes one of how far trainers should meet teachers' expectations and how far they should try to change them. Trainers are aware of how their own approach has changed over the years and such questions are seen as live issues influencing their work.

Most trainers are disappointed with the follow-up to training courses. It depends very much on the interest and concern of the head of the centre where the teacher works. They feel there is a need for continuing support to keep new ideas and attitudes alive, and to build upon and develop the benefits derived from the course. In the absence of this, perhaps more emphasis could be put on ways in which training might help teachers sustain their own development. For example, little mention was made of the role reading might play and how handouts and booklists could help teachers to plan their own learning after their course. One trainer did mention how he put teachers in touch with particular journals and subject-specialist organisations that they may find useful, an idea which might benefit from a pooling of knowledge and information. It has been shown how some courses aim to have teachers analyse and think about situations in a way they can apply to new situations when back at work in their centre. These activities clearly become more difficult to sustain when teachers lose the stimulation of being on a course and of their contact with the people on it. This suggests a need to bring teachers together more often. At present, opportunities are limited, but in Northamptonshire the part-time teachers' association is one example of how teachers have organised to meet their own needs.

CHAPTER 5

Learning to Teach: The Trainees

This chapter is based upon information provided by teachers enrolled on Stage 1, Stage 2 and Stage 2/City and Guilds 730 training courses. It begins with a description of the characteristics of 'trainees', their personal details and their work and experience in adult education. This information is derived from questionnaire responses. The chapter is divided into six sections:

The Trainees

Training Course Organisation

Course Design: Principles and Practice

Expectations and Effects

Further Developments

Overview

Although most of the attitudes and opinions about training and the training courses came from interviews, some use was also made of the written responses contained in the various monitoring schedules completed by some trainees. In this chapter the approach has been that of the 'perceptions of trainees', not necessarily the same reality as that of their trainers.

SECTION 1: THE TRAINEES

This description results from an analysis of questionnaires returned by people enrolled on the 9 S1 and 4 S2 (+S2/C&G 730) courses running in the four counties during the period September 1980 to March 1981. Allowing for people who left the courses or for some similar reason did not receive the questionnaire it is thought that 149 trainees of the 168 enrolled were contacted and 97 returned the document in a sufficiently complete form for subsequent analysis, a return rate of 65%. (See Table 11 below.)

A decision was taken not to subject this material to any analytical statistical comparisons. It was judged that with the relatively small numbers within groups and with the additional restriction imposed by missing data, significant differences were unlikely to be found even if they were present. It was also considered that a simple description would provide a more readable and sensible account of trainee characteristics. Usually only percentages have been given in the text since in most instances they have the same value as the numerical totals. Nevertheless, attention has been drawn to differences between levels of training where it is appropriate; where no such comparisons have been made it may be assumed that no observable differences were present.

Within the sample of 97 who attended, 70% were on the nine S1 courses, 9% on the one S2 and 21% on the three S2/C&G 730. There were twice as many women as men within the overall sample, 67% : 32%, and they outnumbered men by 3 to 1 on S1 courses 75% : 25%, although on the C&G 730 course men outnumbered women exactly 3 : 2 within the total of 20. The average age of all trainees was in the early to middle thirties although trainees on the higher level courses were slightly older than those on S1 courses, typically being nearer 40 than 30.

Table 11: Adult Education Teacher Training Courses in Four Counties of the Survey Region (Not S3)

Course	Enrolled	Questionnaire Distrib.	Questionnaire Return	%	Intr's Completed
Stage 1	9	8	7	88	2
Stage 1	10	8	7	88	2
Stage 1	11	10	9	90	3
Stage 2	12	11	8	73	2
Stage 1	9	7	7	100	2
Stage 1	9	9	4	44	2
Stage 1	12	9	1	11	0
Stage 2/730	13	10	7	70	2
Stage 1	19	19	12	63	3
Stage 1	23	23	12	52	2
Stage 1	13	11	9	69	3
Stage 2/730	14	14	5	36	2
Stage 2/730	14	11	9	64	2
TOTALS	169	149	97	65	27

Table 12: Age of Trainees

20–29 years	30–39 years	40–49 years	50–59 years	60 + years
17%	43%	27%	8%	3%

Seventy five percent of all trainees were working as LEA non-vocational teachers. LEA FE vocational teaching and other LEA functions, youth, literacy, etc., accounted for 3%, a further 3% were employed by other employers, 15% failed to record any present employer and 12% of the total were not currently doing any AE work. The majority of those in FE and other LEA functions were on the S2 level courses with all three of the FE teachers on 730.

The majority of trainees, 60% taught one non-vocational part-time class, though 20% taught two. Of the remainder 8% taught three or more whereas 12% had no current class. Slightly more S2 trainees taught two classes than did S1s. With the exception of the more narrowly defined academic subjects (14%), the other three subject categories were equally represented, Arts and Crafts (26%), Skills (24%), and Sports (24%), as the trainees' teaching subject. Their classes were as likely to run for one term as for two (48% : 52%).

Trainees' total teaching experience taken as a single entity produced a mean value of just over 3 years' part-time teaching. However, a closer analysis showed more interesting features. Of the 91 trainees who recorded their teaching histories, 7% had taught in compulsory age range schools, one still worked in full-time FE, and 9% had taught in part-time vocational FE, 6 of whom were studying for 730. One quarter of the whole sample also indicated that they had taught in a part-time capacity outside the maintained sector and these were typically engaged in private tuition, HM Forces, industrial training and in sports centres or sports coaching. The part-time non-vocational adult education teaching experience of trainees is shown in Table 13.

Table 13: Teaching Experience: Part-Time Non-Vocational A E

	All	S1	S2	730
None	20	9	1	10
Up to 1 year	36	31	2	3
1 to 2 years	13	11	0	2
3 to 5 years	17	11	4	2
6 to 10 years	4	0	2	2
Not stated	7	6	0	1
	97	68	9	20

Two thirds (66%) of all trainees reported that they had had work experience other than teaching in their main subject (paid employment, voluntary work etc.) and this was equally likely to be the case within each type of course.

Asked about their formal qualifications other than those connected with teaching, the vast majority (81%) recorded some certification. The highest percentage (31%) had qualifications ranging from licentiates of societies to National Federation of Women's Institute qualifications. Eleven percent of trainees had a variety of City and Guilds Certificates and 10% had GCEs. There were also 4% who had taken craft apprenticeships and 2% were professionally qualified people. One-fifth of the whole sample were either graduates (16%) or holders of HNC/HND (5%). It was only in these higher qualifications that there were any differences between training levels; of the five HNC/HNDs, four were to be found on 730 courses (20% of the 730 population) with the graduates somewhat more evenly spread with 11 on S1 (15% of S1 population) and two each on S2 (22%) and 730 (15%) courses.

Qualifications and experience within the taught subject were possessed by the majority of trainees. One-third (33%) of the total had had subject training and obtained formal qualifications and 9% had attended joint subject/professional courses. A further 15% had had some form of work experience within their subject though they had not attended a training course whilst the remaining 41% had neither formal qualifications nor work experience in the subject that they taught. These included teachers of subjects such as wine making, beekeeping and like subjects where neither formal qualification nor industrial/trade experience is normally available.

Turning to teaching qualifications, there were only two qualified school teachers in the sample, both doing S2. Nine percent of trainees had subject specialist teaching certificates and 4% had other certificates (craft, cookery, etc.). Three percent of the whole sample had previously begun but not completed AE teacher training.

Asked about their intentions to undertake further training, only 9% answered that they did not intend to take further training, 22% said they did, whilst 64% said 'possibly'. Looked at in terms of course levels: on S1, 7% said 'no', 27% said they intended to continue and 63% indicated that they might. Asked which course they would attend if they took further training, 63% of the S1 trainees opted for S2 and 4% chose subject training. On the single S2

146

course, 22% opted for further training, with one definite 'yes' and 55% 'possible'. The courses chosen were three Stage 3 and one subject course. On 730 courses, there were 10% 'for', 10% 'against', and 70% thought they might attend a course. Of the 20 on the C&G 730, 60% did not know their 'intended' course, 15% chose subject courses and 10% selected additional teacher training though not necessarily Stage 3.

Only a quarter of trainees (28%) appear to have received any support outside the formal training courses. Where examples were given by trainees they were either connected with literacy schemes or subject training and not AE teacher training support. Two or three spoke of the help given by Centre Heads and Area Principals. Of the other trainees, a further 25% recorded that they thought that there was no support or training available and the remainder (45%) gave no answer with an implication that they had not had any involvement. Comparisons between the levels of courses do not show any marked differences though, taken together, S2 trainees are more likely to have been involved in support and training activities than are S1 trainees.

Though there are obvious dangers in putting together a picture of a typical trainee, it is a convenient method of highlighting and summarising some of the data previously described.

An S1 trainee is likely to be a woman and to be in her thirties, teaching a non-vocational AE class for the LEA over either one or two terms. She will have had little or no other teaching experience and will be in her first year of teaching. Her general education is likely to have resulted in some level of formal certification and she will probably have either work experience or qualification (or both) in her teaching subject. She is most unlikely to have had any previous teacher training though she thinks she will possibly go on to an S2 course on completion of the present S1. She is unlikely to have had contact with any form of support or training other than on S1.

The S2 trainee is more likely to be a woman just into her forties. She will be employed by the LEA to teach one subject probably to two non-vocational AE classes either for one or two terms. She may have done some other teaching but she is likely to have been teaching in non-vocational AE work for three to four years. Her general education could be at any certificated level and she is likely to have had some work experience and/or qualification in her teaching subject. She has probably completed an S1 course and is more likely to be a qualified school teacher than her S1 colleagues. She thinks that she possibly may continue with training and where she is aware of what courses are available, it would probably be an S3. She does not seem very aware of other forms of support and training.

The trainee on joint S2/City and Guilds 730 courses is more likely to be a man just into his forties. He will be employed by the LEA and will probably teach one subject, either skills or sport, to a single non-vocational AE class though he might work in an FE College. His teaching experience in part-time non-vocational work is probably about two years and he may have done some other form of teaching. His general education is likely to be at a somewhat higher certificated level than that found in other groups though he is as likely as they to have experience and/or qualifications in his teaching subject. He is less likely, however, to have completed an S1 course than other S2 trainees and, though he equally thinks he may continue training, he is rather unaware of which course he might take. He probably has had more support and training than other trainees.

The next three sections deal with training courses as perceived by trainees. Face-to-face interviews were carried out with 27 trainees selected from amongst those who indicated their willingness. They usually lasted an hour or so and were invariably conducted in private away from the training course. At least two trainees from each course were interviewed and, where possible, a man and a woman were chosen. One S1 course did not provide any representative as no-one was willing to take part. Another S1 course provided three since it normally functioned as three separate sub-groups, coming together only for major activities such as the residential weekend.

SECTION 2: TRAINING COURSE ORGANISATION

Many closely inter-related factors are involved in the organisation and administration of training courses. Staffing and the composition of the student group are of prime importance in the setting up of a course, as are such features as location, format and resources. Each of these factors, either individually or in combination with any of the others, can exert a powerful influence upon trainees and can be crucial in determining their subsequent achievements. Some of the organisational features of courses which are perceived as important by S1 and S2 trainees are discussed in this section.

Recruitment

The initial notification of and recruitment to S1 courses appears to have been somewhat haphazard and there were inconsistencies even within those counties which had a policy of compulsory attendance for their untrained staffs. Some trainees had received letters from the LEA asking if they would like to take part.

> A letter came though the door. When I informed (my Centre Head) that I was going he was quite pleased...but he didn't tell me about it.

Many however do seem to have been told by their Centre Heads or Principals that the opportunity for training was there or rather more bluntly:

> We were told that we'd got to go on it.

There was little resentment over the procedures where trainees had been directed to join the course, even where it was part of the original appointment. The great majority undertook the initial training of S1 quite willingly.

Many S2 trainees knew of their course from previous attendance on S1, though again some had received written invitations.

> I heard about it through the S1 course. When I had finished I was offered the opportunity to start an S2. Stage 1 was very interesting, it made me think more about my work and how I was doing it and what result I was getting, how the students were behaving. So I thought that S2 might even be better. I was encouraged to go...as well as letters arriving at home.

Some learnt through other means:

> A sort of circular in the register...I had been teaching for about seven years at the College — I never knew the course was running...

and there was evidence that some Centre Heads had brought courses to the notice of their staffs. There were other trainees who did not receive all the information that they would have liked and it may well be that the information network is rather imperfect.

I put pressure on the S1 teachers. I kept saying 'I want to do more, I want to do more, where can I go?' I was writing letters all over the place...and telephoning...I did all the chasing myself. I got the impression that S2 was if you wanted to go on and teach more or less full-time. There didn't seem to be much pressure on you to go on to anything else as if S1 were quite sufficient for anyone teaching adults. It would have been a tremendous help if there had been more information...it might have made a few (more) try...

All S1 courses were free to trainees although one county imposed a returnable £5 deposit. All made some sort of charge for residential weekends. Where S2 courses were run in conjunction with City and Guilds courses fees were charged; where they were run alone they were usually free. Little objection was expressed by trainees to paying the minimal fees and out of pocket expenses. Where travel expenses were offered for attendance at Regional Scheme courses, many trainees appeared pleasantly surprised.

Composition of trainee group

No subject-based training courses were visited, as the four East Midlands counties studied were currently providing only general course training within the Regional Scheme. Trainees' attitudes towards general teacher rather than subject-based training were probably influenced by the fact that they were in the process of completing general training courses. Although a fair proportion had experienced a variety of subject-based training courses previously there was little doubt that trainees definitely approved of general training. There was a strong belief that much adult learning and teaching was common to all.

It doesn't matter what the subject...the teaching problems are basically the same.

Moreover, it was considered to be positively beneficial to be working alongside teachers from different specialisms and backgrounds. Great interest was expressed in their differing specialisms and skills, in the problems peculiar to individual topics and in the sharing of solutions by many trainees.

You gain...from so many different viewpoints.

It's been good having a mixture of people on the course...if you had people all teaching the same subject you'd tend to get into the same rut whereas with different people (subjects)...you think well, I could use the same idea in my class.

There was no identifiable difference between S1 and S2 courses on these points and what slight reservations there were came equally from both.

I was the only one in my subject...it could have helped if there had been someone else there who taught my subject...on the other hand, it could have been a drawback.

I like to see language teachers...but I think that mixing is a good thing — to see what happens in all (areas).

There were several comments referring to differences in trainees' actual teaching experiences — some having taught several sessions whilst others were teaching their first class. On the whole they supported this trainee's opinion:

For me the mix in our group was ideal. We had some people who were teaching practical subjects...one had been teaching for several years and not been on a course and some had not taught at all. The fact that we were from different Centres was good too.

Thus it would appear that trainees believed they benefited from general rather than subject training in terms of adult learning and teaching. They judged that they gained from the sharing of knowledge and experience with teachers from different backgrounds and subject specialisms. There was no real evidence as to whether the general training they undertook was consistently applicable to the teaching of subject disciplines or whether such transfer was only occasionally possible. The overall impression given is that positive transfer was more common than not.

Difficulties arising from the course

It was clear from trainees' responses that the difficulties on the course fell into three broadly related categories: adjusting to the role of trainee, learning how to study and fitting in course requirements with family and work commitments.

Despite the fact that many trainees had been students in adult classes before and some currently still were, there were clear indications that levels of apprehension, anxiety and uncertainty were at their highest during the early weeks of most courses, regardless of level. These comments echo how many people felt:

> The first meeting I went to I was very nervous because I hadn't been involved in any formal training for a long time — I didn't know what to expect...but once we got chatting I found I was joining in quite a lot.

> If I hadn't have paid the £5 deposit...I probably wouldn't have gone...I got into such a state about (doing) it.

> I found it terrifying at first...I thought I was making a complete fool of myself, especially as some were much older and knew what they were talking about...I was really lost for a while.

The evidence suggests that the early period of a course is a crucial time for a number of people; it is a time of re-appraisal, re-adjustment and unlearning. The pressures arising from this process during the first few meetings put a great strain on people. Many of them are uncertain about themselves as people and as teachers, they are set in their ways and quite frequently unwilling to change their attitudes and practices in the classroom. It is not only a time of adjustment to fresh concepts and approaches, but also a time for adjusting to different roles carrying new responsibilities. On the one hand there is the role transition from class teacher to trainee, on the other the transition from lay person to professional.

The nature of the adjustment to these new roles was not surprisingly rather varied. However, as a result of the active informality adopted by most trainers, all course members seem to have adjusted relatively quickly and easily. This can be seen from the following typical examples:

> It could have been quite awkward being a student again but the lecturer was ideal in a sense, he put everyone at ease the first evening. It was far more pleasant than I thought it was going to be.

> Adjusting to being a student again...was a difficult situation...but on this course I felt more of a participator, and someone who was giving as well as receiving.

What was clear beyond doubt was that the skills of course trainers were most effectively used in the early sessions when anxieties were allayed and apprehensions assuaged. Time and again at different points in conversation and in response to other enquiries, trainees spoke of the sympathy, empathy and understanding of trainers.

I was put at ease by the attitude of the tutor right from the beginning.

The intimacy of the small tutorial group gave me confidence. My tutor was clear, concise and caring.

The first night...I was made to feel very much at home early on...

Some anxiety was expressed by a few trainees about learning to study. Their major concerns were associated either with producing written work or with trying to understand and assimilate the theoretical and abstract issues with which they were being presented. The problems of those trainees who talked about writing essays appeared to be twofold: first that of disciplining themselves to produce the work and secondly expressing themselves and discussing ideas on paper. Difficulties such as:

Organising myself to do the written assignments.

Trying to do the written assignments. As this is not my thing, I find it difficult to put it down on paper what I want to say.

My main problem in the course was the writing of essays. A problem because my school education was at secondary modern level — and as the essays were of an academic standard — I found the writing of them very difficult and trying, but with the help of my course tutor I have managed to overcome some of these problems.

illustrate the reaction of these individuals. A few trainees expressed frustration at their lack of intellectual skills necessary to come to terms with basic teaching concepts. One trainee well summed up what was involved when she said:

My brain is terribly rusty...it is a struggle to start thinking again.

In the main, however, both sets of problems over learning to study were identified more by S2 students than they were by S1 trainees. There did not appear to have been any major problems at S1 level in terms of intellectual demands or study skills: significantly they were not asked to do written essay assignments.

There were also problems connected with course requirements and family/work commitments. It may be seen from these typical comments that the difficulties were often of a domestic nature:

Having family commitments, especially at the weekend...time is a problem.

Attending on Saturdays is difficult...

and indeed for some there were some travel and attendance problems. Nor was attendance without some sacrifice:

I work one Saturday in three and I have, therefore, had to lose quite a bit of money over the duration of the course. I think it has been worth it.

It is appropriate to note here that the length of training courses, 36–40 hours for S1 and 100 for S2 represent contact hours. The associated activities of private study, homework tasks, class observation, travel and so on are all additional. The majority of adult education trainee teachers teach at least one part-time adult class as well as doing a full-time job within or beyond the home, quite often with pressing family responsibilities. Unlike most in-service education training in the school sector all training for the part-time teacher of adults is carried out in their own time and may even represent lost earnings. There can be little doubt that trainees are highly committed to, and interested in, the activity of adult education and to improving their own contribution to it. It is apparent at least for some, that the transition to the role of professional is not accomplished without effort. New skills of study and expression have to be acquired and attitudes and opinions may need to be modified. Nevertheless the vast majority of trainees appear highly motivated to succeed.

Staffing

A strong thread that ran through many of the conversations with trainees was the importance of the course trainers. Not surprisingly perhaps, they were seen to have a major influence upon the structure and organisation of the course and also upon the whole tenor, atmosphere and ultimate success of it too. In many instances, trainees had worked with one trainer in particular and there was dramatic identification with him or her. This seems to have occurred even where there was more than one 'resident' trainer on the course.

> I think that it was X who made the course...he was marvellous...when we went on the residential weekend, the other two we didn't like at all. When we split up into their groups it was miserable.

> Having met the others (trainers) I think we had the best one.

In fairness, one or two trainees did make the point that it might be beneficial to work with more than one trainer.

> I feel that we'd all have liked it better if we had been taught by more than one tutor...if it had been split between two of them, as well as the guest lecturers.

Yet the lasting impression is that trainees had formed a marked attachment for their own particular trainer and where they offered some criticism of the course and of the trainer, either directly or by implication, they still spoke of him/her in approving and warm tones.

Most interestingly, when trainees talked about the qualities that make for a good trainer, they often used their own trainer as the exemplar. Asked about such appropriate qualities many trainees spoke of the importance of trainers having experience as class teachers of adults.

> They should have vast teaching experience themselves — then they can appreciate the problems that you have.

> A lot of experience of teaching and working with adults.

> He's got to be very patient...the more training that they have, the better the training they can pass on...ability to teach and understand when someone has not caught on or is in a different position.

There was also a strong belief that trainers should treat group members as adults:

> They need to appreciate that we were adults.

> Good rapport with adults.

> Non-authoritarian...not like a school teacher...

and that they should be well versed in subject matter:

Exactly the same qualities as a teacher...knows his subject and puts it over in an interesting way, and to be enthusiastic about it.

The qualities I would expect of myself, a knowledge of my subject, interesting, dynamic, adventurous.

Other qualities mentioned included a sense of humour, good organisation skills and being positive in approach. They should also be adaptable, approachable, even charismatic:

X has a terrific charisma about her. She never loses your attention...her self-confidence...she can treat people as equals and doesn't need to put on this air of authority.

There was a strongly-held view that trainers should have some 'understanding' of the role of trainee.

To be very diplomatic and very understanding about teachers. Some of us have been teaching a long time...he has to tell us how to change in a way without saying 'Don't do that, that's wrong'. I think that (such suggestions) are quite acceptable and they are good ideas. Certain of the points that he made us think about and discuss I think that I can apply them and use them.

Ultimately, he has to be human...he's got to identify with us. I think that X had exactly the right qualities...he was very interested in what we did and became our friend, I think, so that everybody didn't mind talking to him. I liked the way he'd come and sit with us even when we went for a break — there was no going away to look at his papers — he'd come and sit with us and have coffee and talk. That is the key to it, to get on to a friendly basis.

Perhaps this role of the 'interested, friendly human' might go a long way towards providing the 'armature' for the ideal trainer.

Trainees were less satisfied with the support that they received from staff more directly concerned with their part-time teaching, namely Centre Heads and Principals. Apparently some Centre Heads did show concern:

Yes, the Centre Head was very supportive...after Christmas he kept my course going because I was doing the S1.

My Centre Head was very good...he asked me how I got on at the residential weekend...and he had a meeting with X (the trainer).

The Vice-Principal was involved because he knew that the tutor was coming and he asked me how I was getting on. Yes, he took an interest, he asked me about the course, but other than that I don't know anybody else who was.

Where it was given the demonstrated interest was appreciated, but though some Centre Heads were well-meaning all too often they were otherwise occupied.

I'm not saying that he wasn't interested (when I went to see him)...but his work is so involved...people coming in...phones ringing...he just hasn't got time.

Others were quite unconcerned:

No, they were not interested at all...I've had no support at all. We're supposed to have the Principal come and watch us...mine never has, and he's never enquired or anything...he's never mentioned it.

I don't know if anyone is interested...maybe they don't like us doing the course. Do the Principals feel that we are getting support — support from outside their centre? We are going to be a bit more demanding. They are not going to like that.

Whilst the evidence is not abundant there is quite sufficient to indicate that trainees considered that Centre Heads can exercise a desirable supportive role whilst they are on training courses. Unfortunately there were a number of instances where senior staffs' interest and concern was sadly lacking.

The residential weekend

A major feature of most though not all training courses was the residential weekend. They appeared at the beginning, the middle and at the end of courses though there was no evidence from trainees to suggest that one timing was any better than another. Trainees, as with other aspects of their courses, approved most what they knew best.

The weekend was good...we started to really get to know each other. Coming at the end of course it seemed to bring a lot together.

I thought it was good starting with a residential weekend, particularly staying away...for those of us with children...we got to know each other well, we had to talk about each other...we benefited a lot from being together all the time...another residential weekend would have been nice.

Wherever it was placed, the residential weekend played a major part in course structures, particularly where, as in one county, it was the only occasion when the members of the whole course met together since at other times trainees met in three sub-groups. Trainees were less than specific about what they thought the stated objectives of a residential weekend ought to be but they were near unanimous in approving the weekend for its continuity of purpose and intent, its group cohesion (or lack of it in one case), its intensity of learning and not least its social aspect.

A weekend gives time to create a learning situation whereas a couple of hours per week is not so conducive — it doesn't give one time to cut off totally from mundane tasks to enable one to learn so readily.

I think the residential weekend an excellent idea as I was able to devote myself entirely to the task in hand and develop my thoughts.

The opportunity afforded by the residential weekend to get away from the domestic scene was commented on favourably by many:

The residential weekend...that was excellent...more value than the entire course...the variety of staff...the atmosphere was better than the evenings because the evenings were always affected by individuals' domestic things...the social side was good — and it does help the learning, the atmosphere of working together.

Though this S2 trainee, in common with quite a few others, spoke of preliminary upheaval:

The only disadvantage I found was preparing to go. Being in FT employment and running a home, it is difficult to find time to cover a 'free weekend'. Having achieved this only hurdle, the residential weekend was both informative and interesting and well worth the effort. I hope there is another one next year.

Most trainees talked quite positively about the benefits of working closely with others in their group over a period of concentrated time. It is apparent that the experiences that they had had on their weekends and the discussions which took place between students in their groups had a notable effect upon them. A new awareness about inter-personal relationships and individual needs was commonly reported.

I have learnt to evaluate members of the class and be aware of personalities and difficulties within the class.

The interaction and stimulation between students...It enabled my somewhat narrow attitude to be broadened...

One learns to relate to other people and listen to their points of view.

One learnt more about 'people' through this (working as a group) and could apply it to one's own students and be aware that the tutor should lead in welding the group together.

Trainees reported other experiences arising directly from the weekend especially variation of teaching styles, methods and planning of courses. It comes as little surprise that the social aspect of the weekends was rated highly by the vast majority. It should not be thought however that this was all of the 'beer and skittles' variety. Many trainees spoke positively of the benefits they derived from meeting others, thus from S2 weekends:

I enjoyed mixing with people from different walks of life — with different attitudes and ideas — I felt I gained a lot from this.

It gave me an opportunity to meet my colleagues socially — also giving us a chance to talk to each other and understand each other...

and from S1s:

The biggest advantage is that everybody is together in a living and working situation...a real chance to chat on a million and one topics.

I thoroughly enjoyed the residential weekend. I think that I thought I was going to be hurled in with a lot of academic types and it was a relief to find that they were ordinary people all at the same stage as myself. All had been brought into AE perhaps the year previously...I enjoyed the mix, the new ideas and the social side...we all got to know each other.

Not everyone had the opportunity to attend; S2 trainees on at least one course did not.

We would have liked a residential weekend...we were all looking forward to that but we didn't get one. We would have liked one...we all go together...and meet different people...

Every weekend was not as well organised as this S2 one obviously was:

155

> The residential weekend went well — we knew exactly what we were doing. We stuck to the time limits and knew exactly what we were supposed to be doing at a particular moment of the day...

One or two seem to have fallen short in execution if not planning, owing to audio-visual equipment failures, non-appearance of guest speakers due to bad weather, and so on.

> Even the standby things went wrong...they couldn't believe it. In the end they had to play it by ear.

These criticisms notwithstanding, the overall impression from the mass of evidence is that trainees were full of approval for residential weekends and even though for many attendance was quite difficult to organise they believed that they had benefited by going. Those S2s who could not go wished that they could, whilst those who went wanted a repeat in the second year of their course.

> I felt completely drained on Sunday evening, but I had a strong sense of personal and group achievement and realised I had learnt a great deal. I would like it to be incorporated into the second year of the course too.

> I found it very stimulating and the residential weekend was excellent...the best part of the whole course...it brought it all together which is what it was designed to do.

For one S1 trainee at least, it was a success beyond her expectations:

> I have never experienced a weekend of this nature and I was somewhat apprehensive, but once started I thoroughly enjoyed myself and feel I have derived great benefit, both as a person and as a teacher.

SECTION 3: COURSE DESIGN: PRINCIPLES AND PRACTICE

The design and structure of training courses should embrace four key elements, namely: aims and objectives, content, methods and assessment. At the same time this design should be based upon a rationale which reflects sound educational practice and the course adequately staffed and resourced. It is interesting to note that in the Regional Advisory Council's guidelines for its basic training schemes particular emphasis is placed on the principle of adult education as a joint activity between teacher and taught with the intention that trainees should be involved in helping to give shape and purpose to what they are doing.

This section examines the opinions of trainees of how their courses were designed and their experiences of the implementation of some of the major principles.

Objectives

Awareness of course principles was shrouded in general vagueness and uncertainty. Few trainees seemed to be aware of any specific course objectives and there was a lack of clarity in their perceptions and understanding of the distinction between overall aims and specific objectives or for that matter between course syllabuses and topics. Asked directly about course objectives some trainees responded thus:

156

Objectives...I don't think that there were any specific points made. We were given a syllabus for the course.

but many were rather puzzled:

I don't know that we were specifically told what they (the objectives) were.

There was no mention of objectives as such — it would have been a useful introduction for what (was) required.

(Were you aware of any objectives?) Not really, no, that's dreadful. (They weren't stated, written, discussed?) No, no. (Would it have helped...?) Yes, I suppose that it must have done because we would have known what we were aiming for...really there was nothing at the end that we'd got to aim for.

Some S1 courses did provide clear specification of the objectives in a written form:

(We were) sent a sheet of objectives — and they were referred to (later).

We got the objectives written out...

though in this second case the recipient went on to reveal:

I've read them and I tended to ignore them. The only time I referred back to them was when I was doing my own lesson plan to see how they'd done it.

Most Stage 2 course trainees appear to have been rather more fortunate:

At each lesson you were made aware straight away of the objectives that that lesson set out to achieve...and of course, during the beginning of the course you were given a sheet of more or less objectives — a statement of what would be taught during the period of time. There was some alteration...(following feedback from the group)...the odd hour's lesson. It did seem a bit daunting — placed in front of you the first night.

There was a full documentation of the progressive objectives right through the course and the course work and assignments and (we) were given ample time and pre-warned. The course was set down...the objectives going through the time that we were going to spend on it...after the initial meeting, as we went on, we were asked if we would like to modify it, or if we were happy going along with it. So we were given the option to change it if we wanted to, as we wanted to, along the guidelines that were there.

though not all:

The objectives haven't been written down anywhere. He sat us down last week and asked us what we thought the aims and objectives of the course were and we all came up with completely different ideas.

There was no suggestion from trainees on any of the courses that they had been involved in the setting of course objectives, or that they had been consulted. There was no clear evidence whether or not trainees thought that they themselves might give their own students such opportunity to discuss the objectives of the class.

Content

It is less easy to understand why trainees were not more involved in course organisation and planning. Little negotiation appears to have taken place in the first weeks of any course. Well into the course some trainers apparently did:

> ...ask us what we wanted to talk about...

but the impression given is that topics suggested would somehow be slipped in rather than any reorganisation or modification of the programme be undertaken. In the case of two different S2 courses:

> The course was all laid out but they always told us if there was anything we wanted to know specifically they would lay it on for us.

> We asked for certain things and X (the trainer) was very willing to fit them in. We have fitted in as much as we wanted.

The overall sense remains that trainees were not overly consulted about the broad outlines of their courses although for many students this was apparently quite acceptable.

> It was all done and planned...it is better for them to have it planned, (if we had been involved) it would probably have been chaotic.

> He obviously had so many weeks (planned) and I think if we'd started asking things we'd have upset that.

> I don't think that we had the experience to draw upon...you don't know what is required.

There was also a current opinion among quite a few trainees that it was the trainer's job as trainer to plan and direct the course.

> If he's training (the trainer) I expect him to know and I'm quite happy if he says 'Right, you must do this'. I assume, rightly or wrongly, he knows what he is talking about and it's up to me to do it to the best of my ability.

This attitude was not restricted to S1 alone, as this S2 trainee points out:

> I don't think that I'd like to be involved (in planning the course)...I think I've come to be taught and I think it was up to me in particular to sit back and listen to what they had to say...it's nice listening to your peers in discussion...but surely we've come to listen to tutors telling us what we're short of, what you need to be doing in the future to make your lessons better...so less involvement for me in planning and more actual teaching and learning.

Not everyone was quite so sanguine, however and one S2 course trainee had a rather different attitude:

> I've a feeling the course is going to be done in one particular way and we don't seem to have a great deal of say in it really. People have made comments which I think have been filed away...It would have been very different if we had all had our say! If he had taperecorded our coffee breaks...I don't think he's terribly keen to change anything.

There were some occasions when trainees quite radically determined what they were to do but these arose from particular circumstances and not because the principle was recognised by the course tutor.

> I was the blocker one week...I thought we'd done enough (role play) and I spoke out and said that I didn't want to do it. The others agreed with me...we did something else.

A trainee from another S1 course related another incident at some greater length:

> Well when I first started I was very eager and looking forward to doing it...the first week was all right and the second week I thought, well, we did this last week and then the third week I was thinking, well, what am I coming for because it was very boring — we were repeating what we'd done the two weeks before...after four weeks we were looking out of the window and thinking 'whatever are we doing here?'...One of the tutors said 'What are you looking out of the window for, so and so?' and she said, 'because I'm bored out of my mind' and he said 'Oh' and had another think about it. When another tutor came in...he insisted that we did what he wanted and we kept saying 'We can't do it — he wanted to spend three complete weeks on it...(Would it have helped...if the trainers had sat down with you and asked what sort of course do you think you want?) Yes...it might have done because we reached this crisis, when we all sat back and said 'This is not doing us any good', they said 'Right, well, we'll have to sit back and think what we are going to do about it'.

It was also evident that on more than one course trainees usually did not know the outline course structure and were unaware from one week to the next what they would be doing. From their comments, it appeared that there was no sense of continuity between sessions, and topics appeared almost arbitrarily.

> It would have been better with a programme and objectives, some idea of what the course was going to cover, rather than turning up each week and not knowing...he had a framework himself probably...

> One meeting didn't seem to lead on to the next at all, and I didn't know what to expect until I got there. I would have preferred to have been given more tasks...to look at and assess myself at home and then follow it up at the next meeting rather than go raw into a meeting and then sort of say, 'We're going to do this', which you haven't had time to think about.

Even where a programme was provided, not everything went to plan as this S1 trainee pointed out:

> There was a lack of consistency. We were given a programme at the first lesson...but we didn't follow it...I like to know where I'm going and prepare myself for it...

and similarly, on an S2 course:

> It's been very 'itsy bitsy'. We seem to have started something and not actually finished it. We were given to start with a list of aims...I think he's trying to stick with it...but there isn't enough time...so we get half way through and he says 'We'll have to leave that now and perhaps come back to it'. That's happened several times. I'd have liked a bit more continuity.

Aims, objectives, programmes — the evidence provided by trainees indicates clearly that on at least a minority of courses, notably S1s, there is a perceived lack of communication between trainees and trainers about how courses are structured, and indeed why.

Methods

Conversations with trainees about the appropriateness and relevance of the teaching methods they had come across in their training courses led to the identification of several related points. There was general approval of the friendly atmosphere in which practically all the courses were run, a typical comment being:

> I like the informality...adults to adults.

Asked directly about specific teaching methods used on the course, many trainees talked of teaching aids and the physical organisation of classrooms rather than the interpersonal skills such as questioning, explaining, encouraging, reinforcing. Thus:

> The visual thing of the blackboard, that made things a lot more clear than just sitting there discussing. And bringing in things like visual aids and printed stuff was very useful.

That is not to say that trainees were unaware of the teaching-learning skills involved, for the last quotation continued:

> I felt that they needed value for money and wanted to sit there for the whole two hours and listen, which you realise they don't...

Other trainees spoke of the methods they had observed.

> We had a simulated language lesson, and she did it all orally and I've never seen that sort of thing before.

> The way X teaches is great — she gets it out of you, what you've got in you, rather than pushes things into you.

> ...question and answer...he did (avoid) just talking at you for evermore. You were always involved in one way or another. There was practical demonstration if it were possible, and answering or writing down or anything to make sure you were awake.

Mention was made of role play, simulations and, of course, micro-teaching and although some trainees maintained that they had not been introduced to any new teaching methods there were some for whom these were a revelation:

> Apart from the teacher standing with the blackboard and chalk I hadn't even thought about methods of teaching before.

> It gave me a list of possibilities which I had never considered before.

The majority of trainees usually did not identify particular teaching methods in specific terms of appropriateness and relevance yet many described themselves as being satisfied with what they had experienced.

Trainees appeared to hold critical opinions about 'modelling'. There was little doubt that most trainees felt that they benefited from the opportunity to observe other teachers at work, whether they were their own tutors (trainers), their peers on the course, or other teachers. Indeed, several made quite strong cases for being allowed to sit in on other teachers' classes in their own Centres for such a purpose, both as preparation before joining a training course and as a method of continued self-development afterwards. Primarily though it was trainers who were closely observed.

> We learned quite a bit from watching them putting information across to us as adults...it was interesting to watch their methods.

> When they interrupt, or have a discussion, or when we want something else, I am learning in the way that X (the trainer) deals with it. I watch what (he) does when everyone starts arguing, discussing and sometimes (I) sit back and watch and say to myself, 'Where is he going to stop it, what is he going to do?'

Trainees also closely watched the micro-teaching and demonstrating activities of their peers:

> You can learn a great deal, just by seeing how people do things. Some ideas you think 'that's really good...I could give that a try'.

This is not to say that the trainers were unaware of the possibilities for learning that observation of models provides since several courses had programmes which included experienced teachers giving demonstration lessons of one sort or another.

> The Sunday was taken up by two different teachers who came into the class — we were their students. (It was) putting us into the student situation again and showing us two different teachers' ideas of ways of teaching.

> They used a good variety (of teaching methods) and tried to point out lots of ways of getting things over. (Was it a model for your teaching?) Yes, although none of them would say it is how they thought it ought to be done. They thought you should adapt all the various methods you come across to your style. Once you know a bit about the students you've got (in your class), you have to adapt to them — that came across in the course.

But time and again trainees made it clear that it was the trainers themselves who were the models most observed and whilst some provided excellent examples others quite unintentionally provided models of 'how not to do it'. Although there may be some benefit to be gained from observing negative examples, and trainees think unequivocally that there is, it is to be hoped that where the model is a trainer, the example is planned rather than fortuitous.

> One of the tutors was telling us how important it was that all your equipment was ready to go and in perfect order, and he was showing us a film and it snapped, and got all tangled up and it took him twenty minutes to sort this out. During that time he ignored us because he was panic-striken, and that was the real point, that he didn't practise what he preached, that you should always keep your audience entertained if something like this happens, and he didn't, he illustrated the point perfectly by doing it all wrong. (Did he realise after?) Yes, because we told him...it was quite good that, quite funny.

Some sympathy might well be felt for anyone in this nightmare situation, though trainees did report having benefited from such situations.

161

Actually, I've learned more from what I felt were the mistakes they made...it makes you a better teacher by default. In a way I've learned a lot by watching and seeing how others react.

I was aware of the negative elements in their teaching — (to) make sure that I wasn't going to do those. A lot of it had to do with awareness, my awareness in picking-up what I believed to be right or wrong in their way of teaching...

In some instances the 'negative' model was consciously offered:

Saturday night we had an awful lesson, light relief, with all the mistakes. They (demonstrated it) all really, from the very bad to the really good.

There is no doubt that some trainees did feel strongly about the teaching methods that they were exposed to on their training courses. There was a current of suggestion, particularly running through S2 courses that trainers themselves should use a full range of teaching methods, voiced by a few thus:

We've gone through all the teaching methods but I'd like to see one or two of the lecturers use them as well as us being taught about them.

I would have liked to have seen the lecturers use the vehicles they were trying to get over to us...the actual lessons done as examples, it would be more advantageous to us as students than sitting and discussing them.

In addition there were some direct criticism of 'poor' teaching:

Tutors on occasions beat the topic to death and oversimplified it for us, thus appearing to treat us like children and thus rendering the whole topic somewhat tedious.

and more bluntly still:

I don't know that some of them (the training staff) had any teaching methods. I used to think that before I came on this course that my teaching lacked a lot. I still do, but compared to some other people...that taught us on the course, I don't think that it is too bad after all. In fact, some of those (teaching) on the course would be better on the course. Sometimes I just sat there and thought, 'Well I don't know why they are paying these blokes to teach us because I feel that I would be better off at home'.

It is evident that many trainees learn as much from what trainers do as from what they say. The process of training is certainly as important as content. It is also clear that a minority of trainers presented examples, at least at times, which were perceived by trainees as undesirable according to their own precepts. The majority of trainers however, were recognised as presenting positive and helpful examples.

Working with others: the sharing of ideas and experience

Although it has already been noted that trainees did not have a great deal of influence upon the determination of either course objectives or course content, there is little doubt that there was full participation within course sessions and not only on residential weekends. Trainees, particularly on S1 courses, reported that they were greatly involved in activities of micro-teaching demonstrations, role playing, simulation and other group activities. In S1 courses, some of the project work and the preparation of aids and materials were done in small groups. Fundamental to all these particular activities was the informality of the training group, the adult to adult relationships developed and the willingness of the vast majority of group members to talk.

> After each item or topic...we discussed...and everybody could put their views forward, which I thought was very helpful.

> For me (there was) a hundred per cent participation — I gave it all I'd got to give and I really felt part of it and enjoyed it. I think that it made it all more enjoyable.

This was also the case for many S2 courses:

> They involved you all the time...with some dropout as the group got smaller, it was like sitting with a group of friends really.

Though not all:

> There should be more practical involvement on the part of the students...and the aims and objectives...should be made clearer — as he tells us to!

> The major drawback is...very little active teaching by students (trainees)...We haven't had much chance to be in control of the group either — in discussion or something. It's mainly been people talking to us.

But on the whole evidence does suggest the level of practical student involvement in courses was high. A point perhaps best summed up by this trainee:

> Full participation by the course members is there for the taking. The group and individual attitudes are informal and the group/teacher bond is being well-formed.

The willingness of trainees to participate within their groups was quite closely related to the way that training courses drew upon their knowledge and experience insofar as they were able to discuss as full participants of a supportive group. Typically:

> Yes, they kept referring to us to give accounts of what we'd found in our lessons. You did find people who were more extrovert, the same few, giving forth, and the other people sat there quietly but we all had the opportunity to give an account of our experiences.

> He utilised very well various people's subjects and specialisms, their experiences, to show what variety of methods (could) be used for different subjects.

In particular, trainees appear to have greatly valued the opportunity to consider individual experiences especially where others identified with them and were thus able to share directly in the points raised.

> Everyone had a chance to get their problems out — everyone was totally involved.

> He would give his views (on a subject raised by a trainee) and throw it open for general discussion. I'm sure that it was a help to think that other people were going through what they had, or having problems that they had had and how they resolved them.

> (By) discussing their problems...met in their class — that was helpful because it wasn't them who were talking, it was us, the fellow students. You identified with them. 'That might happen to me'...with a general discussion on how the situation could be put right.

It was clear that a very real support function was operating in this particular respect, restated by this trainee:

> Help with class problems...yes, it did, tremendously so. Just because you could talk it out. When I come home my husband is not interested in what I'm doing. I never discuss it with him...he's got his own problems. It's nice to be with a lot of people who do the same thing and talk it out (with them).

Not all experiences brought to the group were of necessity 'problem page' varieties:

> Everyone had their own views and you can pick up a lot from that — and the way that they put their subject over...everybody has a different method and you get a chance to learn from them.

> I am quite happy to be isolated but sometimes it is nice to meet other people. I seem reasonably self-sufficient and self-confident in what I'm doing but it is nice to pass ideas and opinions (on) sometimes, to make a fool of yourself, and, sometimes, to do the right thing...

But the findings:

> There was plenty of opportunity for people to put forward their ideas based on experience, ample opportunity.

> We get together and bring up points of what happened in our courses and what we are doing and I think it is all the time a continuous exchange.

mentioned by S1 and S2 trainees respectively, reinforce the point succinctly that sharing of experiences and ideas within the training group was seen as being of real benefit by trainees.

The development of teaching skills

The direct contribution of the course to trainees' experience of teaching was identified by many as not only deriving from shared experiences but from individual teaching opportunities connected with the course. There were especially the micro-teaching activities which took place on the vast majority of courses and the trainers' visits to classes being currently taught by trainees.

Micro-teaching appeared in several guises in most courses; in some cases it was the four or five minute variety, in others a half-hour type and in one or two cases, both. Regardless of its exact form and nomenclature, and notwithstanding the apprehension it often seems to have engendered in the performers, it was universally approved of.

> The main thing was the little demonstration when we could examine ourselves and each other...that was extremely valuable.

> We had to give a lesson for half an hour...it was quite enjoyable actually. By the time we did it we all knew what we should be looking for.

> We had to do 10 minutes with a visual aid that we had prepared...then half an hour or 40 minutes teaching our own subject and then for the next half an hour that was pulled to pieces. That was useful. (Did people criticise?) Yes, at first they were all very nice. The first person got through easy and got away with it really easy because we were all polite, but then we realised what we should be looking for.

Micro-teaching exercises took place in most S1 and S2 courses though only a small minority made use of closed circuit television. However, as these S2 trainees report, practically everyone seems to have felt they benefited from the whole experience:

> The micro-teaching exercise was good. You were aware that you were in a group of your own peers and that they were going to pick you to pieces...it got you on your mettle.

> We did micro-teaching in the classroom — useful because I set up my own objectives...within their guidelines. It was an excellent piece of work, there was a lot of feedback on it for me.

Where micro-teaching either did not take place within the course or was in some way curtailed, there was a degree of resentment insofar as a valuable opportunity had been lost.

> I would have liked to have done more...with everyone taking part, not just those who X had volunteered.

> Sometimes we are given a problem and asked how you would solve it in your particular area of work. I don't think that we are used really — if we had more micro-teaching and more chance for each person to have their say instead of just answering questions, then you'd probably gain more.

The other major contribution to trainee experience was the supervised 'teaching practice'. In the case of S2 courses there is a requirement of 30 hours teaching practice with the proviso that the trainee be visited either by a trainer or some other member of the field staff (such as a Head of Centre). Many S1 courses also included at least one visit by the trainer to group members' classes and in practically all cases, trainees expressed approval.

> He came round on two of my lessons and he reviewed the class and gave me a report — it was reasonably favourable.

> We've had four visits. They give you a lovely report...they go through everything, your syllabus, scheme of work, presentation, your attitude to your students...

However, it was the S1 trainees who spoke most enthusiastically about visits.

> He came to see our actual classes and watched us teach. It was a bit unnerving — but he was obviously taking mental notes because he wrote back and complimented the class and also pointed out one or two things that perhaps I had not thought about. His comments were very useful because he was able to sit down and evaluate as an outside observer.

> It was really useful because he became one of the students and he discussed me with them, really — he asked them what they thought...he was good, he wrote to me afterwards — said the points that he'd noticed — things that he felt were good and things that he felt could be improved upon.

> He came to see me teach — he went round all of us...when he first said that he was coming I was horrified...so I planned carefully and hoped that everybody would turn up and that I wouldn't forget anything or fall over. He was very unobtrusive...he gave me a very good report — I've gained a tremendous amount of confidence.

165

Not everyone was quite so satisfied with the results, mainly because of the lack of comment from the person observing them. It was the quality of subsequent discussions and comment which was seen as the crucial element. A minority of trainees reported:

> He came to see me teach — he didn't comment and I didn't ask!

> I would have felt a lot happier if he'd had a proper talk (with me) afterwards and said 'You did this right, you did this wrong, and not just walked out (saying), 'You were great'.

> He came to watch us teach but he never said what he thought — we'd have liked some feedback.

Some trainees on one course did not get the opportunity:

> (Did he come to watch you teach?) No, he said he didn't on purpose. I think that it would have been useful if he had, he would have been able to tell us honestly what he thought, which would have been useful. You are bound to make mistakes and if they are pointed out to you it would be good.

though the majority did. Thus there was clear evidence of the value of teaching whilst observed by peers and certainly in the more natural surroundings of a weekly class with a trainer present. What is also apparent is that constructive criticism either in written form or verbally is considered an indispensable part of the whole activity.

Assessment

For many trainees, assessment equated with marking. The general expectation amongst S2 trainees was that assignments that they had completed would be marked and returned, as indeed a good proportion of them seem to have been.

> He gives us marks on the written work we do...he puts comments at the end — that it misses the object of the question, tells us where it has gone wrong. It's useful.

What evidence there is from S1s however, indicates that rather little attention appears to have been paid to the assessment of even the small amount of written work that most trainees were given.

Assessment was recognised as having a feedback function and mention has already been made of the different responses to the 'assessments' made on teaching practice where some trainees were provided not only with a full written critique but also given the opportunity for tutorial discussion afterwards. Thus:

> We'd built up a relationship and the class was going well. He gave me a very lengthy (written) criticism, mostly constructive — a negative part was the use of the blackboard. It was positive because I learned from it. It was a pleasant experience.

> The report from the class visit...was useful — as a confidence boost for me because it was a good report.

Many trainees however viewed assessment in the context of a general form of continuous monitoring rather than as specific responses to written work and teaching practice. In their view, this was made not just by the course tutors but also by their peer group.

We were all 'assessing' each other all the time...

> We used to discuss quite a lot what each other was doing and say what we thought about it.

With respect to their trainers as assessors many commented thus:

> I think they were assessing us all the time.

> I feel that the course was a constant assessment, I think, on the individual's performance. Also, when he came to see us teach, I think that was an assessment, and of course on the weekend — I must have failed miserably on mine. But I think there was a general assessment because he got to know people.

> I suppose that he is watching us all the time. My judgement is that he is very sharp, he is very alert and I think that he is judging us all the time. Not just the written work but the way we react to every subject that we deal with...I think that is good...

Apparently it wasn't always clear to some trainees what was being done.

> (Were we assessed?)...I don't know...not by X (the trainer) specifically, though the group did...At times it was as if he were a fly on the wall...I thought 'Maybe something is missing and he should be doing more'.

> Well, apparently we were assessed as we went along, but I wasn't told how we were getting on...(I wasn't conscious of it), no.

Many trainees appeared to be saying quite clearly that they wanted the results of assessment — comments, feedback, constructive criticism. One trainee in answer to a question about reasons for attending the course in the first place gave a cogent statement which reflected the views of many of her peers:

> They were something about learning something about teaching...to test my own ability as a teacher. I had nothing to measure it against...all I got was feedback from students, and they might not be telling the truth all the time, but I know that I'd be coming to a situation where I'd meet greater honesty.

On some courses she wouldn't have received this in the way she wanted.

> The only thing was that he didn't bother checking it...didn't bother marking it. When you'd done it, that was the only thing that bothered me — why had I done it? I suppose really it was to get you to think and did it matter that anybody read it anyway? But it wasn't what I was used to...It would have been nice for him to have discussed what I'd written. Occasionally, he'd go through it — but he'd only go through it, he wouldn't look at it, he'd talk generally about it...Did I mention it to him? No, not really, because I felt that he didn't have time.

> We had to produce a course plan. We didn't get it back — only a little feedback. He looked at it (and said) 'Yes, that's more or less right'. I didn't get it back with written comments on it. I think they bent over backwards not to judge or not to be seen to judge. There was a feeling from the group that they wanted to be told 'That's right' or 'No, that's wrong'.

This last contributor may well be a great deal closer to the truth than he might suppose about the effect of non-judgemental attitudes to training. What is clear is that trainees both expect to be criticised and accept criticism and they set great store by it. They would doubtless prefer the complimentary sort but there is an awareness that criticism of any kind is essential to the work that they do.

Course requirements

There were clear distinctions between S1 and S2 courses in terms of the requirements of individual study, both reading and written assignments. In S1 courses there appears to have been very little reading outside the course and even where it was recommended it was very much as an 'optional extra'.

> We were shown titles of books that we could pick out from the library if we wished.

> We were given a book to read and I assumed that we would follow it up but we didn't — it was never referred to again (Jennifer Rogers 'Adult Learning').

A minority of S1 trainees held a different standpoint:

> There was a lot of reading from handouts...maybe it should be cut down but then it's useful for reference. It stimulated me to find out more.

perhaps reflecting the differing demands made by some S1 courses. Similarly with written work: S1 courses usually asked for a minimum of written contribution but none required anything of a formal essay-type assignment. Some trainees were asked to keep diaries of their own day or evening class and at least two groups wrote individual 'course progress' diaries. Many trainees were required to prepare specimen course outlines/structures and lesson plans and several course tutors requested 'project work', thus:

> We all had a project to do which we thought would help us in our particular field, to take to class with us...so I did a series of posters. The pottery people did (one of) lots of different glazes to show how the finished thing looked.

When and where such assignments were employed they were practically all of direct and immediate relevance to the trainees' role of teacher. There was little or no adverse comment from trainees about the individual work they were asked to do and none seems to have found it unduly onerous. But the unmistakable impression is that the expectation made of trainees, with regard to reading and written work were low, and that few demands were made upon them.

S2 courses, on the other hand, did make clear demands:

> A considerable amount of reading was expected of us...and written work...something like a dozen essays.

> A lot of reading...the college arranged for the library to be open for us in the evening. I think my essay writing has improved over the year.

> We had handouts...an open library where you tick off and take books out and I had about six books...there was written work...courses and assignments.

Practically all S2 trainees spoke of the demands made upon them by their course in one way or another, occasionally with the inevitable consequences:

> I realised that it would be a lot more intensive than S1, which it was...some people found it too much and dropped out...

168

Reading and particularly written work were quite often cited in this context.

> I expected to be involved in writing essays...I expected the course to be trying and very time-consuming but I didn't realise how taxing and time-consuming.

> I find the written work helpful...it is a problem I have to separate myself from the family completely and get on with it, do the reading...

and some found it difficult:

> The written work requirement was excessive and caused difficulty in completing it.

> ...as I have gone on I found that I initially had problems (of writing) but after a while I found it about right. He always gave us breakdowns...he points...out the errors that he acknowledges you have made or things that you could have added in.

If the course was found to be hard-going it was nevertheless felt to be appropriate. There seemed to be general acceptance of course demands, expectations were clear and trainees responded accordingly.

Course evaluation

There appear to be two approaches to course evaluation in current use by trainers: continuous or 'on-going' evaluation and that which takes place at the end of a course. Some S1 and S2 courses employed continuous evaluation insofar as they either encouraged evaluative comment throughout or they actually included programmed evaluation sessions.

> We had several periods set aside for course evaluation so we could direct the direction of the course...just generally talking about the course and what directions we would like to see it going. I held nothing back...the people I was most in contact with felt quite confident enough to say what they thought...and there were slight changes and alterations — that's all we wanted.

> It was important to him that he knew how we felt...he tried to find out constantly what we thought about what we were doing...

> Every fifth or sixth week we get counselling and we sit down and talk about (the course), that's when they ask if you are happy with it and if there is anything more that you want to learn. (We are quite frank), they've encouraged that throughout the course.

Other courses predominantly relied upon the traditional last evening evaluation session, though some trainees did not report these occasions with any great enthusiasm.

> At the end...I felt that we were able to say what we thought.

> We were asked at the end to say whether or not the course had fulfilled what we'd hoped. Most of the criticisms put forward were trivial, there was nothing of any real significance that would have altered the way future courses were done.

The participation of trainees in course evaluation appears to have taken place on all courses with the certain exception of one.

> We were to have a plenary on the final day but we didn't because the tutors weren't there. I was very disappointed at that. I think that it would have been rather super to sit down with the tutors and discuss everything.

One or two comments were of a rather desultory nature:

> Involved in the evaluation?...not really, we weren't conscious of it.

> (Are you involved in evaluation?) Not really. He asks us occasionally what we think, but it doesn't affect the course — maybe it will affect next year's. He evaluates the course through the assessments of individual students.

and the impression given by these and other similar comments was that at least for a few courses the evaluation session lacked clarity and purpose. At least one trainer bowed to the inevitable; perhaps he got his feedback later:

> (Did we evaluate the course?) Not really...our opinions would be something to take note of, to use as a reference...perhaps on the last evening we may well have been (about) to be asked (but) he got waylaid and no-one would take him seriously so we all adjourned to the pub...he did have a list of things that he intended to get through...but I'm afraid he (had to) put (it) away...

The evidence suggests that quite a few trainees leave their course with no clear understanding of the concept of course evaluation or the skills to carry it out in practice.

Trainees had a lot to say about the design and practice of their training courses as they experienced them. They were asked about, and freely commented upon, course objectives, planning, participation and so on. They were not specifically asked during their interviews whether they thought that they in their turn should involve their students in such discussions, negotiations and evaluations of their classes. There is, therefore, no clear evidence on this point though there were indications from at least some of the trainees that they would introduce the practice in their own classes. Some clearly intended to take rather greater account of their students' needs as adult learners than previously, tempering their own teaching accordingly. Whether there will be significant change in class participation in planning, organisations and evaluation is beyond the scope of this research to establish.

SECTION 4: EXPECTATIONS AND EFFECTS

Largely because of inadequate means of assessment, we still know very little about the effects of professional training upon teaching behaviours. The identification of exactly how individuals are affected or changed as a consequence of their training remains a problem. This is particularly difficult with a basic course of 36 hours such as Stage 1. The observations of trainers concerning the changes brought about by S1 and S2 courses were examined in Chapter 4 and what now follows is an analysis of trainees' comments upon the same issue. These provide evidence of how they perceive their training to have influenced their own attitudes and teaching behaviours. Some clues about this process emerge from an attempt to match trainee expectations with their perceptions of what they have achieved and from the exercise which required trainees to list their criteria for good adult teaching.

In the original project design there was a built-in intention to attempt some match between trainees' expectations of their training courses with their subsequent perceptions of what they had in fact received from and achieved on their courses. With this intent specific questions were included in the written monitoring schedule which it was hoped would be completed by all trainees. It has already been pointed out in Chapter 2 that there was a very disappointing rate of return of this written matter and there were very few complete sets of the documents from particular individuals. Since those that were returned show a disappointing spread in breadth and depth of response the comparisons originally envisaged could not realistically be carried out.

Nevertheless some quotations from what was provided in this written form may prove of value in giving a flavour of trainees' attitudes. The following quotations are responses made by S1 trainees to two linked questions, "What did you expect to get out of the course?" and the second, which immediately followed it: "Did you in fact get this?" Thus, from some individuals:

I had no expectations.   — I got the ability to communicate more easily with strangers. I got confidence in myself.

I don't really know.   — It did serve to confirm what I hope were my own assumptions of working with adults.

A few trainees were more forthcoming:

Qualification to teach adults in non-vocational classes.   — Anticipating, yes.

Some idea of what was expected of a teacher of adults.   — Yes.

I thought it would... make me a better teacher.   — Yes.

General information which would give me a better understanding of teaching.   — I consider that the course has been helpful and thus given me greater confidence to teach my subject.

Others were more specific in their expectations:

Confidence in teaching adults.   — Yes.

The actual method of teaching, putting over one subject and handling the class.   — Yes, pretty well.

Some ideas on how to improve my teaching method and/or test my ability to teach.   — Yes, e.g. I have a better idea of how much content for two hours plus a growth in personal confidence.

Very little, due to having six years' FT vocational teaching.   — I gained more than I expected though it was of more value to the less experienced.

I hoped it would help me to decide how to approach my students — whether or not I was talking too much and not letting them join in — was I planning the course right.   — Yes, I think so. The session on course planning and the one on visual aids I have found of great benefit, especially the use of OHPs.

One trainee in common with many others stated that she did not know what to expect but in her case, she was quite clear what she got.

> I gained...an infinite amount of knowledge on teaching methods and an awful lot of self-confidence, being reassured that not all teachers are already intellectual whizz-kids.

In the case of S2 trainees, however, there were much clearer statements of expectations and very few indeed had 'none'. In some cases, trainees referred directly to the obtaining of the course certificate and/or future employment.

> To increase my ability as an instructor plus a worthwhile paper qualification when I leave the RAF. Yes, but a little question mark about the value of the certificate in terms of finding a job.

> Additional knowledge of adult students and how best to teach them...better understanding...practice...and career counselling.

> I fancy a job in FT education and the City and Guilds Course will help me get to the Poly, if I want to go for a teacher's ticket.

In the main, expectations made reference to improvements in and development of trainees' role as teachers.

> To learn the refinements of teaching and enable me to make the best of resources available.

> An individual-based course on how to teach...plus a great deal more experience of practical teaching.

> To teach me how to prepare lessons and AV aids and how to teach correctly...I am finding it very helpful with the teaching sessions I am doing at the moment.

Several had obviously given thought to the demands of the course as for example this trainee:

> I expected the course to be trying and very time-consuming but I didn't realise how taxing and time-consuming. Yes, I did get this but I also gained the fellowship and friendship of the course tutors. Also, their unstinting help and advice in doing the course tasks. I also had the pleasure of receiving written comments on written work which have been very useful.

He was not alone in making reference to the perhaps unexpected behaviours of trainers:

> The same sort of information I had been given on my S1, but at a higher level. Yes, and more besides. I find the course far more stimulating than I thought it would be. Part of this is probably due to our course tutor, X (who) makes things interesting and puts information over so well. I also find the course assignments interesting.

There were very few respondents who believed that they had gained little from the S1 courses though one or two stated that they were quite experienced and in consequence the course served only to confirm what they already knew. The group of trainees who were all teachers of the same subject exclusively attending one S1 course, and had all previously attended a training course run by their subject association were less than enthralled though some of them did report 'confirmation' of what they had already been taught.

It is not possible to designate the effects of the courses too categorically but they do seem to fall into quite neat groupings. Of these, 'preparation and planning' was often cited:

> I've learnt how to plan a course and plan individual lessons.

> Much more professional than I used to be...and I now plan my course week by week, what particular aspect I'm going to do in addition to what students ask me. I used to tend to let the class go along and muddle through but now I plan it out, try to cover less. I used to think that I ought to be everything...

'Methods' and 'approaches' were also often mentioned:

> The importance of good preparation of lessons coupled with flexibility of approach...

> (It caused me to) think about the way I was putting things over.

> How problems can be identified and subsequently tackled.

In addition, quite a few trainees typically thought that they would:

> Be able to think 'in front' and always be prepared for the unexpected.

> Know the tips and tricks you can employ to make a class run more smoothly.

> Organise the room: make sure the chairs would be in the right place.

> Use more visual aids — especially the overhead projector and so on.

Indeed, many trainees were unaware of the advances made in educational hard and software and the overhead projector was very often seized upon as a novel and valuable teaching accessory.

> The visual aids — I find them very useful. The overhead projector...we had tuition in how one went about making diagrams and so on. I found that very, very useful.

> (There was) nothing I hadn't come across before but certainly things I hadn't used before — the overhead projector...the blackboard which I had used (before) but according to X, very badly. It opened up avenues and pointed me in a direction in which I hadn't been inclined to go.

The opportunities given to develop specific teaching aids and materials relating to individuals' subject areas were also valued, particularly where these led to group evaluation and discussion.

> We had to demonstrate the visual aids we'd chosen and I found that useful with the constructive criticism.

It was noticeable that in talking about the effects of the courses there was a considerable amount of comment relating to students in particular to teaching awareness of their difficulties, their individuality, their needs and their learning.

> I think more about the social aspects and relationships with students to each other and to me.

> Awareness of the feelings and possible attitudes of the students.

> I think about the level...I have got to be aware of the varying needs of students in the class...I have go to stand back a bit from the subject and...be careful...and think.

It helped me deal with awkward students and to teach straight to people and not down to them. And to make yourself know that they've understood what you've said...I'd never thought of that. I was interested in the teaching but I wasn't quite so interested in if they were learning anything. I was so worried about what I was teaching...I (now have) found out what they were learning.

But in the words of one trainee:

It made me review what I was doing...it gave me confidence and I think that it must have shown (to her own students). It has done me a lot of good actually because I went on the course feeling, not inadequate, but fairly unsure of myself...a lot of people were just as nervous as I was and it's reassuring, because you tend to think that teachers are very self-assured and you realise that a lot of them are not. I didn't know what to expect from the course . . . I didn't think that I'd learn as much as I did. . . there's a lot of aspects of teaching I'd never thought about...(the course) makes you look at what you are doing and it gives you the opportunity to stop and think and maybe do things in a different way. That would be of benefit to any teacher, established or not, and for new people like I was, it's going to give you confidence.

The single most cited effect of training is quite unequivocally — confidence. Time and again trainees used this description of change both about themselves in their training group and in their subsequent teaching. These quotations are typical of practically all trainees' response:

People became far more confident. . . we had to give a lesson...it really broke down the barriers. I felt that he had manipulated us into being more confident and more able to discuss things. I noticed at the beginning...asked a question...nobody answered. At the end it was a discussion, it was as though we were pals. We never bothered thinking about 'Will I make a fool of myself?' It worked tremendously well, I thought.

...I think that teachers would be well equipped (by going on an S1 course)...they would gain a lot of confidence...and the confidence would be gained by the fact that there were a number of people in the same boat that they were...and find that they had common problems...this would give them more confidence for teaching.

In a way I lack self-confidence, though I'm told that it doesn't show...inwardly I feel — am I capable of teaching? I suppose that is another reason why I went on the S1, as well as doing a revision, a way of boosting confidence. I think that it gave me extra confidence.

This is not to say that there was a unanimous rise in confidence. A small minority like the trainee quoted below appear to have regressed though it is to be hoped that she soon after experienced an upturn.

My confidence has sadly dropped. I feel slightly inadequate after listening to and seeing all the aids, planning and lesson preparation.

Nevertheless, the vast majority seem to have benefited markedly and as these two observations illustrate, that confidence has been put to good effect.

I suppose that I'm (now) fairly confident which is what I've got from X (the trainer), so I'm hoping that the students will notice that and it rubs off on them...I have seen a difference in a lot of ladies from how they do things because they are confident, so it is

174

rubbing off which is marvellous...it all comes back to confidence because I know what I'm doing...I put it over with confidence.

I have boosted my confidence because I'm now going into my class with new ideas and I feel an excitement at trying to give a better all-round performance. I am already analysing myself much more critically.

Much the same pattern is to be found amongst the S2 trainees. Again, confidence is cited as a major result of the course, though not to quite the same extent.

I don't feel so isolated, I'm part of a group...I have been able to talk to other people. Support, moral support. I now question the way I use the time...the way I use books...look at students...the time I give them, the amount of work I give them...

My confidence as a teacher has been greatly enhanced. I feel more able to undertake and be responsible for planning and teaching of a course.

Again there was a small minority who experienced an initial lessening of confidence but the indication was that this diminution was beneficial.

My confidence has diminished, leading me to learn more. It is now growing after an initial breakdown.

Looking at the other effects reported by trainees, planning, organisation and student feedback are all typically cited.

I have found it very useful and I don't think there is enough emphasis on S1 about...a definite aim and objective, a definite system to work to for each lesson. Now I realise how important (that is)...I hope that it's made me stop and consider all the different ways I can teach...all the different methods.

I think more than anything, lesson planning and trying to get feedback...and the stating of objectives.

...how to set an essay, how to deal with adults on evening courses, how to teach them, how to get through to them, how to help them. . . In every way, it has given me more confidence.

I tended to teach on the basis of what I thought students should learn and probably didn't go into finding out exactly what the student was learning. I (now) try to do a bit of assessment on what was learnt through the evening...how am I putting it over.

Perhaps this final example neatly summarises much of what S2 trainees were saying:

I'm better organised in the way that I teach, I've a lot more visual aids. We use the OHP a lot more than I used to. I try to get examples...and bring them to the class so that they realise what the final thing they are learning about looks like. I think that's the problem when you are teaching, you tend to think that everybody's on the same wavelength as yourself...That's what the course has taught me — to try and get feedback each night and work out whether they are learning what I'm trying to teach them. I think that it's widened my outlook as a teacher — what I should be teaching, how I should be teaching and the standards that I've got to try to meet...

SECTION 5: FURTHER DEVELOPMENTS

Recommendations and suggestions for their own future development outside the Regional Scheme were made by some trainees, though they tended not to be couched in terms of specific LEA provision. It has been noted elsewhere in the report that a number of teachers felt rather isolated in their work and comments like:

> More contact with other people who are teaching...it's difficult round here — you have none —

were not uncommonly made by trainees too. There were also comments about Centre Heads:

> More support from the Centre Head, but I think that I'm fairly unlucky in that respect...

There is evidence to suggest that she might not have been as exceptional as she thought, but that aside, there does seem to be quite a strong feeling that support from colleagues at all levels of the profession would be beneficial.

There was also a quite widespread opinion that having received some training, experience 'on the job' was a *sine qua non* for development.

> I feel at the moment (that) in teaching the class...I do I learn as a teacher. Situations arise and you think about it — you develop and learn all the time.

> The best thing for me would be more teaching practice...even now I would like to go to a Centre and see someone else teach. I tried asking the other art teacher but she wouldn't have it.

> I only think we are going to learn to teach by teaching. I think we will learn only by experience (now)...

One or two trainees made tentative suggestions about day schools and conferences and both subject-based and general teaching contents were mentioned but there was little consensus.

> More courses...refreshers and one-day courses...anything to keep teachers up to date with new ideas.

> I would like (occasional) lectures or meetings...of language teachers or all adult teachers...to get together and to have some link...(to break down isolation)...

Quite a number of trainees did express interest in, if not direct intent, to proceed to further training, either S2 (or C&G 730), as a direct result of having taken S1.

> I shall go on and do Stage 2...I shall still have X's example since she teaches the S2 course.

> I feel that (S1) has just touched the fringes and I want to do more. I want to know more. I'd like to do S2.

> I'm toying with the idea of doing a full-time course at the Poly. It's at the back of my mind...I'm thinking about it.

I'd like to feel it was leading somewhere, on to a higher course. I definitely feel I need to carry on, but I'll have to knock on doors again to find out what is available. My ultimate aim now is to become a full-time teacher.

At least two trainees recognised personal benefit from the process of training.

...the need to continue to study from a personal point of view. To continue and do a Stage 2 or do something else actually involved in AE, because I'm actually at a stage where I am fairly flexible as far as career and job are concerned, so it is a good re-examination. It has affected me a lot, thrown a new light on me which I didn't think existed before...it has changed my way of teaching (too).

I like the present training scheme (where) you've got the progression through and I like the idea of being able to come right from the bottom and come right out at the end, right at the top end...I like the idea of everybody being able to take a second chance. All right, so I was a late learner but if it hadn't been for AE, how could I have got on. The scheme as it is is quite good. I'm sure that there are things that could be added in to improve it, given the facilities and the cash, time and willing tutors to do it. (I should like to see) courses carry on as they are doing...and specialists brought in to see teaching in specialist subjects (like swimming)...to give advice...if not assessment...I'd certainly consider a S3...but again it's difficult...I've got to work full-time and I can't get day release...especially if it could be ongoing from the end of this course, straight into the next...you lose momentum...if you drop off (for a while)...

The theme of personal development was taken up by several trainees in discussion of the value of LEA investment in training and resulting benefits.

I think it is essential (that the LEA should offer training courses) if they want teachers who are not just good teachers but who have a responsibility to society. I think that money is well spent...it makes the teacher a better person, it creates an improvement in teachers and students...

This is not to say that all trainees felt that training should be made compulsory, or indeed that it was always desirable or necessary. There was a belief that if an untrained teacher was recognised as knowing his/her subject and could be seen to be teaching in an acceptable manner to the satisfaction of the class, there was little need for training.

If they've been asked to teach...and they've done a damn good job...surely you're trained well enough if you're doing an adequate job.

If someone is proving that they are good as teachers and people are coming to their class and the Head of Centre notices that what is being taught is not the same from year to year, then I don't think it is necessary if they are doing their job properly.

Nevertheless, the majority of trainees did acknowledge the need for at least basic training and no-one denied that other levels should be available to those who wanted it. Opinions were expressed from the hard line:

The LEA benefit — they get better teachers. There should be more training...S1 should be compulsory and if S2 isn't made compulsory, then perhaps S1 should be longer and S2 shorter.

through to:

> We benefit and I should say education benefits from it and the students benefit through it. If I improve my style of teaching (then) surely it is beneficial to students.

> I think (the time and money spent are worthwhile) if it's going to make better teachers and going to give customers value for money.

SECTION 6: OVERVIEW

There is a tendency in an undertaking of this kind to dwell upon the striking, to identify differences even when they are small and to relate the entertaining at the expense of the more fundamental generalities. As a result basic patterns may become muted. To redress this imbalance it needs to be clearly stated that the overall impression to be gained from trainees is one of general satisfaction with what they have experienced upon their courses. They appear largely satisfied with their achieved results, the promotion of understanding and of effective practice. They enjoy and value their courses and moreover they are often unwilling to criticise their trainers in professional terms, let alone personal ones. In the vast majority of cases trainees have developed a deep respect and liking for their course staff and have learnt a great deal from working with them. Yet paradoxically, it is necessary to bear in mind that the very informality, even cosiness, so carefully fostered by trainers might quite unintentionally prevent trainees from fully developing the freedom of critical judgement that they are thought to possess. It remains true that most do not have sufficient experience and skill fully to evaluate their own training or the perception and knowledge to consider alternative organisation, methods and curricula.

To summarise the major findings cited in this chapter; trainees' participation in the training course appears to have been largely controlled by trainers. All courses encouraged full trainee participation in discussion about adult students, class experiences and teaching problems. Group participation also appeared to have been encouraged in discussion of individual teaching activities, variously described as micro-teaching, demonstrations and practice lessons. There was however rather less participation in the management of the courses, though some trainers had invited suggestions for the modifications and inclusion of different topics. There appeared to be practically no participation in the determination of course aims and objectives. As far as trainees were concerned these were predetermined by trainers and 'rightly so' according to some. Less defensible was the apparent ignorance of many trainees of what the objectives of their course actually were. Aims and objectives remained mysterious to some, this confounded the expectation that within the context of the training of teachers of adults an awareness and understanding of objectives would take precedence over most other activities. This deficiency would appear the more critical since it seems that trainees are influenced in their teaching behaviours by the model presented to them.

Trainees believed that there was a positive benefit to be derived from a training group composed of a variety of subject teachers and having mixed adult teaching experience. Though the majority had only had experience of general training they held the view that the skills and problems associated with adult learning and teaching transcended subject boundaries. Indeed there was clear evidence that much was learnt from peers, in particular, knowledge and experience derived from their different subject backgrounds and experience. There were however marked differences even within LEAs in the ways that teachers were initially contacted and informed about the training scheme. Evidence from other sources, notably from untrained teachers, indicates that by no means all teachers knew about courses let alone what was involved and the benefits to be derived from attendance.

178

One major benefit that becomes increasingly apparent during the training course was that of reassurance, in particular, the awareness that trainees were not alone in their task. The discovery that other teachers who ostensibly radiated confidence and efficiency, experienced similar problems and difficulties was for many a revelation. The discovery that colleagues were also apprehensive and doubtful about their role was equally comforting. Participation within a training group, in essence here a self-support group, allowed for the exploration of these very real concerns. Moreover, the opportunity to discuss with other relatively inexperienced teachers and to compare both effective and practical aspects of their teaching role resulted in a lessening of the feelings of inadequacy and self-doubt.

This is not to say that the trainers had no part to play here, indeed the reverse is true. They had the obligation initially to create an informal welcoming atmosphere, to generate expectations and subsequently promote and develop non-threatening exchange within the group. They had to recognise that at least initially they were perceived as the all-knowing expert and the undisputed controller of the group with all the effects upon group dynamics that that entailed. The majority of trainers referred to in this report appeared to have played their parts to good effect; most trainees felt secure and able to share within the group from an early stage — by implication they felt approved of and valued.

A fundamental and discernible effect of training at both S1 and S2 levels was the growth of trainees' self confidence. Though closely allied to reassurance there is evidence of a projection beyond the confines of the training course. A majority of trainees spoke of a growing self-confidence within their own classrooms as well as a greater freedom to participate in training course activities. Some believed that their 'new' confidence was observable by others, students and class visitors alike, and they had no doubt that the effect was wholly beneficial. The overall impression is that there had been an increase in general all-round confidence which includes the range of adult teaching skills — planning, methodologies and relationships — rather than a specific growth of confidence in a particular skill. A variety of factors appear to have led to this change but micro-teaching and supervised teaching practice are certainly involved as are the sharing of experiences with others and perhaps an increasing mastery over the prerequisites of good teaching, preparation and planning.

There does not seem to have been any serious problems of readjustment to the 'student' role. For some at least the experience of being a trainee led them directly to a much greater awareness of the problems of the adult student. There is little doubt that many trainees on both levels of training course had reason to look afresh at the classes they taught and reassess the needs of these students. Group participation, particularly where it involved micro-teaching and simulation and role playing activities must have aided this process of student awareness quite apart from direct teaching and discussion of the topic. Not everyone may have been affected to quite the same extent however as this trainee points out:

> Trainers tend to think of (AE) as the most fantastic thing in the world that ever happens to anyone, they tend to feel...that teachers...should be solving (student) hangups and things, which I think is nothing to do with teaching whatsoever. I only think that it is important that somebody is coming to your class. I don't think that you should delve into the reasons as to why they are...why people are lonely...I really don't think that's relevant because I'm there to do needlework and I'm not there to solve a social problem. They are solving it by the fact that they are coming to the class...they are solving it for themselves, but there was a lot of emphasis on that, the reasons why people come. My own objective is to teach them what they want and what I think they need, these are my two...I think all these other things are irrelevant."

There was further evidence of change in the way that trainees perceived students' learning. Because they were much more aware of how such learning might be organised, facilitated and assessed trainees were less concerned with their own teaching.

Trainees were quite convinced of the part played by assessment and feedback systems in developing their teaching skills as adult educators. They might well subscribe to the view that criticism needs to be sympathetically tempered to the circumstances and personality of the individual but the impression given is that very few would support a non-judgemental approach. Trainee teachers expect and want constructive criticism of their contributions to the training activities and in particular of their work in the classroom from those they believe to be experts, their trainers. They want objective opinion as to what is considered to be 'good' and 'not-so-good', confirmation or otherwise of their own approach to tasks and the opportunity to consider any proposed modifications and revisions. It may be safely presumed that they would agree that for self-evaluation to be viable there is first a need of a yardstick based upon objective criticism and evaluation. A fair proportion of trainees received constructive criticism from their peer groups, they all wanted it from their trainers as well.

What they did get from their trainers were examples — examples of practice of varying quality. The evidence points unequivocally to the conclusion that trainees learned from what their trainers actually did as well as from what they said. It would be difficult to apportion relative importance to these two activities. Yet the finding is clear that process as well as content is of importance in the business of learning about teaching and can be ignored only at some peril. The related aspect of 'designed models' is also of importance here. There was quite a positive response to the observation of experienced teachers at work, both within the course and in Centres, and though there are dangers the 'how not to do it' exemplars were greatly appreciated and facilitated much learning.

Support for trainees was available within most training courses but less so in Centres. There did seem to be a lack of concern for trainees by some Centre Heads and only a minority appear to have been actively engaged in facilitating staff development. Once trainees have left their course Centre Heads might reasonably be expected to provide continued support. Some suggestions about day conferences and courses were made as suitable ways to provide for trainees' subsequent development as teachers, thus:

> They certainly showed interest...he even tried to get a circle going afterwards so we could meet and talk over what was going on...but three of us went three times and we drafted a letter but we got no response (from the others).

Relatively few ideas or innovations were offered. Perhaps the point of completion of an arduous training activity is not the time to seek views about future additional activities. Nevertheless there was a degree of interest from a substantial minority for a continuation of individual training within the Regional Scheme.

For a few trainees the training process involved readjustments in self-knowledge and actualisation:

> I think that my academic standard has gone up...I've raised my IQ and I've raised my standard of education. I've filled in some gaps in my education...I couldn't read and write at 18. I've had to teach myself reading and writing, my academic qualification was very low, it's only through AE that I've been able to get on...and now I'm a (trained) teacher.

For some it involved a mastery of a "survival kit" of basic skills. For many it provided an opportunity to reassess, refine and develop existing sets of skills acquired either 'on the job' or from previous training courses. Most were well disposed:

> I would just like to comment that I have thoroughly enjoyed attending this course and I feel I have gained a lot of knowledge about teaching methods. I feel that I must mention our course tutor who I think made the whole course enjoyable and interesting and he was very understanding.

a few were disillusioned:

> I said to the tutor 'Well, the only reason I'm coming is to get my bits of paper, that's the only reason I'm coming'...I didn't feel that I was learning anything.

and one was pragmatic:

> "They say that unless you are qualified they won't offer you a job in the future but in actual fact the majority aren't qualified...they haven't got that big choice of teachers to choose from so if they can't get a qualified one they are quite happy with an unqualified one"

Despite the caveats the majority seem to have found that:

> The course is generally very interesting and helpful. More adult education part time teachers should be made aware of their existence and the helpfulness of such courses and encouraged to attend.

CHAPTER 6

Conclusions and Implications

The original aims of the project focused upon the training of part-time teachers of adults in the LEA field. We set out to provide an account of the variety of training provision, to describe those groups of people involved in the training process and to examine their qualitative assessment of training and its benefits within the East Midlands Region. The fundamental concept which gave direction to the research was that training is primarily concerned with the modification of the behaviour and attitudes of trainee teachers. The process of change is the manner in which these changes are brought about and its outcomes or benefits are the consequences of such training. As a result of our research, we now know something of the intentions of those who provide training opportunities and the extent to which those who train and those who are trained value the training process. We also now know about the perceived benefits of training from several different standpoints, including those of trainees who are on, or have just finished a course, of teachers who have completed a course and are now teaching, and of those who teach on training courses.

It would not seem appropriate in a conclusion to rehearse in detail all the opinions given to us or all the attitudes expressed. Our respondents have spoken for themselves and we hope we have given due weight to these expressions. Instead we will restate the more significant benefits of training and highlight some of the strengths and shortcomings which may be affecting this process.

There was a degree of consistency among the benefits identified by trainers, teachers and trainees. Moreover they were generally consistent with the results of previous research in this field.[1] Interestingly, some of the benefits were the same as the qualities which students looked for in their teachers. (A tabular comparison of perceived benefits is shown in Table 14). Though it is not easy to measure change, it is evident that teachers *had* changed. There was evidence of:

— an increased confidence in teaching and ways of working in the classroom

— a growing awareness of the needs of adult learners coupled with an increased sensitivity to their learning difficulties

— an increased awareness of the importance of different teaching approaches and methods

— an appreciation of the current provisions and purposes of adult education and their own role as teachers within this.

Of these perceived benefits, increased confidence was most often cited as a major effect of training. It is an element of effective change which may be an important basis for other, subsequent, attitude modification. It also appears to be fundamental to many enactive achievements of trainee teachers. For example, confidence was identified as a basis of:

---

[1] K.T. Elsdon, "Some Practical Implications for Training and Professional Development", in Explorations in Adult Learning and Training for Adult Education, Proceedings of a DES Conference, Cambridge, January 1970 pp 89-103. In the late 60s the work of a group of part-time tutors who had been trained in one region were assessed "before" and "after" attending these courses. The results from this method of identifying the effects of training significantly matched those derived from the approach adopted in this study.

Table 14: Tabular Comparisons of Perceived Benefits against RAC Objectives

RAC SCHEME Course Objectives	TEACHERS	TRAINERS	TRAINEES
To foster his enthusiasm for teaching and throughout it a deeper professional involvement;		It refreshes teachers with the subsequent increased enthusiasm for their work, more likely to enjoy it and do it better.	
To stimulate his enthusiasm for his subject and a continuing interest in it and the emergence of new ideas;			
To enable him to analyse his own personal educational experience and what can be learned from it in relation to the whole range of educational experience;			
To provide him with the capacity for organising his knowledge and selecting appropriate methodological techniques to produce effective learning situations;	Appreciation of the advantage of preparation and planning. Aware of value of using visual aids especially technical equipment;	Use a wider range of teaching methods.	Preparation and planning; attempting new methods and approaches including use of visual aids and materials in relation to subject areas
To enable the teacher to recognise opportunities offered by his own subject, not as an end in itself but (a) as part of a continuing educational process for both teachers and students (b) as part of a continuum of knowledge that involves other subjects, and (c) for students overall personal development:			
To develop in the teacher a sensitivity to the individual student and to the group in terms of background, motivation, expectations and goals leading to appropriate relationships and teaching methods;	Perceive students as equals who can be used as valuable resources in the classroom: more concerned with students' learning difficulties than own teaching problems; increased awareness of student potential; awareness of how individuals are affected by groups and the different types of interaction in class.	They show a greater awareness of students' needs and of the situation in which they are teaching; in particular they become more sensitive to students reactions and to their needs and come to see them as people in their own right.	Increased awareness of students' needs and feelings, of their difficulties of their individuality and learning
To help the teacher to identify the expectation and responsibilities of his role in the educational system with particular reference to the educational setting within which he will work;	Changed the perception of the overall nature of adult education. Helped see teaching in a wider perspective and to understand their place in this;	They come to perceive their class and themselves within a broader context of adult education. This brings about: – a sense of belonging to a larger professional group – increased awareness of resources and support that should be available – increased awareness of purposes and functions of adult education	
To offer opportunities for practice as a teacher with an assessment which will provide adequate assurance of progress and achievement;			

Table 14: (Continued)

RAC SCHEME Course Objectives	PREVIOUS RESEARCH (1970)	STUDENTS	LEA
To help teachers with self presentation, including the importance of dress, manner, voice and speech;		They become more open minded and self critical	Increased confidence
To provide information on resources and materials available to him locally and nationally;	Increased confidence in own teaching ability	An increase in confidence, increases self-esteem	
To reinforce the desire for training and to establish a critical attitude to his own teaching performance and an awareness of the importance of continual in-service training;	Hold class together Transmit confidence to teachers	Personal growth and self-development	
To foster his enthusiasm for teaching and throughout it a deeper professional involvement;			Increasing their understanding of the philosophy and ethos of the adult education service by making them more aware of the implication of how they work, especially for the students and by helping them to improve the structure and organisation of classes
To stimulate his enthusiasm for his subject and a continuing interest in it and the emergence of new ideas;			
To enable him to analyse his own personal educational experience and what can be learned from it in relation to the whole range of educational experience;		A professional attitude; preparation and making demands on people.	
To provide him with the capacity for organising his knowledge and selecting appropriate methodological techniques to produce effective learning situations;	Using a greater variety of teaching methods adapted to changing situations and individuals had learnt to prepare schemes and syllabuses and to make visual aids		
To enable the teacher to recognise opportunities offered by his own subject, not as an end in itself but (a) as part of a continuing educational process for both teachers and students (b) as part of a continuum of knowledge that involves other subjects, and (c) for students' overall personal development;			Benefits for LEA — number of and range of courses on offer — of students attending — numbers of complaints received — helping provide value for money — improve quality of teachers

Table 14: Comparisons of perceived benefits against RAC objectives (Continued)

To develop in the teacher a sensitivity to the individual student and to the group in terms of background, motivation, expectations and goals leading to appropriate relationships and teaching methods;	They were investigating the needs of their students when starting new courses and planning the courses more flexibly and imaginatively than before to meet those needs.	Ability to create relationships with students Treat students as adults in class and are sensitive to their learning needs and difficulties
To help the teacher to identify the expectation and responsibilities of his role in the educational system with particular reference to the educational setting within which he will work;		Aware of social needs of students Qualities: understanding, sympathetic and caring, ready to listen
To offer opportunities for practice as a teacher with an assessment which will provide adequate assurance of progress and achievement;		
To help teachers with self presentation, including the importance of dress, manner, voice and speech;		
To provide information on resources and materials available to him locally and nationally;	Many tutors had matured in the sense of becoming more aware of themselves and the skills they were employing and a desire to continue the training process individually and above all in co-operation with colleagues.	
To reinforce the desire for training and to establish a critical attitude to his own teaching performance and an awareness of the importance of continual in-service training;	Made them more confident as teachers and in ways they were conducting their classes.	

- feeling more self-assured in the classroom
- being more self-reliant and feeling more able to use different teaching methods
- dealing with students' difficulties and problems
- transmitting confidence to students
- sharing and communicating new ideas with others
- making a personal re-assessment of one's work

We do not *know* that reported rises in confidence actually lead to improvements in classroom performance, but everything would suggest they do. Perhaps some teachers continue to teach badly but with greater confidence.

It is clear that teachers do not all benefit in the same way. However, it is significant that heightened awareness of adults as learners as well as increased confidence in teaching come consistently high in the order of benefits as stated by trainers, teachers and trainees. Nor should it be expected that there will be instant, fundamental, change in trainees' teaching behaviours. It is more likely that major modifications will appear over time as a synthesis of training, further teaching experience and subsequent professional support beyond the training course.

At this stage in our thinking about the outcomes of training we do not have any definite answers to a number of critical questions about the nature and extent of this attitude change. For example, do trainees express the opinions of course tutors without personally holding them; are newly acquired attitudes reflected in a teacher's work in class; do they undergo further change again once the teacher is 'on his own' in the classroom? The evidence we have shows that the attitudes expressed by adult education trained teachers some time after their training courses are consistent with those encouraged and engendered *during* training, and the inference is that much affective change is relatively permanent. We therefore draw the conclusion that current training practice has been successful in modifying some of the key attitudes of trainees.

Training is not only concerned with modifying attitudes, it is also concerned with increasing professional and academic knowledge. These elements set out to help teachers understand some of the principles and concepts which underpin teaching and they are taught by drawing on the theoretical disciplines of sociology, philosophy, history and psychology. An analysis of the programmes of training courses suggests emphasis is given to the assimilation of conceptual material. Yet it is interesting to note that cognitive achievements were not so readily perceived as major discernible benefits as were affective gains. This is not to imply that trainees failed to acquire such knowledge; on the contrary, they did gain in understanding, especially in some of the basic concepts underlying such important factors as 'student learning', 'teaching methods', 'course and lesson planning', and 'teaching skills'. This became more evident when trainers spoke of trainees demonstrating improved levels of skill in their teaching 'in micro-teaching activities' and more importantly in their own classrooms. Evidence was offered which suggested that lessons were better planned, greater varieties of methods were employed and the trainees' whole approach was more suited to adult students. These changes were in line with trainers' intentions and the Regional Advisory Council's objectives. (A tabular comparison of trainees' responses to trainers' intentions as expressed by training course process is shown in Table 15.)

In short, there was a general consensus of opinion that training was valuable and relevant. Taking the evidence together we conclude that training helps teachers of adults approach their work in a much more knowledgeable and professional manner than before they were trained.

186

We now turn to what we see as the strengths of the East Midland Regional Training Scheme, and the principles upon which the more effective courses are based. The account given of the history and development of the RAC Training Scheme fails to do justice to the impact that it has had on the thinking and practice of LEA part-time tutor training in Britain. Whilst others can claim to have been the originators of the scheme, the East Midland Regional Advisory Council has pioneered a viable, progressive and tiered approach to training which has proved to be a major innovation in adult education. The crucial factor which emerges is the way that the scheme has evolved organically, beginning with development of resources to ensure the quality of provision, before going on to establish the next stage with a parallel development of assessment and moderation. One of the unique features of the whole initiative has been the co-operation of LEAs, the Universities and later the Polytechnics. Despite the different histories and traditions of universities and local authorities, the scheme has indicated that functional co-operation does work. Given a common commitment, philosophy and mutal respect, all concerned found it natural to work together at different levels of the course programme to worthwhile ends.

The results of this endeavour are the regional courses currently provided.

Stage 1 is a practical everyday course run on county lines but a with a broadly similar content. Most teachers with any but a passing commitment may be expected to undertake it ultimately, though it may be too idiosyncratic to be recognised as other than a local qualification. Nevertheless it can provide a fundamental opportunity for the less experienced teacher to gain confidence and to discover and apply some of the basic skills of adult teaching.

Stage 2 (and Stage 2/City & Guilds 730) can be recognised as a more significant qualification, since there are rather greater demands made upon trainees and the presence of moderators ensures regional equivalence. It may, therefore, be expected to be taken by anyone wishing to be seen as a 'regular' on the books. This level of training, though covering much of the same ground as Stage 1, does so at a more intense level and introduces a more critical analysis of the concepts of adult learning and teaching.

Stage 3 appears to make rather more rigorous demands upon teachers and it is unlikely to appeal to many besides those making a career in teaching adults.

Table 15: Tabular Comparison of Trainees' Responses to Trainers' Intentions as Expressed by Training Course Process

Aspects of Course Process or Structure	Trainers	Trainees
Expectations	More confident: become better teachers: self-development: improve chance of employment: look at work more critically: look at work through students eyes: provide broader view of adult education.	Give confidence: provide qualifications which will improve chances of employment: improve teaching: help to understand student.
Academic Content	Tends to be standard on most courses: little evidence of change.	
Aims and Objectives	Not in forefront of their thinking: no clear distinction between aims and objectives: some found them useful, others not.	Awareness shrouded in vagueness and uncertainty: only a few were aware of training course objectives, lack of clarity in their thinking about differences between aims and objectives. No involvement in setting up course objectives.
Methods	Discussion, case study, lectures: on the whole favoured informal methods which create friendly co-operative atmosphere. Faced with dilemma: committed to student centred learning but felt tendency to be directive.	General approval of informal methods: helped people adjust to the course: encouraging and supportive. Valued and enjoyed practical involvement in discussions and other tasks. But critical of trainers who did not employ the methods they were advocating. Tutorials were considered most helpful.
Course Work and Individual Study	Little mention of written work, especially at Stage 1 level; Idea of study rarely referred to. Reluctant to make demands in terms of written and reading work. Expected more at Stage 2. Careful not to overburden people. No evidence of much advice about returning to study.	Few demands made in the form of reading and written work at first stage. At Stage 2, expectation much clearer and they responded accordingly. Where written work was asked for, it was source of worry to many people.
Residential Weekend	Generally regarded as significant part of a course.	Universal acclaim: tended to be one of the most outstanding features for them.
Learning Through Being a Student	Active steps taken to encourage this: small minority of trainers use experiential methods: majority cautious about this approach	No evidence of their reaction to experiential methods: but clearly developed insights into students' feelings from their own experience.
Sharing Ideas and Experiences	Aware that trainees can bring considerable experience of teaching and of being students. Courses were structured to draw upon and share this.	Considered to be most beneficial to be working with other teachers, especially from different specialisms and backgrounds: particularly valued chance to share experiences and problems.

Table 15: Comparison of trainees' responses to trainers' intentions as expressed by training course process (Continued)

Aspects of Course Process or Structure	Trainers	Trainees
Learning From Teaching	Two kinds of opportunity provided: micro-teaching and teaching one's own class. Very little evidence of observational visits to other teachers. Perceive process of visits to teachers in terms of support and guidance, instead of assessment. Would value help and support of Centre Head.	Micro-teaching universally approved of. Also approval of class visits by Trainers — but considered that constructive criticism was an indispensable element of this process: not always given Less than satisfied with post-course support in Centres.
Applying the Course in Practice	Conscious of the need to relate course to the needs and the real world of teachers. Attempted to make courses flexible: however no trainers gave trainees a major say in how their courses were run but many gave trainees scope to follow individual interests.	Little involvement in course planning: not consulted about major elements of their courses. For many this was apparently successful but not so for others.
Helping People to Teach their Subjects	Aware of the need but were uncertain about exact purposes and methods: appeared to be an area of low priority.	Many hoped for subject-based element which would help match general principles of teaching and learning to what they teach.
The Course As a Model for Good Practice	Were conscious of the need to "practice what they preach": but not fully aware of the importance of course process.	Course process exerts a powerful influence upon them: closely observed and analysed trainers as models of teaching. For many trainees this appeared to be as important as formal content.
Evaluation (i) course itself	Informal, unstructured methods: conscious of the need to improve their techniques and to be more objective. Only rarely was the need to evaluate the subsequent effects of training mentioned. No-one distinguished between process and outcomes	No clear understanding of the concept of evaluation or the techniques required.
(ii) assessment of trainees	No standard approach at Stage 1 level but more agreement for Stage 2: no real awareness of purposes of assessment: unhappy about the concept of "grading".	Expressed strong views that all work should be assessed: strong expressed need for comment, feedback and constructive criticism: expect to receive critical judgements about their work.

An innovation of this nature cannot work without professional and committed staff. The vast majority of training staff within the scheme were just that. Compared with school teaching, social work or youth work, adult education is the only area where the functions of line manager and trainer are combined. This duality allows adult education trainers to meet the crucial criterion of being up-to-date practitioners. There can be no doubt that practically all trainers were perceived by trainees as being highly credible; they were recognised as having substantial involvement in adult education and experience as teachers of adults. There was, moreover, a positive relationship between effective courses and the ability of trainers to apply to training key principles derived from their own practical adult education experience. The more significant of these would appear to be:

— the use of informal, co-operative methods which allow for maximum active participatory learning

— the use of the whole range of teaching approaches

— the provision of opportunities for trainees to apply different methods to what they teach in order to assess the relevance to their subject

— an emphasis within teaching approaches upon student learning rather than teacher performance

— the provision of opportunities for practical teaching in order that trainees may put into practice what they have learnt

— the promotion of a constant inter-play between theory and practice of adult teaching and learning

— the establishment of an atmosphere where mutual and constructive criticism could become a natural part of the course

— the avoidance of abstract approaches

— the promotion of a mutually supportive group

— the exploitation of the experience available in a mixed group of teachers with different backgrounds and subject expertise

Our research indicates that many of these principles were being applied much of the time on the majority of training courses within the region. We draw the conclusion that there are worthwhile and valuable training opportunities provided within courses for the part-time teacher of adults.

There was a general awareness among trainers of the over-riding principle that a training course should be a model based upon sound adult education practice and that they themselves should 'practise what they preach'. Many attempted to apply such a model and some were clearly successful. However, the evidence shows that there was some lack of perception of the full extent to which trainees observed, evaluated and critically analysed them as models of adult teaching. Although differences in trainers' awareness of the importance of process is perhaps one of degree there were other more fundamental shortcomings apparent in training courses.

Stage 1 and 2 Courses may be described as being rather traditional and prescriptive; trainers frequently determined trainees' learning needs and designed the content and methods in the light of these. Whilst trainers did exercise flexibility in their teaching and course management, on the whole it was apparent that courses were designed so that they usually decided not only what trainees were going to study but also how they were going to do it. What this model frequently lacks is an involvement of trainees in the relevant decision making process about course objectives, subject content and methods of assessment. It may be argued that trainees are not initially able to make substantial contributions in some of these areas though a basic assumption of the RAC Scheme is that attention should be given to:

> The extent to which students may have been involved in decisions on the objectives and activities on the course

It must be recognised that this does pose a genuine dilemma for anyone trying to implement such participation.

The Regional Advisory Council 'subject' objectives, especially at Stage 2 level, are founded on the assumption that training should assist the trainee teacher to think more critically and imaginatively about the subject taught and about the principles upon which it is based. The purpose of this element is not simply to 'update' or 'extend' subject knowledge but to introduce trainees to the concept of 'subject' as well as to the skills required to realise its full potential within the classroom. However, for a variety of reasons — need to fulfil other course obligations, the relative importance of the concept in trainers' thinking, the uncertainty of how to approach it, and the lack of more detailed guidance from the Regional Advisory Council — little time appears to have been devoted to meeting this objective.[1] This is an area of the RAC Scheme which may need to be re-examined along with a number of other shortcomings listed below. Examples of these are:

— a lack of observational visits to adult classes

— a reduction in opportunities to attend residential weekends

— a lack of detailed monitoring and assessment of 'supervised' teaching practice

— rather modest reading and writing requirements

— ambiguous attitudes towards, and understanding of, aims and objectives

— low levels of constructive feedback, both of teaching activities and students' course work

— uncertain methods of course evaluation

— a less than clear distinction between training course process and its outcomes in terms of trainees', and their students', benefits

— a wariness of making too great demands upon trainees' thinking and assumptions about their work as teachers

— an absence of an adequate conceptual analysis of adult teaching and criteria of professional competence

It should not be judged that these shortcomings were found in each and every course, though they did appear to a greater or lesser extent in many. Some of these problems may be a reflection of a weakening of the RAC machinery and the regional network. Others, particularly where they depend heavily on resources are certainly due to public expenditure cuts. Among the serious consequences are the abolition of the sub-committee responsible for the supervision of the scheme and the assessment of course standards, and the present lack of opportunity for trainers to share experiences and to learn from each other. Other shortcomings may be a result of the somewhat ambiguous manner in which the expectations

---

[1] In the year following the Research, one county has in fact re-introduced complementary subject based 'modules' at Stage 1 level run as additional provision to the 36 hours.

and objectives of the scheme are expressed. Yet some do remain the responsibility of those who are involved in the planning, organisation and teaching of training courses. The continued success of the Regional Training Scheme may depend not only upon curriculum change but also upon the creation or restoration of organisational structures and the development of initiatives which will lead to improvements.

One central issue raised throughout our discussions with the field was the singular lack of counselling and support for part-time teachers beyond their training courses. In a service in which the thin crust of full-time staff and the large substratum of part-time teachers are becomingly increasingly professional, the Centre Heads and others with similar responsibilities are the crucial link. Yet it is clear that little is being done to enable them to do this vital aspect of their job, for it could be said that "the service hinges upon them, but there is no hinge". Suggestions were made by trainers that Centre Heads should be included in course training teams as well as receiving concurrent training themselves. Whatever the outcome, our findings assert that teachers continue to develop and acquire skills after formal training ends. They need encouragement and support in this crucial process and moreover their experiences of isolation need to be mitigated.

Interestingly, although the Responsible Bodies do not have a clearly formulated policy for training their part-time staff, they claim to be strong in offering individual guidance and support to them. Indeed their whole training effort seems to lie in this direction, for there was no evidence of formal training activities. The specialist subject bodies appear to span the two approaches; they not only provide training courses but they also offer an appropriate back-up and support system for their members. One of the striking features of many of these organisations is their insistence upon, and maintenance of, high standards of subject competence. There can be no doubt that all the major providers have something to learn from each other in this as in other areas of training. The Regional Scheme would benefit from an approach to training which utilise *all* existing resources in a more co-ordinated manner. We believe that there is a need for co-operation and exchange of training information between relevant agencies in the field.

Few teachers were opposed to training *per se* though some did speak of its irrelevance to their needs. Where they had prior experience of training and of teaching they believed that they did not require the same intensity of exposure to basic teaching skills as did untrained teachers. Where they possessed high levels of subject competence they were less willing to take up the general training offered by the LEA, preferring the support offered by their subject organisations. The group of teachers who were totally resistant to training were those who taught a subject which was also their full-time employment. These reactions suggest that different groups of teachers may indeed have different training needs. We conclude that a regional training scheme should not assume that all teachers should be trained in the same way regardless of their background and experience.

Our findings suggest some definite pointers for future training policy and practice. These are set out below.

It should be recognised that the acquisition of teaching competence and expertise does not arise simply from attending training courses. Learning to teach is a continuous process of development which consists of a number of inter-related elements beginning with interview and selection. Appropriate support and training must be readily available to a teacher throughout his career. This requires a policy of staff development which, laying proper claim to resources, can embrace the continuing and changing needs of all adult educators. All else springs from this.

The Regional Advisory Council

The East Midlands Advisory Council was a pioneer in developing and establishing a viable and realistic training scheme for part-time teachers of adults where little else had previously existed. This major achievement is now well recognised and valued but the initiatives established should not be eroded even in times of economic stringency. To maintain the momentum, there is need to

— evolve clearer and unambiguous statements of the Scheme's expectations, aims and objectives

— re-examine the infra-structure which manages, co-ordinates and monitors the standards and quality of the total scheme and provide means by which these may be properly maintained

— consider both inter-regional equivalence and recognition of Stage 2 qualifications and intra-regional equivalance of Stage 1 courses

— develop and encourage progressive, innovative and experimental ideas and practices

— forge and co-ordinate links with subject specialist training agencies in the field

— become part of an information resource and forum to allow trainers and teachers to keep up-to-date with and share methods, ideas and materials

The scheme should, overall, allow for maximum flexibility and interpretation consonant with the maintenance of standards, to meet the ever changing role and needs of adult teachers.

The Local Education Authorities

There is a need for a more comprehensive and well defined LEA adult education staff development training policy encompassing not only training course development but also the provision of additional support. Such a policy should reflect improvements in the professional status and expertise of all personnel involved in the service. Elements of this policy should include:

— better information and communication about training policy and the provision and availability of training activities and support for all teachers of adults

— co-operation between LEAs in providing publicity and in optimising the provision and location of courses, etc. These might be jointly provided but they need to be made available when and where the demand is apparent, particularly at Stage 2 level.

— the continued use of full-time, experienced, practising adult educators as trainers

— a proper recognition of trainers' commitment to training, with formal acknowledgement in their job specification of the time and work involved.

The regional network of trainers is one of the fundamental strengths of the scheme. To achieve its full effect it needs, continuously, to provide opportunities for new and existing trainers to develop their knowledge and practical skills. This could be achieved by the provision of a variety of opportunities to:

— induct relatively new trainers for each stage into the knowledge, understanding and skills required for the task

— allow all trainers to develop their training skills to a more advanced level

— promote the exchange of innovation and expertise

— employ qualified and experienced part-time teachers as members of training schemes.

Local Support

There is need for a fundamental reassessment of the training role of Centre Heads and others responsible for local management of adult education for the full benefits of training to be realised. It would seem necessary to:

— involve them in active dissemination of information about training policy, provision and the recruitment of trainees

— develop their supervisory, counselling and support skills

— encourage their direct association and/or involvement in training courses

— recognise their staff development/training functions with formal acknowledgement of the time and work involved.

Curriculum and Methods

Without rehearsing all the observations and conclusions made about curriculum and methods, we highlight several points concerning training courses themselves. They are that:

— informal participatory methods should continue to predominate

— a 'mixed' group of teachers possessing different specialisms and experiences should continue to be the norm

— there should be a greater awareness of the fundamental importance that process has upon trainees and the impact that the 'trainer as model' has upon them

— constructive criticism of trainees' teaching and learning activities should be offered as a matter of normal course practice. Moreover, it should be recognised as a necessary and vital precursor to the establishment of trainee self-evaluation

— re-examinations of the purposes of assessment of trainees and of the evaluation of courses should be undertaken

— a reconsideration of the principle of trainee participation and involvement in course decision making should be made

— more attention be given to the application of general principles to the practice of specialist teachers

— further consideration should be given to the liberalising of trainees' attitudes, particularly with regard to subject specialisms

— the potential of experiential learning should not be neglected, though it is not presently recommended as a principal component of training.

CONCLUSION

Taken as a whole, this research project has demonstrated growing skills and sureness of touch in many areas and in many respects of training. It has also shown that there are some departures from expected standards and from the requirements of the scheme. Nevertheless we are left with the overriding impression that training has proved to be beneficial to those who undertake it. There are positive increases in teachers' academic and professional knowledge, modifications of their attitudes to adult students and to teaching, and changes in their classroom practice.
The consensus of the value of training provided was universal; therefore, such training should become general and should be further developed.

The timing of this enquiry may seem unfortunate when resources are short and morale in the service is low, but it is perhaps easier to raise the quality of teaching when quantity is limited because all are aware of the importance of 'value for money'. When expansion comes, it should be from a base line of high quality.

In the final analysis, a training scheme such as the one we have investigated could not succeed without the enthusiasm of part-time teachers. They derive no material advantage from training yet they give generously of their time and often make real financial and personal sacrifices to attend. Above all, they have a strong desire to improve the quality of their work as teachers. The comments they made over and over again convey the sense of commitment to something which is simply more than a job. Where training is regarded as being relevant to both personal and professional needs, the part-time teacher will respond positively to, and derive benefit from it. The present regional scheme has demonstrated the validity of this premise.

SOME IMPLICATIONS FOR FURTHER RESEARCH

The completion of this project has uncovered several further issues connected with teaching and training which would justify and profit from further research.

One worthwhile area of investigation would be the careful monitoring and evaluation of the change process as it is happening. This might employ a longitudinal approach beginning with a group of intending teachers of adults and following them through the training process. This 'before, during and after' investigation would allow not only the identification of change, but also the change agents and critical incidents that may promote it. A comparison with a matched group of teachers not undergoing training would provide some measure of the magnitude of such change and determine the relative effects of training plus experience against experience alone.

A second likely area concerns practising teachers of adults. Whilst there may quite rightly be disagreement with the four categories of teachers employed in this report, there is, nevertheless, clear evidence that there are different groupings of adult education teachers. They have different backgrounds and experience and they have different training needs.

Further research could elucidate a detailed and perhaps more appropriate classification and description, and determine the particular training needs of those involved.

It is axiomatic of all adult education teacher training that the major beneficiary must be the adult student. Doubtless, the trainee teacher derives personal value and satisfaction from training, both as person and educator, but the final arbiter must be 'what does teacher training do for the student in class'? We have still little real understanding of how the outcomes of teacher training affect adult students. Thus, a third important area of study requires that a variety of analytical and evaluative techniques be employed, calling upon appropriate contributory disciplines, to identify the critical factors involved. Since learning is about change we need to discover precisely what aspects of modifiable teacher behaviour lead to student change and best facilitate learning. Such a determination of outcomes, by observation, by report, by analytical techniques, would help guide further thinking about the nature and process of training. It would not only evaluate what is current practice but also point to the necessary modifications.

A further area of research interest is the role and functions of Centre Heads and others responsible for the local management of adult education. There is a need for a much more detailed investigation than we were able to undertake into the attitudes and opinions of Centre Heads towards training, the constraints that act upon them, their current practice, their future commitment, and so on. It is evident that teachers need support and guidance in their centres and Centre Heads have an important part to play. We, and they, need to know how this support can be most effectively and efficiently provided.

REFERENCES

ACACE (1981) *Specialist training for part-time teachers of adults,* April 1981.

ACSTT (1978) ACSTT II: *The training of Adult Education and Part-time Further Education Teachers: Second Report.*

DES (1970) *Explorations in adult learning and training for Adult Education.*

DES (1981) *The Provision of training for part-time teachers in Further Education in relation to the recommendations of the second report of the Advisory Committee on the Supply and Training of Teachers* (FE Sub Committee)

Elsdon, K.T., 1970, "Some practical implications for training and professional development" in: *Explorations in Adult Learning and Training for Adult Education,* Proceedings of the Cambridge DES Conference, Jan. 1970.

Elsdon, K.T., 1973, The East Midlands' Scheme, *Adult Education,* 46, 4.

Elsdon, K.T., 1977, "Some possibilities of regional co-operation in Adult Education", unpublished paper for *DES Course N88,* 11-14 July, 1977.

EMRAC (1978) *The role and training of the part-time Head of Centre.*

NIAE (1966) "Recruitment and training of staff for Adult Education", *Adult Education.* 38,6.

NIAE *Teaching Adults — A practical training aid for part-time tutors.*

NIAE (1982) "Training the educators of adults", NIAE Monograph, in: *National Institute review of existing research in Adult & Continuing Education*

Rogers, J., (1969) (Ed), *Teaching on equal terms,* BBC

Rogers, J., (1969) (Ed) *Adults in Education,* BBC

Rogers, J., (1977) *Adults Learning,* O.U. (2nd Ed).

Sullivan, T., and Daines, J., (1981) "Economic Analysis and Training of Adult Educators" in *Policy and Research in Adult Education,* B. Harvey, J. Daines, D. Jones and J. Wallis (Eds), Dept. of Adult Education, University of Nottingham.

GLOSSARY

ACACE	Advisory Council for Adult and Continuing Education
ACSTT	Advisory Committee on the Supply and Training of Teachers (FE Sub-Committee)
ACSTT II	Second ACSTT Report (1978)
ATO	Area Training Organisation
B Ed	Bachelor of Education
CBA	Cost Benefit Analysis
CGLI 730 C&G 730	City and Guilds of London Institute, Course 730 Certificate for Teachers of Further Education
CGLI 942	City and Guilds of London Institute, Course 942, Certificate in the Teaching of Adults
DES	Department of Education and Science
East Midlands	The Counties of Derbyshire, Nottinghamshire, Lincolnshire, Leicestershire and Northamptonshire
EMRAC	East Midlands Regional Advisory Council
EMRIAE	East Midlands Regional Institute of Adult Education
FE	Further Education
HE	Higher Education
HMI	Her Majesty's Inspector
LEA	Local Educational Authority
PGCE	Post Graduate Certificate in Education
RAC	Regional Advisory Council
RB	Responsible Body (for the provision of Adult Education) — the Universities and the WEA
WEA	Workers' Education Association
SPSS	Statistical Package for the Social Sciences

THE APPENDICES

1   "CBA — Collecting the Data"

2   List of Organisations written to by the Project

3   *Extracts from:* Regional Advisory Council for the Organisation of Further Education in the East Midlands. 'Regional Scheme of Training for Part-time Teachers in Non-vocational Adult Education'.

4   *Extracts from:* The Second ACSTT Report. *The Training of Adult Education and Part-time Further Education Staff.*

5   Subjects taught in Adult Education Classes

6   Examples of Training Course patterns

7   Examples of Training Course Syllabus

APPENDIX 1: "CBA — COLLECTING THE DATA"

The original proposal included the use of Cost Benefit Analysis as an evaluative technique to test the efficiency and effectiveness of training. This appendix sets down the reasons for the abandonment of this analysis.[1]

In order to test a series of hypotheses on the influence of training by means of this technique, a measurement of both costs and benefits had to be obtained. Costs were taken to be the capital costs of setting up the training schemes plus the total operating costs. Benefits were taken to be the willingness of students to allocate time, effort and finance in order to obtain the services of adult education classes. At its simplest, it was hypothesised that students received more benefit from being in classes taught by adult trained teachers rather than untrained teachers.

Costs: The first return from LEAs on costs of training and training courses showed that there were obvious difficulties involved in the identification of specific and precise costs within the totals of the adult education budget. Capital and operating costs probably could have been derived from other less direct sources but in the event, the inability to collect the data on benefits made further enquiry superfluous.

Benefits: Measurements of individual student's willingness to make various payments for attendance at classes were to be obtained by means of a questionnaire applied in the class. Whilst a small scale pilot only hinted at the problems, it became dramatically apparent from visits to several adult classes that students (a) had difficulty in making responses to certain items, particularly hypothetical questions relating to present and future class attendance, and (b) though quite amenable, were unwilling to devote much of their paid-for class time to research.

The project did not have the necessary resources in time or manpower to develop relationships with relatively large numbers of classes which might have facilitated data collection, let alone undertake individual interviews. Consequently, it was decided that this element of the overall research design would have to be abandoned.

---

[1] For a more detailed account see:
Sullivan, T. and Daines, J., (1981) "Economic Analysis and Training of Adult Educators", in *Policy and Research in Adult Education,* B. Harvey, J. Daines, D. Jones and J. Wallis (Eds), Department of Adult Education, University of Nottingham.

APPENDIX 2: LIST OF ORGANISATIONS WRITTEN TO BY THE PROJECT

Amateur Fencing Association
Amateur Swimming Association
Badminton Association of England and Wales
British Amateur Gymnastics Association
British Horse Society
British Judo Association
British Red Cross Society
British Theatre Association
British Wheel of Yoga
City and Guilds of London Institute
College of Handicrafts
College of Preceptors
Co-operative Union
English Basketball Association
English Bridge Teachers Association
English Golf Union
English Schools Badminton Association
Football Association
Guild of Professional Teachers of Dancing
Institute of Iyenga Yoga
Institute of Linguists
International Dance Teachers Association
Keep Fit Association
Lawn Tennis Association
Liverpool Craft Teachers' Certificate
National Council for Proficiency Testing,
　　National Agricultural Centre

National Federation of Women's Institutes
National Federation of Young Farmers' Clubs
National Joint Council of Approved Driving
　　Instructors' Organisations
National Marriage Guidance Council
National Playing Fields Association
National Union of Townswomen's Guilds
Physical Education Association
Pre-Retirement Association
Pre-School Playgroups Association
Royal Automobile Club
Royal Life Saving Association
Royal Scottish Country Dance Society
Royal Society of Arts
Royal Yachting Association
St. John's Ambulance
Samaritans
Slimnastics Association
Sports Council
Swing Into Shape
Squash Rackets Association
Workers' Educational Association
Yoga for Health Foundation
Young Men's Christian Association
Young Women's Christian Association
Youth Leadership, Brunel University

APPENDIX 3: EXTRACTS FROM: REGIONAL ADVISORY COUNCIL FOR THE ORGANISATION OF FURTHER EDUCATION IN THE EAST MIDLANDS

REGIONAL SCHEME OF TRAINING FOR PART-TIME TEACHERS IN NON-VOCATIONAL ADULT EDUCATION

In May 1971 the Regional Advisory Council recommended to the Constituent Local Education Authorities and Responsible Bodies in the Region the establishment of a REGIONAL SCHEME OF TRAINING FOR PART-TIME TEACHERS IN NON-VOCATIONAL ADULT EDUCATION.

It had been recognised for some time that the training of such teachers in the Region was desirable. It had been recognised also that many Local Education Authorities in the Region already made provision in various forms for the training of part-time teachers in adult education. It became apparent that it would be valuable for there to be co-ordination of the provision of training within the Region and for that training to admit of a form of certification that not only would be valid within the Region but also could have currency elsewhere.

At that time it was felt there existed no form of training leading to national certification which was suited entirely to the needs and interests of part-time teachers of adults in non-vocational adult education, nor one which, in many cases, would take account of their particular qualifications and experience. Moreover, it was felt that within the Regional Scheme there should be sufficient flexibility to allow modes of assessment which would take account of such factors as well as of the especial objectives and motivation of the teachers concerned. In order to accommodate such varying experience, needs and motivation of part-time teachers of adults within the Region, therefore, the Scheme as a whole was conceived as comprising three consecutive stages.

As the basis for courses for STAGE I and STAGE II within the Scheme certain objectives have been defined and a Course Syllabus proposed. It should be noted that it has been assumed that those part-time teachers of adults admitted to State I or Stage II Courses would have satisfied already, or would be in the process of acquiring, certain requirements of their employing bodies in respect of their subject knowledge and/or skills.

STAGE I COURSES — It has been agreed that it is appropriate for Local Education Authorities individually or in association to provide Stage I Courses in accordance with their perceived needs and resources and to be responsible for the awards which they carry. It was suggested, however, that any form of Certification issued by a Local Education Authority in respect of its Stage I course might contain a reference to its having been designed to include at least the fulfilment of the requirements recommended for a Stage I course within the Regional Scheme of Training. In the proposed Course syllabus Module 'A' is intended to indicate what might be included in a Stage I Course so that it might form the basis of a Stage II Course. Insofar as it seems possible to suggest a duration of Stage I Courses it is felt that something in the order of 36 hours of tuition would seem to be a minimum. It seems likely that some part-time teachers of adults will not wish to proceed further than the completion of Stage I Course of Training.

STAGE II COURSES — It has been agreed that Stage II Courses also should be provided by Local Education Authorities either individually or in association. In the case of such courses, however it has been agreed that they should lead to the award of a REGIONAL CERTIFICATE IN ADULT EDUCATION. Stage II Courses of training are seen as requiring a greater degree of commitment on the part of those part-time teachers of adults who elect or are selected to take them. Although, as in the case of Stage I Courses, it does not seem either possible or desirable to prescribe a precise length for Stage II Courses, 100 hours of tuition are regarded as presenting a reasonable guide. Since Module 'A' is covered normally by Stage I Courses, for most entrants the content of Stage II Courses is expected to include that in Modules 'B', 'C', 'D' and 'E'. In some cases evidence of alternative preparatory study would be required. To advise on matters such as those concerned with selection procedures, standardisation and staffing of Stage II Courses the Council has appointed an ASSESSMENT OF TRAINING SUB-COMMITTEE through its Consultative Committee for Non-Vocational Adult Education. Members of this Sub-Committee are to be restricted to a relatively small number of persons with specialist expertise in adult education in the sector of either the Local Education Authorities or the Responsible Bodies. (A copy of the Terms of Reference of the Assessment of Training Sub-Committee is attached to this document as Appendix B). It has been recognised that Local Education Authorities and Responsible Bodies in the Region would welcome guidance on the procedures recommended for adoption in providing Stage II Courses and, in particular, on the issue of moderation. Similarly, because of their involvement in a new and important area of work, the need has been recognised to assist moderators in carrying out their task.

Just as some part-time teachers of adults were expected to wish or to be advised to go no further than Stage I Courses, so it was thought likely that it would be appropriate for a further number not to proceed automatically to Stage III Courses.

STAGE III COURSES — It has been agreed that Stage III Courses should lead to the award of INSTITUTIONS OF HIGHER EDUCATION in the Region. The entry requirements to such courses are seen as those which would be determined by such Institutions. The successful completion of a Stage II Course of training is expected to grant exemption from some parts or part of Stage III Courses.

Alongside the recommendation that there be established a Regional Scheme of Training for Part-time Teachers of Adults the need has been appreciated to ensure the adequate training and supply of those responsible for effecting the training of the part-time teachers of adults concerned. Whenever there has appeared sufficient demand, therefore, the Regional Advisory Council had invited an Area Training Organization to mount in association with the Department of Education and Science TRAINING OF TRAINERS COURSES.

It will have been clear that the Regional Scheme of Training for Part-time Teachers of Adults essentially has emerged from and called upon the collective experience of Local Education Authorities in the Region in providing training for part-time teachers of adults. At the same time, however, representatives of the Responsible Bodies have been involved in the discussion and planning of the Regional Scheme and have expressed interest in and support for it. Furthermore, the Regional Scheme has evolved in response to the needs of part-time teachers of adults employed by Local Education Authorities in the Region and will continue to change if those needs and other considerations make change desirable.

May 1976

GENERAL OBJECTIVES

To help the teacher:

(a) to understand the purpose of Adult Education as it at present exists (this may include a knowledge of its history);

(b) to understand the organisation so that he may work better with people in the system, e.g. the Principal, the Caretaker;

(c) to teach the subject liberally; and

(d) (the most important objective): to understand his students better; to be sensitive to them as individuals; to be responsive to the whole range of their needs; to be more aware of them as students with learning problems; and to be responsive to them as a group with all the possibilities that this offers for more exciting and stimulating situations in the classroom.

COURSE OBJECTIVES

(i) to foster the teacher's enthusiasm for teaching and through it a deeper professional involvement;

(ii) to stimulate the teacher's enthusiasm for his subject and a continuing interest in it and in the emergence of new ideas;

(iii) to enable the teacher to analyse his own personal educational experience and what can be learnt from it in relation to the whole range of educational experience;

(iv) to provide the teacher with a capacity for organising his knowledge and selecting appropriate methodological techniques to produce effective learning situations;

(v) to enable the teacher to recognise opportunities offered by his own subject, not as an end in itself, but (a) as part of a continuing educational process for both teacher and students, (b) as part of a continuum of knowledge that involves other subjects, and (c) for the student's overall personal development;

(vi) to develop in the teacher a sensitivity to the individual student and to the group in terms of background, motivation, expectations and goals leading to appropriate relationships and teaching methods.

(vii) to help the teacher to identify the expectations and responsibilities of his role in the educational system with particular reference to the educational setting within which he will work;

(viii) to offer opportunities for practice as a teacher with an assessment which will provide adequate assurance of progress and achievement;

(ix) to help the teacher with self-presentation including the importance of dress, manner, voice and speech;

(x) to provide the teacher with information on resources and materials available to him locally and nationally; and

(xi) to reinforce in the teacher the desire for training and to establish a critical attitude to his own teaching performance and an awareness of the importance of continued in-service training.

CHARACTERISTICS OF TRAINEE TEACHERS

It is assumed that the following behavioural characteristics of entrants would have been identified at selection:—

(i) a craft competence;

(ii) adequate motivation to teach and enthusiasm for their teaching;

(iii) a reasonable degree of articulation and audibility;

(iv) a sense of order which might show itself in a logic of approach i.e. they would have a reasonable capacity for an ordered approach to their teaching; and

(v) a recognition of the need for training and a willingness to seek help.

The following were identified as the kind of weaknesses that untrained part-time teachers might exhibit:-

(vi) a tendency to look back on their most recent educational experience as a guide to their future activities in the teaching situation;

(vii) a concentric attitude to the subject which they are teaching, i.e. an attitude which is inward looking and syllabus bound;

(viii) a narrowness of methodological approach;

(ix) an under-estimation of motivation and aspiration of their students;

(x) an inability to relate adequately to students as people and to the life and work of the institution;

(xi) a lack of personal confidence in their own ability as teachers, and

(xii) an ignorance of resources and materials available to them.

PROPOSED COURSE SYLLABUS

MODULE A.

Induction

The induction period should touch briefly on all element of the course and should aim at establishing a common vocabulary. It should, therefore, include discussion and analysis of the personal educational experience of the group and particularly those which are relevant to adult education; it should enable intending teachers to consider by means of visits and discussion the place of adult education in contemporary society and the environment in which non-vocational adult education is operating; it should establish the fundamental principle of adult education as a joint activity between teacher and taught and the importance of human relationships.

MODULE B.

The Student

The social and economic background of the individual students, their expectations, motivations, needs, interests and activities;

Individual and group behaviour; inter-personal relationships;

The class as a human group and relationships between students, class, centre and community;

Adult learning processes and unsupervised learning; and

Assessment, evaluation and the place of tests, examinations and records.

MODULE C.

The Teacher and the Teaching Method

Motiviation and expectations of the teacher;

The teacher's job, his role in the learning situation and the need for continuous self-assessment;

Teacher/student relationships in the light of adult learning processes;

Good teaching: what are the criteria?

Observations of a variety of adult classes;

Discussion of common and individual observation, success and problems;

*The organisation of syllabuses and schemes of work;

*Lesson preparation, methods of presentation;

*Preparation and use of teaching aids;

Preparation and participation in practical teaching exercises for analysis and discussion;

Self-presentation, including the importance of dress, manner, voice and speech;

*Resources and materials available to the teacher; and

Opportunities for further in-service training.

*Arrangements should be made for teachers of specialist subjects to receive help and guidance in the application of general teaching principles to their particular subject.

206

MODULE D.

The Organisation of Adult Education

The tradition, aims and purpose of adult education and the educational and social aims of an Adult Centre;

The place of Adult Education in the general educational system;

A comparative study of the local organisation including the range of facilities available, the roles of the personnel involved, the place of the part-time teacher in the structure and his professional position; and

Adult education and society at home and abroad.

MODULE E.

Probationary Teaching

Under the guidance of an experienced tutor an intending teacher should undertake a period of successful teacher practice.

The specialist subject tutor should meet the student periodically to discuss the progress being made. A report could be made after eight class meetings and at the completion of the module. The meetings need not be consecutive, e.g. where a teacher has offered six-meeting courses, assessment would be made during the second course.

INTRODUCTION AND INDUCTION COURSES

Local Education Authorities may wish to consider the establishment of two other elements in addition to the modules outlined above:

"TASTER" COURSES

These might well form part of the Authority's selection procedures and would give potential teachers some idea of what is involved in teaching Adult Education classes without any commitment or guarantee of employment. It would help them to decide whether they were sufficiently equipped to undergo a course of teacher training while at the same time offering the Authority an opportunity of deciding whether they were suitable for employment.

INTRODUCTORY COURSES

These would be for teachers newly-appointed to their first teaching post and needing some guidance and help before they had any class contact. Guidance on lesson planning, teacher-student relations and what to expect when teaching adult students should be essential parts of such a course.

May 1976

ASSESSMENT OF TRAINING SUB-COMMITTEE: TERMS OF REFERENCE

(i) to receive and consider applications for the recognition of Stage II courses;

(ii) to review the methods of assessment on such courses and to appoint moderators;

(iii) to recommend the approval of exemptions from part or parts of Stage II courses and to make recommendations on the entry qualifications for, and the admission of students to, such courses;

(iv) to receive and consider assessments of candidates on Stage II courses and to recommend the award of Certificates;

(v) to maintain a register of those who have successfully completed Stage II courses or individual modules of Stage II courses;

(vi) to maintain close links with the LEAs, Universities and other appropriate bodies on the relationships of Stage I, Stage II and Stage III courses;

(vii) to review panels of trainers for Stage II courses and to make recommendations on their qualifications and on the need for training of trainers courses;

(viii) to report annually on the progress of the Regional Training Schemes for part-time teachers of Non-Vocational Adult Education in the Region.

October 1976

NOTES FOR GUIDANCE ON THE RECOGNITION OF COURSES LEADING TO THE REGIONAL CERTIFICATE IN ADULT EDUCATION

Objectives and Content:

The Regional Advisory Council has accepted in principle the objectives outlined in the attached document. The outline course syllabus appended to the document is recommended as the basis for the content of courses of training within the Regional Scheme of Training. Courses submitted for recognition should be related to this outline syllabus.

Duration:

Whilst not wishing to lay down a specific minimum of hours, the Council might generally expect that approximately 100 hours, extending over one year, of learning in groups will be necessary in most cases. In addition, a considerable amount of time will need to be devoted by students to directed private study and assignments. Supervised practical teaching should be an integral part of the course of training and will require time above that already indicated.

Course Directors/Tutors:

It is expected that those employed as course directors and tutors will have had considerable experience of teaching adults and will possess those qualities expected in persons involved in the training of teachers. In addition, it is desirable that they themselves participate regularly in appropriate courses for tutors.

Moderation:

It is envisaged that the Council's primary role will be to assess a course of training and only where necessary to assess an individual student. The Council, therefore, will look for evidence that a particular course of training has been, is being and will continue to be conducted in such a way as to give reasonable assurance of the achievement of:

    (i) the objectives of the course;

    (ii) standards comparable with those of similar courses provided in other parts of the region;

    (iii) the fair and proper assessment of students.

The Regional Advisory Council will appoint moderators and will look to moderators for reports on courses. A copy of such reports will be sent to the Local Education Authority concerned.

It is expected that moderators will be professional adult educators from within the region, selected because of their involvement in the Regional Scheme of Training.

It is important that moderators should maintain common objectives and that they should attend meetings of the Council's Assessment of Training Sub-Committee as necessary. Moderators should also have opportunities to discuss any matters concerning a course with its director and tutors and to visit the course at various stages.

Fees and expenses of moderators will be met as part of the costs of training incurred by the Local Education Authority providing the course. A moderation fee and appropriate expenses for travel and subsistence, as agreed from time to time between Local Education Authorities, should be paid by a Local Education Authority to the person(s) appointed to act as moderator(s) for its course(s).

The Council, therefore, expects that a Local Education Authority wishing to provide a course of training leading to certification by the Regional Advisory Council will need to ensure the following:

A. Before the commencement of a course

    (i) the propriety of the objectives, syllabus, modes of recruitment and assessment, appointment of directors and tutors and general arrangements of its proposed course;

    (ii) the submission, at least one term in advance, of the expected date of commencement of the course, of formal application for recognition of the course for the purpose of moderation and the award of certificates;

    (iii) the agreement of the Council to any exemptions, which are felt to be appropriate for particular students, from part or parts of the course.

B. During a course of training

    (i) the maintenance of appropriate standards of tuition, supervision, assessment and arrangements for practical teaching;

    (ii) assistance to a suitably appointed moderator in fulfilling his responsibilities and payment to that moderator of an agreed fee and expenses;

(iii) due regard for such suggestions as the moderator may make for ensuring the validity and comparability of standards between courses;

(iv) the opportunity for course directors and tutors to attend relevant meetings and courses;

(v) notification to the Council of any changes in circumstances which might be regarded as affecting recognised courses;

(vi) the availability of suitably recorded evidence of the performance and progress of individual students.

C. Following the completion of a course

(i) submission of evidence that a student has attained, to the Local Education Authority's satisfaction, an appropriate standard in all parts of the course and is recommended for the award of the Regional Certificate;

(ii) the availability of an opportunity for any student referred in whole or part to prepare for re-assessment within a reasonable period of time.

October 1976

APPENDIX 4: EXTRACTS FROM: THE SECOND ACSTT REPORT. 'THE TRAINING OF ADULT EDUCATION AND PART-TIME FURTHER EDUCATION STAFF'.

Stages of Training

19 Training for part-time teachers should be arranged in three stages, each stage offering a range of modules to meet the differing needs of part-time teachers concerned with different subjects, different levels of work and different age groups.

20 The first two stages, involving some 100 hours of course attendance and at least 30 hours of teaching practice, should be widely accessible and should be taken by all newly appointed part-time teachers who have been recruited for regular teaching in further and adult education and who are not already qualified as teachers in schools. Consideration was given to whether a shorter period of training might be suitable for those teaching only two or three hours a week, but it was agreed that the requirements of this group were basically the same as those with heavier teaching loads.

Stage I

21 Stage I courses should provide a brief initiation into basic teaching skills. This should preferably precede a part-time teacher's first "live performance", but where this is not possible it should take place during the first two terms of service. It is not the intention to be prescriptive about the content of this stage, but the following suggestions about possible topics will illustrate the general scope of what is intended.

(i)   Motives and expectations of teachers and students.
(ii)   The setting of aims and objectives.
(iii)   An introduction to learning theory.
(iv)   Planning learning situations.
(v)   An introduction to teaching aids.
(vi)   An introduction to lesson evaluation.

The treatment of these topics will naturally need to be appropriate to the age groups and context concerned.

22 Since the principal objective of this stage is to develop skill and confidence, active participation by course members is essential and at least 36 hours of attendance would be required.

Stage II

23 The new part-time teacher requires a degree of training in the pedagogical skills beyond that which can be given in the first stage and this should be provided by means of Stage II in-service modules, involving at least 60 hours of attendance and 30 hours of supervised teaching practice. Here again it is not the intention to be prescriptive about the content or method of organisation of these modules, but some suggestions are given below for purposes of illustration, it being important to note that the content and

treatment will need to be related to the age groups and objectives of the students with which the teachers in training are concerned.

(i) Objectives — an introduction to course design: consideration of the aims and objectives of courses, how to carry out tests, their reliability and validity.

(ii) The psychology of learning in the post-adolescent stage of life — an introduction to the classifications and explanations of learning and their relation to classroom teaching and learning; study of the physical, psychological and social constraints upon learning.

(iii) Teaching methods with post-school students — consideration of different approaches to teaching based upon learning requirements: exposition, demonstration, discussion, the uses of questioning, projects, assignments, role-playing, case-studies and programmed instruction.

(iv) Audio-visual aids — practical instruction in the use of aids and consideration of their applicability in different teaching situations.

(v) The teaching of particular subjects — a module based on specialist needs.

Stage III

24 On the completion of Stages I and II, part-time teachers should have the opportunity to undertake further in-service training leading to full certification, by means of Stage III courses of some 300 hours and appropriate teaching practice. Stage III courses, while designed for the part-time teacher, should, together with the preceding Stage I and II courses, be fully comparable in the demands they make to the courses for full-time staff described in the Sub-Committee's first report, and should reach comparable standards. Their duration needs to be adjusted to provide a comparable duration for the course as a whole. Thus, if Stages I and II together are of some 100 contact hours, then Stage III would require a minimum of 350 contact hours and a further 100 hours of supervised practice. These courses should be provided at centres with a substantial nucleus of experienced staff who have completed courses of advanced study in education and whose major commitment is to the professional education and development of teachers at the post-school stage. In appropriate cases it should be possible for part-time teachers to transfer (possibly by means of a bridging course) to the full-time teachers training scheme.

Transition courses for qualified school teachers.

25 School teachers taking up part-time teaching in further and adult education should be encouraged to undertake selected modules from the stages outlined above.

THE TRAINING OF TRAINERS

34 If training is to influence the subsequent behaviour of student teachers it should itself exemplify the teaching and organizing characteristics and attitudes it aims to develop in those who are being trained. This is so whether the training is part or full-time and at any level. The quality of the training courses suggested in this report would depend primarily on the calibre, experience and training of the staff responsible for conducting these courses. The skills, knowledge and understanding required at all stages of the

scheme are considerable. It is therefore of key importance that trainers must possess these before they plan and launch their courses. They therefore need specialist training themselves in the first instance as well as personal experience of the area of further education concerned. It is most important that theory is linked to practice. Specialist training is potentially available in a number of areas and centres but not in all regions. This availability must be exploited and coordinated. Very great importance needs to be given to the establishment of appropriate "training the trainers" courses and it is imperative that these are based at institutions which understand the skills and knowledge required. There are examples of the co-operation of university departments in this connection which have been highly successful. Only appropriate institutions should provide such training.

APPENDIX 5: SUBJECTS TAUGHT IN ADULT EDUCATION CLASSES

Major Categories & Classification	Examples of A.E. part-time Classes
ARTS/CRAFTS	
Flowers	Flower arranging, Pressed Flowers
Food and Drink	Cake decoration, Wine-tasting, Cookery
Textiles	Dressmaking, Creative Embroidery, Quilting
Beauty	Beauty Care, Hair Care
Hobbies	Macramé, Fabric Printing, Soft Toys
Art	Life/Portrait Painting, Oil Painting
SKILLS	
Car	Car Maintenance, Advanced Driving
Secretarial and Office	The Small Business Office, Shorthand, Simple Accounts
Garden and Rural	Gardening, Beekeeping
DIY Outside	Bricklaying, Welding
DIY Inside	Cabinet making, Soft Furnishing, Radio/T.V.
Music	Brass Instrumental, Guitar
Social	Public Speaking, Lip reading
Hobby	Photography, Dog training
SPORTS/EXERCISES	
Exercise	Slimnastics, Swing into Shape, Men's P.E.
Racket	Badminton, Squash
Ball	Cricket, Volley ball, Ladies Games
Water	Canoeing, Yachtmasters, Swimming
Martial	Karate, Fencing, Judo
Dancing	Folk, Ballet, Ballroom
Other (Individual)	Archery, Golf, Horse Riding
ACADEMIC	
Language	Dutch, Russian, Welsh
Writing	Writers' Workshop, Action Writing
Appreciation/Criticism	Art Appreciation, English Literature
Natural History	Geology, Woodland Ecology, Wild Flowers
Technology/Science	Computing, Human Biology, Electronics
Social Studies	Local Government, Child Development
Pastimes	Bridge, Genealogy

APPENDIX 6: EXAMPLES OF TRAINING COURSE PATTERNS

Stage 1 Courses — 3 Separate Counties

Weeks 1 — 8 Evenings
Vacation
Weeks 9 — 11 Evenings
    12 Residential
        Weekend
    13 — 14 Evenings
12 Evenings + 1 Res. Weekend
	Weeks 1 — 7 Evenings
	Vacation
	Weeks 8 — 16 Evenings
	
	16 Evenings
		Week 1 — Residential weekend
		Week 2 — Whole Day
		Week 3 — 2 Whole Days
		Week 4 — Whole Day
		
		4 days + 1 Res. Weekend

A Stage 2 and a S2/C & G 730 Course — 2 Separate Counties

Weeks   1 — 2 Evenings
          3 Saturday
     4 — 5 Evenings
          6 Saturday
     7 — 8 Evenings
          9 Saturday
Vacation
Weeks 10 — 11 Evenings
        12 Saturday
   13 — 16 Evenings
        17 Saturday
   18 — 19 Evenings
        20 Saturday
Vacation
Weeks   21 Evening
        22 Saturday
   23 — 24 Evenings
        25 Saturday
   26 — 28 Evenings
(20 Evenings + 8 days.)
	Weeks 1 — 14 Evenings
	Vacation
	Weeks 15 — 16 Evenings
	        17 Residential Weekend
	   18 — 28 Evenings
	Vacation
	Weeks 29 — 35 Evenings
	(34 Evenings + 1 Residential Weekend)
	Year 1 of 2

APPENDIX 7: EXAMPLES OF TRAINING COURSE SYLLABUSES*

*(as distributed to course trainees)

A Stage 1

Introduction — Elements and requirements; Aims and Objectives; Recommended reading

Adult Education — Types of A.E. provision; A.E. within the framework of F.E; Aims and purposes of F.E. and A.E; The Management of A.E.

The Teacher in Adult Education — Role — Functions and Tasks. Student Teacher Relationships. Criteria of Good Teaching

The Adult Student — Characteristics, Background Expectations, Motivation

Adult Learning — 1 — How do Adults Learn? Different types of learning. Different Types of Teaching

Adult Learning — 2 — The Individual Student — a basic psychology. The Idea of Group Behaviour

Teaching/Learning Aids (x2)

Mini-Lessons

Teaching Methods (x3) — Exposition/Lecture — Demonstration Discussion — Case Study etc. — Introduction to Micro-Teaching Task

Preparing a Course — Aims and Objectives — Syllabus — Scheme of Work

Preparing a Lesson — Aims and Objectives — Planning and Organisation — Groups — Preparation for Micro Teaching

Class Visits — Report and Evaluation

Group Work — Preparation and Planning for Micro-teaching

(16 weeks + 1 Residential Weekend — 2 days)

A Stage 1

Objectives
1. To be able to diagnose the needs of a student group with reference to an adult education provision
2. To be aware of the potential development of their subject
3. To be able to construct a syllabus, scheme of work and lesson plan
4. To be able to take a class using basic techniques
5. To recognise the need and express a wish to continue self-development

Content
1. The Student — needs, wants, motivation profiles
2. Subject development
3. Course and lesson construction
4. Basic teaching methods
5. Learning aids
6. Education Provision and Resources

(16 weeks)

A Stage 2/C & G 730 (1 Year Course)

Enrolment details and requirements of course
The organisation of Further Education
Survival Kit Teaching Practice/Observation
The Qualities of a Good Teacher
Principles of Lesson Planning
The Use of the Library and Textbook resources
The Local Adult Education Service
Principles of Learning and Motivation (x4)
Why Students Attend Further Education
Adolescence
Adulthood
Learning Resources (4)
Communication (x3)
The College Vice Principal
Course Planning and Design (x2)
Aims/Objectives — Lesson Planning (x4)
Lesson Planning
Principles and methods of assessment
Lesson Planning and Revision
Principles and methods of assessment (x2)
Assessment schemes linked to Lesson Plans
Methods of Teaching (x6)
Methods of Teaching Micro teaching situation
Presentation of Learning Resources
The College Principal
Careers Provision in Further Education
Micro Teaching Day/Assessment (x2)
Schemes of Work & Lesson Planning — progress
Adult Education — Characteristics of Adults
Schemes of Work and Lesson Planning — progress
Presentation of Method (micro teaching)
Revision of Teaching Method
Case Study — Teaching Problems (x2)
Revision of Principles of Learning
Revision of Teaching Strategy (x2)
Learning Resources practical
Learning Resources — OHP to group
Course Work Revision (x2)
Adult Education — differences in teaching!
Communications Revision
Course Review and Criticism (x2)

(67 Sessions — 1 year course)